Y0-BVO-683

Towards a New Europe?

Towards a New Europe?

Structural Change in the European Economy

Edited by

Ash Amin
Centre for Urban and Regional
Development Studies
University of Newcastle upon Tyne

Michael Dietrich

Department of Economics
and Government
Newcastle Polytechnic

Edward Elgar

Published by
Edward Elgar Publishing Limited
Gower House
Croft Road
Aldershot
Hants GU11 3HR
England

Edward Elgar Publishing Limited
Distributed in the United States by
Ashgate Publishing Company
Old Post Road
Brookfield
Vermont 05036
USA

CIP catalogue records for this book
are available from the British Library
and the US Library of Congress

ISBN 1 85278 415 6

Printed in Great Britain by
Billing and Sons Ltd, Worcester

Contents

Tables

Contributors

Ash Amin lectures in the Centre for Urban and Regional Development Studies at the University of Newcastle upon Tyne.

Thomas P. Boje is Associate Professor in Social Science at the Institute of Economics and Planning at the Roskilde University Centre in Denmark.

Benjamin Coriat is Professor of Economics at the University of Paris, 13.

Michael Dietrich lectures in the Department of Economics and Government at Newcastle upon Tyne Polytechnic.

John Grahl lectures in economics at Queen Mary and Westfield College, University of London.

Colin Haslam is Principal Lecturer in the Department of Business Studies at East London Polytechnic.

Pascal Petit is a CNRS Research Fellow at CEPREMAP in Paris, an institute affiliated to the French Planning Ministry.

Klaus Semlinger is Research Fellow at the Institut Für Sozialwissenschaftliche Forschung (ISF) in Munich.

John N. Smithin is Associate Professor of Economics in the Faculty of Administrative Studies at York University in Ontario.

Paul Teague lectures in economics at the University of Ulster at Jordanstown in Belfast.

Vivien Walsh is Senior Lecturer in Innovation at the Manchester School of Management at UMIST.

Klaus Weiermair is Full Professor of Economics at the Faculty of Administrative Studies at York University in Ontario.

John Williams is Professor of Economics and Social History in the Department of Economics at the University College of Wales in Aberystwyth.

Karel Williams is Senior Lecturer in the Department of Economics at the University College of Wales in Aberystwyth.

Preface

In 1988, at an historic meeting at Mansion House in Grim's Dyke (North London) between American institutionalists and heterodox European economists of different persuasions, a decision was made to launch a new European association which could develop a sustained and influential alternative to the analyses and policy prescriptions of the neoclassical orthodoxy. This is how the European Association of Evolutionary Political Economy (EAEPE) was born. Today, the Association has over 350 members in different European countries and the US. The membership of economists from the East European countries searching for an alternative to both the centrally planned and the market economy, has also grown rapidly since 1989.

This volume is one of two of the first publications of EAEPE, based on the second Annual Conference of the Association, which was held in Florence in November 1990. The conference, with its ambitious title 'Rethinking Economics: Theory and Policy for Europe in the 21st Century', was a great success, eliciting, as it did, a wide range of papers and active discussion on questions of economic theory (the subject matter of the companion volume) and on patterns of restructuring in Europe.

To the pleasure of the organizers, the conference produced a surprisingly high level of consensus over the issues discussed; a consensus rooted in a political economy drawing upon the work of such antecedents as Marx, Keynes, Polanyi, Veblen, Commons, Myrdal and Kaldor. It was widely felt that this, at the very least, would secure the longevity of the Association and, with it, prospects of a broad heterodox alternative to neoclassical economics. The building blocks of such an approach are evident both in this volume on the dynamics of structural and institutional change in Europe and in the accompanying volume, *Rethinking Economics*.

Ash Amin
Michael Dietrich

PART ONE

The Terms of Structural Economic Change

1. Deciphering the Terrain of Change in Europe

Ash Amin and Michael Dietrich

It is now commonplace to hear of a new, and very different, European economy in the making. Shifts in trade and foreign direct investment patterns between East and West are anticipated as a consequence of the economic reforms associated with the collapse of central planning in Eastern Europe. Similarly, the completion of the Single European Market (SEM) and monetary union are expected to alter the existing distribution of resources, growth potential and balance of economic power between the regions and nations of the European Community (EC).

More difficult to anticipate are the precise contours of the new map of Europe likely to be drawn as a result of these two major institutional transformations in the economic and regulatory environment. Which industries and countries in the East will be the beneficiaries of new export opportunities to the West? How will new investment from South East Asia, the US and the EC affect individual countries? How will the opening up of borders affect European macroeconomic stability and the dynamics of growth? These and other questions are still very much a matter of speculation. The same can be said of the direction and scale of damage or growth likely to be expected by individual regions and countries of the EC.

This uncertainty, to be sure, is not the result of inadequate or faulty forecasting methods and tools. It is more real, reflecting, as it does, difficulties in predicting future developments such as the direction and final outcome of reforms in the East (for example, the scale of liberalization, deregulation and privatization in each country, levels of institutional modernization and political stability) as well as the response of companies and governments in the West to the reforms (for example, the criteria for choosing between exports, joint-ventures and direct investment as a strategy for grasping new opportunities in the East). In addition, changes in the composition of the EC itself, with the re-

3

unification of Germany and the membership intentions of Poland, Hungary and Czechoslovakia compound these uncertainties.

In marked contrast to the acknowledged uncertainties surrounding these transformations in Europe, much of the literature on the economics of the '1992' project has been more confident about the future dynamics and geography of change within the EC. The most trumpeted, neo-liberal, position is also the clearest in terms of its naïvety, offering an optimism which is almost as simple as the economics upon which it draws. It assumes the possibility of friction-free trade, perfect factor mobility between sectors and regions, minimum 'interference' from the public sector as well as from historically embedded social, cultural and institutional traditions and perfectly 'rational' and information rich behaviour from economic actors. Unfolding wittingly or unwittingly, from the '1992' project, it anticipates a 'rational' and equitable distribution of resources and revenues between sectors and nations, once the full-scale effects of the enlarged and unified European market are realized, given appropriate entrepreneurial behaviour and institutional supports.

Fortunately, the European Commission itself is less convinced by the argument that equity and efficiency are the natural outcome of market expansion and, more importantly, the market as the only mode of regulation. Although it shares the neo-liberal optimism regarding the expected growth in demand and output associated with the completion of the SEM, it also accepts that the economic benefits are likely to be unevenly distributed, and in the favour of the larger and most competitive companies, regions and nations. Recognizing the dangers faced by smaller firms and the more peripheral regional and national economies, it proposes the possibility of ensuring equity through the provision of active support from different Directorates of the Commission in order to improve the competitive position of the weaker players.

Thus, here too, uncertainties regarding the anticipated benefits of '1992' and their fair distribution, are dispelled through the promise of such incentives as, on the one hand, tighter controls on the actions of the stronger players (for example, via Europe-wide enforcement of tighter merger and competition policy) and, on the other hand, the provision of incentives to the smaller or weaker players for improving competitiveness through technological and infrastructural renovation and up-grading of skills and training. Though differing from the neo-liberal position on the respective roles of the state and the market mechanism, this position, too, remains not only optimistic, but certain about the shape of things to come in the new EC.

But, how justified is this certainty? Equally, what are the grounds for optimism against evident centralizing tendencies in the European economy, both in terms of geography and corporate power? Why should the market not continue, as it has in the past, to favour the most efficient and well-organized firms and core regions? Might it not also be the case that the corrective incentives offered by Brussels are insufficient to counter-balance the scale advantages and market opportunities offered to the core players by economic and monetary union? What also of the distinct possibility that, like any set of formal rules, the regulations governing conduct under the SEM might never be fully enforced or compiled with or that, as in the past, they might be manipulated to serve the interests of the dominant firms and economies? In the rush for accurate predictions of the future, such basic questions concerning the scale of influence of the new institutional and regulatory changes on existing, *inherited* patterns of economic behaviour and uneven balances of power, appear to have been lost.

It is not only this issue which makes the task of writing about economic scenarios within the EC problematic. Much of the futurology on Europe is oblivious to the debate which has been raging since the early 1980s on the significance of the scale of contemporary structural change faced by the advanced economies; a debate which talks of a profound and system-wide transformation of the very structures and norms of production, consumption and exchange in the advanced economies. The implication of this debate is that the nature of the material foundation for profitable production and exchange, itself, is under question, thus casting further doubt on the authenticity of futurology regarding the likely outcomes of the present institutional reforms.

At least three competing theorizations of structural change in the advanced economies have become well known. One, perhaps the least equivocal about the future and also the most controversial, derives from the work of Michael Piore and Charles Sabel (1984), who describe the present as a major historical divide between a past dominated by the structures and patterns of mass production and mass consumption and a new era of 'flexible specialization', governed by the principles of non-standardized demand and vertically disintegrated production. Pointing to the proliferation of market fragmentation, customized demand and market volatility and also the increasing availability of generic and highly-flexible technologies, these authors and their followers, for example, Hirst and Zeitlin (1989), argue that the present may be a propitious time for 'returning' to craft-based and decentralized forms of organizing production within both large and small firms. 'Flexible specialization', that is, the division of tasks and responsibilities to loosely inter-connected units, is anticipated to be the most efficient and quickest way of turning out good quality goods for ever-changing markets.

Implicit in this interpretation of structural change is the replacement of the dominant institutional forms and patterns of the past, such as 'giantism', monopolistic forms of competition, vertically integrated production and centralized or universalistic forms of regulation and collective bargaining. The new economic landscape is likely to be more like a confederation of product specialist, self-contained, regional economies with their own regulating structures, trading with each other on a neo-Smithian basis (Sabel, 1989). This will replace a unified landscape of regions and nations conjoined and dominated by the needs of giant firms or the most powerful national or supranational governments. If this vision of change is related to the European agenda, what can be anticipated is a 'Europe of the regions' composed of locally governed, 'flexibly specialized' economies which, probably, can stand without the guarantees and rules offered by Brussels. Europe would have no obvious economic reality but would exist as a political or administrative constraint on restructuring processes already under way in the economy.

A second, and more wide reaching design for the changing macro-economy is less celebratory and less fixed about the future than the first position. It is the approach pioneered by the French Regulation School (see Chapter 2 for detailed references). Through the work of, among others, Aglietta, Lipietz, Boyer, Coriat, Petit, Delorme and de Bernis, the present can be seen as a period of crisis and transition from one long cycle of economic growth ('regime of accumulation') and institutional support ('mode of regulation') to another very difficult cycle. Regulation theory refers to the crisis of Fordism, a system of macroeconomic development which characterized the post-war economy and secured unprecedented growth on a national basis to the most advanced industrial economies. This was growth based on a productivity raising synergy between, in particular, three pillars: the deployment of appropriate techniques and labour usage patterns for mass production; the sustainability of mass consumption through global market expansion and growth in disposable income; and, through 'monopolistic' forms of regulation (for example, Keynesian policies, collective bargaining and welfarism), a series of norms and policies to ensure congruence within the mass production–mass consumption norm.

This description of the present as a period of transition rather than achieved change is important. It is recognized that rising out of the ashes of Fordism are the elements of an entirely new macroeconomy composed of both new structural tendencies as well as continuities from the past. Some of the new tendencies which are emphasized include: the modification of the mass production principle via the extensive deployment of new information and communication technologies and novel patterns of vertical disintegration in production; the use of more individualized forms for managing industrial relations and extensive usage of flexible working practices and wage contracts; the emergence of new growth sectors in the service industries and the greater informatization of manufacturing; and greater experimentation with neo-liberal and market-led forms of economic governance. Elements of continuity include: the persistence of both mass production and mass consumption in the global economy; the internationalization of 'Fordism' through notably the activities of multinational corporations and transnational banks; and the persistence of monopolistic forms of regulation through, for instance, the forces of financial and industrial concentration.

Thus, while the elements of the neo-Fordist economy are in place and also quite different from Fordism, the overall shape and dynamics of the new macroeconomy are not clear because of the contradictory and uncertain nature of structural change today and because the 'systemic' aspects of the new regime have yet to consolidate. As far as the future of the European economy goes, the Regulation School would tend to conclude that the institutional reforms in Brussels or in the East will have to measure up to very different foundations and codes of conduct in the macroeconomy itself, from those in the past. However, and this is the point, the nature of the division of labour between regions or nations, sectors and firms, and the balance of power between different institutions and social groups remains very difficult to predict because of the incomplete nature of structural change in the macroeconomy.

A third school of thought, which anticipates a new Europe, again, on the basis of structural rather than institutional change, is the neo-Schumpeterian one, see, for instance, Freeman and Perez (1988). Its analysis of the dynamics and direction of contemporary change in the macroeconomy is not dissimilar to that of more recent writing in the Regulation School. One key difference, however, is the central emphasis placed by neo-Schumpeterians on the role of technical change in shaping a long-term 'techno-economic' paradigm and in influencing the transition from one paradigm to another. Splitting long cycles of economic development into up-swings and down-swings of productivity growth, Freeman and Perez argue that microelectronics and more generally information technology and biotechnology will be the bearers of a new up-swing of economic growth in the emerging techno-economic paradigm. According to Freeman and Perez, successful restructuring, however, requires a match-up between new technological developments and institutional forms which are conducive to the full diffusion of the potential of the new technologies across the economy. In other words, the new macroeconomy requires new institutions for its full realization.

The key question for Europe which arises from this perspective on change, is whether the present major institutional reforms on offer are the appropriate ones for renewed economic growth. The answer to this question is probably a negative one, given the incongruity between the neo-Schumpeterian emphasis on the need for imaginative, co-ordinated and active public intervention on both the supply-side and in markets, and the lack of any real appreciation of structural change in the thinking behind the present Europe-wide institutional reforms. On the other hand, the neo-Schumpeterian framework is more appropriate for capturing abstract restructuring processes. However, with regard to this abstract level it has to be said that technology can only be taken as the pivotal factor in understanding restructuring if it is given a prior asocial existence removed from particular institutional circumstances. It is clear that technologies are developed, adopted and adapted by people not abstract economic agents. Hence detailed application of the neo-Schumpeterian position to European restructuring would have to recognize the idiosyncrasies of institutional arrangements.

Taking the above lines of argument, it is difficult to characterize a generalized, discontinuous process of restructuring divorced from particular circumstances and particular histories. The logic of the argument so far, then, is that, from a dual perspective, it is premature to forecast the precise future of the European economy, both as a whole and in its parts. The first uncertainty derives from the unknown outcome of how individual agents – firms, countries, workers, managers – will respond to the reforms. The second relates to the larger question concerning the changing nature of the very requirements for profitable production and exchange within the capitalist economy; movements in directions which are, for the moment, imprecise and subject to major controversy.

CHANGING MACROECONOMIC, ORGANIZATIONAL, LABOUR AND MONETARY REGIMES

It is the desire to strike a fine balance between exploring the possibility of a European economy undergoing profound structural changes and retaining sensitivity to questions of continuity, difference and diversity, which unifies the chapters in this volume. Inevitably, in taking such an approach, the book will disappoint those hoping for a complete or total view of the implications of the current institutional reforms in the EC. The reasons for this absence should have become amply clear from the preceding discussion. This is not to say that the thesis of the book is to propose that the future is entirely open-ended. The aim, rather, is to propose that the future will be shaped by the central processes of restructuring which have been under way within the advanced economies at least since the 1970s.

What, then, does the book have to say about the European economy? The volume is more concerned with changes in the EC than with the reforms in Eastern Europe. Also, with the exception of the last two chapters on the implications of monetary union within the European Community, the book is not about the '1992' project. Instead, it explores the dynamics of key aspects of change within the advanced economies which will shape and be shaped by the emerging institutional reforms. In addition to its focus on money, processes of restructuring in three arenas in particular are examined: the macroeconomy; industrial organization; and the labour market and industrial relations. The common analytical thread which runs through the chapters on these different themes is that of a non-orthodox political economy which is sensitive to the idea of structural change but also recognizes the importance of institutional continuity.

In one of the more ambitiously forward looking analyses of the Regulation School, Benjamin Coriat and Pascal Petit attempt to speculate on the characteristics of the emerging post-Fordist regime of accumulation. This is achieved by reinterpreting the process of de-industrialization and tertiarization common to all the advanced economies as a key aspect of changing inter-sectoral relations in the new macroeconomy. Following a review of the deindustrialization debate, the authors argue that the phenomenon cannot be reduced to inadequate adjustment policies on the part of national governments or to aberrations in the business cycle. Sectoral restructuring, for these two authors, is an aspect of the transition from the Fordist regime of accumulation, dominated by mass manufacturing, and centralized management in industry and government, to a new, 'information' and 'knowledge' based, economic regime.

Focusing on one aspect of emerging changes in the social division of labour, namely the relationship between manufacturing and services, the authors illustrate the nature of new synergies and complementarities between the so-called secondary and tertiary sectors (for example, the rise of business services, the embodiment of information in products, industry as a source of training and skills for high value-added services, the growth of services as an outcome of vertical disintegration in manufacturing and the use of telematics in industry). The analysis of these new relationships leads Coriat and Petit to conclude that the growth of such 'intermediate' activities may help to facilitate the consolidation of the post-Fordist regime of accumulation. They are seen to enhance the potential of at least three of the central pillars of the new regime: the diffusion of information technology; the potential for flexible, high-volume production and the internationalization of markets and production processes. The chapter concludes with a warning against defensive or short-term adjustment policies which fail to create a strategically planned and protected environment enabling the fullest and most equitable development of the new macroeconomic regime.

The section on organizational change which follows the chapter by Coriat and Petit is composed of four chapters on contemporary changes in the intra-firm and inter-firm division of labour in European industry. Chapter 3 sets out the terms of debate on the changing balance between organizational disintegration and integration in the economy. It draws upon EC-wide data on merger and joint-venture activity and market concentration levels as well as the results of more qualitative studies of corporate restructuring in different industries, to explore the direction of change in the organizational and economic power of large firms.

In demonstrating the continued importance of size and the growing reach of large firms both in markets and global production, the results of this chapter sharply contradict assertions emanating from the theory of flexible specialization regarding the imminent transition to disintegrated and smaller-scale production, the localization of economic activity and more competitive markets within the next phase of capitalist development. The chapter does not, however, argue the case of no change in the corporate economy. It accepts that networking forms of intra- and inter-firm organization on a global basis, are replacing traditional forms of 'hierarchy' as a means for increasing product and functional flexibility in increasingly uncertain markets. But, in contrast to the networking literature (examined in more detail in Chapters 5 and 6) it proposes that the bid for organizational and operational flexibility on the part of large firms is concomitant with an extension of oligopolistic control on a Europe-wide scale.

The contribution by Klaus Weiermair, in Chapter 4, approaches the issue of organizational restructuring from a different perspective by examining the nature of the increasing Japanization of European industry. He points out that while Japanese investment has been growing, it is overwhelmingly restricted to a few service industries, particularly finance and insurance, and to a lesser extent manufacturing activities such as transport equipment and electronics. Hence, at this level, journalistic threats of Japanese dominance of the European economy appear to be partial to say the least. On the other hand, it is Weiermair's thesis that characteristic organizational innovations, with associated new forms of competition, are becoming increasingly dominant in the advanced economies. At the same time, however, such change is not, according to Weiemair, unidirectional because of country specific characteristics and blockages in the arena of organizational innovation. This does not reduce, of course, the significance for Europe of Japanization. Just as the American challenge dominated restructuring in the 1960s, so will the Japanese challenge, as a hegemonic competitive formula, into the 1990s.

Chapters 5 and 6 are both contributions which attempt to go beyond the market-hierarchy dichotomy in industrial organization theory, which, according to the authors, fails to explain key aspects of current European corporate restructuring. Klaus Semlinger, in Chapter 5, approaches the problem by focusing on new developments in subcontracting. His argument is that many mass producers in Europe, confronted with the threat of market saturation and intensified competition, are reducing in-house production in favour of new subcontracting arrangements. In the new market circumstances, outsourcing is said to reduce costs, speed up work-time, enlarge product scope, increase flexibility and improve the incentive as well as the control structures of hierarchical organization. Semlinger's main point is that outsourcing has become a strategic, and possibly also a lasting, organizational option which combines the advantages of market-based incentives to innovation, with the organizational cost efficiencies of asset specificity within individual firms and the adaptabilities afforded by loose firm coupling.

It is the chapter's emphasis on the strategic intentions of the actors involved as well as the uneven power relations of autonomy and domination between buyers and suppliers, which is perhaps the most novel aspect of this addition to the burgeoning literature on the existence of organizational forms in between market and hierarchy. This approach is used to criticize both the transaction cost approach, with its emphasis on efficiency and rational expectations and also the emphasis placed on such concepts as trust and mutual benefit in new writing within organizational sociology to describe the growth of networking between firms. Semlinger's analysis is a refreshing antidote to much of the literature on networking eager to anticipate a new Europe with flatter and more egalitarian inter-corporate relations.

In Chapter 6, Vivien Walsh shifts the analysis of networking to the study of inter-firm technological alliances. The mere existence of such links poses an interesting question: why, in market economies, where firms are expected to compete, should they co-operate? The answer suggested by Walsh is that increasingly, commercial opportunities involve cross-fertilization of ideas and knowledge from different areas, hence multidisciplinary research is needed to obtain any commercially exploitable breakthrough. However, given the human and other barriers inhibiting such diversified development within the context of any one firm, inter-firm agreements represent a means of co-ordinating a large number of complementary knowledge inputs.

Walsh develops this approach in detail through an analysis of inter-firm alliances in the field of biotechnology. Two conclusions in particular are worthy of note. First, the development of links involves not only the private sector but also a pivotal role by the public sector. Secondly, large companies frequently dominate smaller partners within these network alliances because of market power and asset advantages (for example, established marketing systems). As a result of this domination, linkages between small and large firms can compromise the independence of the former; a conclusion which is strongly echoed by other chapters in this section.

The section of the book on labour is composed of two contributions, both of which build upon the preceding analyses of structural change in the macroeconomy and new patterns of organizational restructuring. In Chapter 7, Thomas Boje examines the main developments in the labour markets of the advanced economies during the last decade, focusing his attention on the relation between labour flexibility and the fragmentation of work in Denmark. The chapter seeks to explore the implications of new demands for organizational flexibility and fragmentation, on working conditions and industrial relations. Drawing upon both qualitative and quantitative evidence on part-time work, the rise of different types of temporary work and the nature of tasks externalized by firms, it reaches the conclusion that central to current experimentations with labour use are the dismantling of internal labour markets and job demarcation, a weakening of the bargaining power of organized labour and growing inequality in the conditions of employment.

Boje's conclusions contrast sharply with theorizations of the 1960s and 1970s which highlighted segmentation and dualism in labour markets which were stable, internal and regulated by collective bargaining. Boje claims that labour markets now are much more unstable and diversified, as a consequence of the greater demand by firms for flexible working arrangements. The chapter also provides a sober antidote to an emerging consensus on labour flexibility, which equates organizational decentralization with better working practices and terms of employment. Boje, who makes a serious attempt to examine the available empirical evidence, is less celebratory about present labour market restructuring than those extolling the virtues of a 'flexibly specialized' post-Fordist Europe.

In Chapter 8, John Grahl and Paul Teague push the discussion on labour restructuring forward by examining its implications for the labour movement, notably in terms of the institutional parameters of worker representation. They argue the case for a negotiated settlement, a sort of New Deal, between labour and industry, as the basic condition for a new regime of accumulation which can combine both social equality and renewed economic growth.

Echoing in particular the recent work of the French Regulationist Alan Lipietz (1989), who distinguishes between offensive and defensive forms of corporate restructuring in the 1980s, Grahl and Teague argue that at the micro level of the firm, there is ample evidence of the practice and success of worker involvement. The problem, then, is not one of establishing the legitimacy of industrial democracy in the individual work-places. Instead, the key issue in Europe, for Grahl and Teague, is that of identifying the mechanisms and agencies for an economy-wide settlement in the present context of increasing labour fragmentation. The chapter explores the agendas which the trade unions and the labour movement need to explore to enable such a settlement without resorting to the centralist or corporatist unionism of the past. The authors argue that one solution could be the promotion of active industrial citizenship, a sense of worker engagement in as wide a sphere of activities as possible, with the unions playing a central role in this process. The chapter envisages that the EC Social Charter could actively contribute to furthering such a vision across the European territory by providing framework to workers in different countries, industries and work-places.

The final two chapters of the book concentrate on the implications of European monetary union. Both contributions conclude that the standard monetarist analysis in this area is at best naïve and at worst a recipe for reinforcing the cumulative advantages of the most successful areas of the European economy. John Smithin, in Chapter 9, locates the key link in the drive for monetary union, not in any economic argument, but in the political objective of European integration. He interprets monetary integration to be a means to this greater end. But he argues that this subordination of economic factors has stifled any serious debate, with the exception of monetarist inspired analysis which ignore the effects of monetary policy on the real economy. As an alternative, Smithin situates his analysis in a post-Keynesian framework, developing upon Hicks's concept of a 'monocentre', the institution around which a financial system operates (usually a central bank in a national context).

In a European context the monocentre will be the Bundesbank, thus implying that a system of irrevocably fixed exchange rates in the EC will settle around its actions and policies. The existence of this dominance need not be problematic for individual economies, if similar economic conditions prevail throughout the EC. That this is not the case is obvious, in which case the deflationary bias exhibited by German monetary policy will not bring universal benefits. In short, for Smithin the EC is not an optimal currency area.

A similar scepticism about the likely economic success of European monetary union (EMU) is also evident in the final chapter. John Williams, Karel Williams and Colin Haslam examine the Delors proposals and argue that they, paradoxically, represent a political shift to the Right compared to the Cecchini position, which, at least, retained some sense of a residual liberal collectivism. Fiscal policy has now become subordinated to rigidly defined monetary objectives and there is an overwhelming prejudice against redistributive expenditures. In the Delors plan national policies are defined in terms of a neo-liberal, supply-side agenda of non-intervention, which meshes into an EC framework of 'sound money'. Convergence between players and countries of different strengths will be guaranteed if economic actors grasp the opportunities.

The authors are not convinced by the Delors plan. They argue that by ignoring differing economic structures and national institutions, the burden of adjustment towards the new Europe will fall on the output and employment of the weaker peripheral economies. The central problem, according to Williams, Williams and Haslam, is that identified by Keynes in the 1940s, namely that a symmetry of adjustment which affects the strong as well as the weak is required. Given the virtual non-existence of regional policy initiatives this must involve revaluation at the Centre. But within the neo-liberal vision which dominates current policy prescriptions, there is little space for institutional corrective measures against the intensification of uneven development. For instance, one neo-liberal assumption is that if the 'sound money' policies carried out by German authorities are generally applied, Germany's economic success will be replicated due to a generalized reduction in the rate of inflation. In this vision, there is no recognition of supply-side idiosyncrasies and the role played in the economy by German institutions. The conclusion drawn by Williams, Williams and Haslam is that the main problem with EMU, which prevents the development of a more equitable Europe-wide monetary strategy, is, first and foremost, the exploration of an alternative political agenda for building a strong, democratic, federal European government. Without such an effort, serious discussion of how to maximize the spread of economic benefits from EMU is hampered.

TOWARDS A NEW EUROPE

The contributions in this volume paint a picture of multifaceted restructuring in the EC. Taken as a whole they offer a fairly bleak perspective. The restructuring has reinforced the dominance of large firms, even though the traditional safeguards offered by the corporatist culture and institutions of Fordism are either no longer present or blunted by the various processes of change. At the same time, it is clear that the neo-liberal agenda cannot restructure the supply-side of the European economy in a way that counters the centralizing effects of market forces. In addition, this agenda, along with the Commission's evident neo-mercantilism, appears to have little conception of current structural economic restructuring. Thus a major issue for a new debate on economic policy would be that of developing a new agenda which, at once, recognizes the diversity of the European economy as well as its unity but without marginalizing the public sector to being simply a guardian of 'sound money'.

The arguments presented in Chapters 9 and 10 highlight a destructive side to the monetary union project because of its artificial homogenization of a very diversified economic space. The knitting together of monetary and political union in a neo-liberal sense will have destabilizing implications for the latter if a monetarist framework is adhered to. The *realpolitik* of European union is likely to result in a deflection away from the naïve neo-liberal position on EMU. Any deflection of this sort is to be welcomed in order to avoid the internationalized economy from playing out its own centralizing tendencies within an arena of a disintegrated political infrastructure in Europe. European monetary union, through its neo-liberal variant, is very likely to promote political disintegration as the disgruntled national economies disengage from the project. In reality, however, we are still likely to be left with a momentum towards a highly politicized monetary unification, with all its difficulties for the weaker players.

Following Coriat and Petit, it can be suggested that the strategic objectives of European economic policy should be that of encouraging the consolidation of a post-Fordist regime. The structures or elements involved coalesce around three factors: a pivotal role for information technology; flexible high volume production; and the internationalization of economic activity. In turn, these objectives are contingent upon an avoidance of short-termism because of the required strategic shifts in corporate behaviour and investment in human and other assets. In this respect the current trajectories of European regulatory reform are clearly failing and diverting attention away from the strategic issues. Market unification will, of itself, increase short-term competitive pressures especially in peripheral and non-dominant activities. The consequences are obvious. On the one hand, companies will be forced into defensive positions involving, among other things, labour shedding and the contracting out of non-core activities to promote short-term cost reductions. On the other hand, an increase in economic centralization is likely to result either from liquidation or defensive merger activity.

To avoid this scenario, one option, which the Commission itself embraces, might be to tie the agenda of union to greater European regional and industrial policy initiatives. The main problem with this option is that it echoes a 1960s corporatist philosophy and fails to acknowledge the major organizational changes that have been occurring. The centralization of Fordist macroeconomic control, as characterized by, for example, tri-partite consensus, has broken down. Now, greater emphasis is being put on firm-level activity as labour markets become more fragmented, particularly by gender, occupation and region. Therefore, while a 'top down' policy framework to facilitate network development and influence the activities of leading firms – the current EC stance (Dietrich, 1991) – may appear to be inevitable in a world in which multinational companies play such a leading role, this strategy has its shortcomings. The required EC co-ordination would lead to a bureaucratic nightmare, because of the diversity and complexity of the European economy. Furthermore, EC policy initiatives which operate through existing corporate structures will reinforce the existing relative disadvantage of smaller and weaker players. Finally, a centralized policy stance cannot accommodate the complexities of the diverse restructuring processes.

It follows, therefore, that in addition to a centralized 'top down' policy framework, a 'bottom up' approach is needed to exploit particular advantages and needs and to develop and buttress a new settlement between labour and industry. To some extent the emerging forms of the required new agenda are present. For example, as Grahl and Teague point out in Chapter 8 the EC Social Charter sets out a framework, which could develop decentralized initiatives for implementation. In addition, because of the traditions of particularly trade union activity, this implementation will of necessity involve a central role for the public sector if gross economic and social inequities are to be avoided.

More generally, however, the appropriate economic framework which maximizes the spread of growth and industrial democracy across Europe appears not to be developing. The general contours of this framework are evident from earlier discussions. Local and regional level activity could well promote specialized production and the development of external economies and synergies. But self re-generation is unlikely because of market failures, the dominance of leading firms in the most dynamic sectors and short-term perspectives resulting from competitive pressures. Thus, of central importance is the development of a Europe-wide, protected, strategic environment, which includes a central role for public sector policy. This, in particular in the arena of developing strategic services, such as marketing and research and development (R&D), is likely to be central for post-Fordist growth.

It is clear that a new agenda for Europe requires a multilevel framework of intervention from local, through national to EC activity, one which recognizes institutional diversity and does not rely on an individual initiative constraint. It is equally clear that such a framework has regional and national fiscal implications which appear not to be accommodated by the current momentum towards monetary unification which hinges on central control of the individual deficits. To return to the concerns set out at the start of this chapter: European regulatory reform appears to be lumbering in naïve innocence towards an uncertain future. The elements of an alternative scenario can be gleaned from the individual contributions to this book.

REFERENCES

Dietrich, M. (1991), 'European Economic Integration and Industrial Policy', *Review of Political Economy*, October, **3**, (4), 418–40.

Freeman, C. and C. Perez, (1988), 'Structural Crises of Adjustment, Business Cycles and Investment Behaviour', in G. Dosi, C. Freeman, R. Nelson, G. Silverberg and L. Soete (eds) *Technical Change and Economic Theory*, London, Frances Pinter: 38–66.

Hirst, P. and J. Zeitlin, (1989), 'Flexible Specialisation and the Competitive Failure of UK Manufacturing', *Political Quarterly*, **60**, (3), 164–78.

Lipietz, A. (1989), *Choisir L'Audace*, Paris: La Decouverte.

Piore, M. and C.F. Sabel, (1984), *The Second Industrial Divide: Possibilities for Prosperity*, New York: Basic Books.

Sabel, C.F. (1989), 'Flexible Specialization and the Re-emergence of Regional Economies' in P. Hirst and J. Zeitlin (eds), *Reversing Industrial Decline? Industrial Structure and Policies in Britain and her Competitors*, Oxford: Berg.

2. Deindustrialization and Tertiarization: Towards a New Economic Regime?

Benjamin Coriat and Pascal Petit

INTRODUCTION

Over the past fifteen or twenty years, the share of manufacturing in the industrialized economies has been declining with regard to both employment and output. Occurring in a period of considerable slow-down in the growth of these economies, between 1975 and 1985, the relative decline of manufacturing industry has been isolated by some as one of the major reasons of this slow-down. There has been a controversy over the causes and effects of deindustrialization ever since the mid-1970s. Fifteen years on, it may be possible to take a new look at this issue in the light of the current extensive restructuring of production systems, the growth of a huge business services sector and the greater integration of the developed economies into the world trade system.

This chapter reassesses the arguments on deindustrialization within the context of these developments and reconceptualizes the debate within a Regulationist framework. Today, major questions concerning the role of the so called renewed manufacturing sector remain unanswered. Does this sector continue to remain a dynamic force within the economy, constituting, as it did in the heyday of Fordist mass production, the engine of growth in the developed economies? Manufacturing industry now has to meet the twin challenge of sharper international competition and swifter technological progress. In an economic system in which the division of labour between firms has been considerably extended, how does the manufacturing sector relate to other sectors? Which forces govern its performance and competitiveness?

These are central questions to any attempt to decipher the dynamics of a post-Fordist regime. Two possibilities can be hypothesized. Either a new type of regime of accumulation is unfolding, accompanied by major

18

changes in patterns of productivity and demand formation; or it is simply the case that national economic policies and institutions have been unable to adjust to sectoral shifts in the economy quickly enough. In the latter case, minor institutional rigidities and policy errors would account for the slow-down of growth and the large rise in unemployment in some countries during the past decade.

Current approaches to deindustrialization reflect this dichotomy, in tending to address the issue either as part of a wider process of structural change, or as a continuing problem of policy and institutional adjustment. If, in the past decade, the tendency has been to stress the structural nature of the crisis, this then raises the question of the nature of the new growth regime. The aim in this chapter is to go some way towards addressing this latter question by focusing on aspects of structural change linked to the new division of labour between firms, more precisely that between manufacturing and service sector firms. An understanding of many of the issues related to the future of the developed economies in the new Europe, requires an assessment of this key question.

The first section summarizes the main arguments upon which the debate of deindustrialization has been grounded. This is followed by a survey of the two approaches to deindustrialization, to conclude in favour of a structural explanation. The third section examines the nature of emerging relationships between firms in manufacturing and services. The final section goes on to outline the main features of the new economic regime stemming from this new mix of service sector and manufacturing activities.

MAIN INDICATORS OF DEINDUSTRIALIZATION

It is worth reiterating the broad 'facts' which underlie the deindustrialization controversy. Economists have related the decline of manufacturing industry since the late 1970s to three main indicators: trends in employment; trends in output; and trade performance. For the industrialized OECD countries,[1] the most striking feature has been the progressive decline in industrial employment since 1973 in most countries, both in absolute and relative terms (see Table 2.1). This is an unprecedented reversal of an upward trend dating back to the beginning of the industrial age.

Deindustrialization has meant a slow-down in activity in mainly manufacturing industry. On average the pace of economic growth has been remarkably slow since 1973: GDP for instance, which grew at a rate of 5.1 per cent a year in the OECD during the 1960s, grew by only 2.7 per

The Terms of Structural Economic Change

cent a year in the 1980s. This slow-down affected industry, especially in manufacturing, more than it did the rest of the economy. Growth rates in manufacturing output, which earlier had outpaced growth in the rest of the economy, lagged behind after 1973[2] (see Table 2.1). This turn around in growth differentials is all the more disturbing since it has coincided with slower overall economic growth and a general rise in unemployment.

Table 2.1. Indicators of deindustrialization in selected OECD countries

	Employment growth in industry (%)		Industry as a share of total employment* (%)			Growth in industrial output (%)	
	1960s	1980s	1960	1973	1988	1960s	1980s
Australia	2.1	0.3	38.9	35.1	26.4	5.3†	3.1
Austria	0.4	0.0	40.3	42.3	37.4	5.0	1.4
Belgium	0.2	−2.5	45.0	40.2	28.0	4.6	1.3
Canada	2.5	0.5	32.7	30.5	25.6	5.9	2.7
Denmark	1.7	−1.0	36.9	32.3	27.2	5.1	2.3
France	1.1	−2.0	37.6	39.4	30.3	6.9	0.5
Germany	−0.2	−0.9	47.0	46.7	39.8	4.3	0.4
Italy	0.8	−1.2	33.9	39.3	32.4	7.1	1.9
Japan	4.0	0.8	28.5	37.0	34.1	13.7	5.3
Netherlands	0.7	−1.0	40.5	35.9	26.4	6.5	0.8
Norway	1.0	−0.3	35.6	34.3	26.4	4.7	4.5
Sweden	0.7	−0.5	40.3	37.0	29.5	5.1	2.1
Switzerland	1.5	−0.2	46.4	44.3	35.1	—	—
UK	−0.3	−2.7	47.7	42.0	29.8	2.7	3.7
US	1.9	0.0	35.3	32.5	26.9	4.4	1.8

* Manufacturing and utilities.
† 1968–73.
Source: OECD (various years)

In the 1960s, growth in the industrialized countries was largely powered by a trade surplus in manufactures. A third sign of deindustrialization would hence be a reduction in this surplus. However, since a large share of trade occurs between the industrialized countries, it is to be expected that the trade balance of some countries will improve when that of others worsens. In fact, differences in manufacturing surplus began to become marked after 1973 between, on the one hand, a small selection of industrialized countries whose surpluses kept growing (Japan, Germany and, to a lesser extent, Belgium) and, on the other hand, countries whose surpluses turned into deficits (France and Spain) or whose deficits widened (the UK, the US and Canada). These various observations show that signs of industrial fragility, with national differences in timing and intensity began to show in nearly all the OECD countries after 1973. The phenomenon thus appeared to be at once both universal and strongly national in character (see Table 2.2). The severest form appears in the upper corner of Table 2.2, and concerns the UK, France and Australia. The Federal Republic of Germany, owing to its successful trade record in manufactures, and the US, in which industrial employment has remained buoyant, do not appear in this group.

The shortcomings, however, of relying on purely quantitative

Table 2.2. Terms of apparent deindustrialization in 15 OECD countries

Period 1973–1987	Industrial employment decline								
	Below average			Average			Above average		
	+	0	−	+	0	−	+	0	−
Value-added slow-down — Above average		USA CA			NO	FRG	NE	FR UK AUS	
Average				DK		BE		AUT	
Below average	JA	GR	IT	FI					

Evolution of trends in trade in manufactures 1984–89

USA	— United States	AUT	— Austria
CA	— Canada	DK	— Denmark
FR	— France	BE	— Belgium
UK	— United Kingdom	GR	— Greece
AUS	— Australia	FI	— Finland
NO	— Norway	JA	— Japan
NE	— Netherlands	IT	— Italy
FRG	— Germany		

measures are obvious. They do not help much to understand how the above symptoms have affected individual economies. Is there, for instance, any threshold beyond which economic growth is strongly hampered or destabilized? Accordingly, in the following section, we shall review the various theoretical approaches which have made an attempt to make sense of the above symptoms, before going on to explore the significance of new growth patterns in assessing the role of manufacturing industry in the economy.

DEINDUSTRIALIZATION: STRUCTURAL CRISIS OR INADEQUATE ADJUSTMENT POLICIES?

Two conflicting sets of ideas have been proposed in the past decade to account for deindustrialization and its effects on economic growth. One questions the internal, structural, factors which caused the preceding growth regime to stagnate, while the other questions the role of policies in various countries enacted to adjust to external and structural changes. In the terms of Regulation Theory, the first refers to a crisis of the Fordist regime of accumulation, while the second is more concerned with mismatches regarding the formulation of government policies within the mode of regulation.

Breakdown of the 'Industrial Engine' of Growth?

The structural approaches to deindustrialization can be placed within the conceptual framework of the cumulative causation model, as developed by Kaldor (1966, 1972 and 1975[3]), in which industry plays the role of the engine of growth. The growth of industrial markets is supposed to foster an increased division of labour both inside the firm (an idea already promoted by Adam Smith) and outside, via subcontracting and specialization between firms and branches, which stimulates increases in productivity. This industrial momentum is mainly conveyed to the different components of demand (the consumption of goods and services, investment and exports) through some sharing of productivity gains between prices, wages and profits. The ensuing expansion in demand, in turn, leads to further increases in productivity. The outcome is thus a virtuous circle of growth, in which market expansion and increased productivity gains follow on from each other cumulatively. Numerous studies[4] have confirmed the empirical validity of this scheme up until the mid-1970s and its breakdown thereafter. See Michl (1985) and Boyer and Petit (forthcoming).

Three basic sets of reasons have been identified in the literature as constraints on the cumulative causation process: an exhaustion of the sources of dynamic returns to scale; blockages in the formation of external demand; and transformations in the labour market. The first set of reasons is concerned with slow-down in the inner dynamic of productivity, also referred to as the productivity regime. This dynamic has been thoroughly transformed but it is unclear whether, overall, it will go on delivering high productivity gains. Some sources of dynamic returns to scale may have reduced their contribution, such as for example, the necessity of Taylorist forms of work organization and management, or enlargement of the size of equipment and machinery. At the same time. i⁺ is likely that a wave of new technology, centred around the microprocessor and telecommunications, has made a positive contribution by increasing both embodied technical change and learning processes.[5] This probably explains why the second two sets of reasons concerned with the 'laws' of demand formation (that is, the demand regime), have been given more consideration in the deindustrialization debate.

The blockage of external demand, or its incapacity to grow in pace with the target needed to reach full employment, occupies a central position among explanations of deindustrialization. See Singh (1977, 1987). The argument here is that first, exports of manufactures are an independent component of effective demand, second, imports of manufactures are directly related to GDP growth and, third, in the medium term, exports and imports of manufactures have to balance out in terms of growth, Thirwall (1982). The theory linking deindustrialization to external demand implies that the industrial sector should be capable of adapting to trends in the world trade in order to ensure a certain level of growth. For Kaldor, the capacity is strictly dependent on appropriate repositioning in expanding markets (that is, the right specialization rather than price-based competition).

Insufficient GDP growth may thus be attributed to stagnation of world demand and an increase in the propensity to import and/or a reduction in the capacity to take advantage of world demand. That there has been a slow-down in world demand is fairly obvious. Whereas between 1960 and 1973, total OECD exports grew at an annual rate of 9 per cent, the rate was down to 5.2 per cent between 1973 and 1976 and a mere 3.4 per cent between 1979 and 1987.[6] This slow-down certainly explains some of the indicators of deindustrialization noted earlier. It is very likely that the pressure of stagnating world demand served to expose deficiencies in the adjustment capability of manufacturing industry in some nations.

If the trade specialization of an economy does not shift in accordance with the trends in the international division of labour and in the patterns of demand, the economy in question will see its relative position deteriorate. Recent studies on 'the end of established advantages'[7] show that many developed economies, far from improving their position in fast growing markets, allowed it, in fact, to slide between 1970 and 1980. The reversal in position of western Europe and the US in the world market for high-tech products (for example electrical and electronic equipment) is not very different to that which has occurred in the automobile industry and even in ailing sectors such as textiles. This inability of manufacturing industry to come to grips with the new conditions governing world trade has remained largely unexplained in the debate.

The importance of this second explanation of deindustrialization, of course, is ultimately conditioned by the role of the industrial surplus in the balance of payments of individual countries. Rowthorn and Wells (1987), rightly point out that one should distinguish between four groups of countries in accordance with the relative importance of their trade balance in manufactures.[8] These national differences regarding the importance of trade in manufactures, however, does not fully account for the various types and levels of deindustrialization displayed in Table 2.2.

Turning to the third major cause of deindustrialization, namely that relating to changes in the labour market, decline in industrial employment can reduce the leading role of key industries as shapers of industrial relations and wage conditions. This weakening paves the way for changes in the conditions of employment (see Chapters 7 and 8), which can have detrimental cumulative effects on employment at a local level, thereby destabilizing the build up of domestic demand as well as blocking the development of new and more productive forms of work organization.

The labour market approach to deindustrialization has tended to focus on two specific issues. The first concerns growth potential at a regional level: the loss of structure in local labour market areas has a cumulative effect that leads to underdevelopment. As a result, jobs in declining industries, together with those governed by the income level of the local population, are jeopardized. This, in turn, has an adverse effect on local investment and house prices. Such knock-on effects are well known, and can only be countered by public restructuring programmes aimed at encouraging economic regeneration. During periods of strong growth, such efforts, assisted by the general economic climate, proved to be effective. However, during periods of sluggish growth, with large numbers of areas being restructured, and with limited funding available from local and national bodies, the success of such efforts is by no means guaranteed. Consequently, some sectors may enter a long period of decline. There are many examples of this phenomenon, one particularly detailed analysis being that of derelict areas in the US by Bluestone and Harrison (1982).

The second approach is concerned with distortions in the overall distribution of income resulting from changes in the labour market, notably the decline of middle-income groups. The argument, following on from the preceding one but more macroeconomic in nature, is that job losses in industry and related effects on wage formation in other sectors, tend to polarize both wages and family income. This results in a dualization of patterns of household consumption, which has a deleterious impact on mass consumption markets and opportunities afforded to national producers.[9]

To summarize, the structural approaches, taken together, marshall a powerful explanation for deindustrialization. Each one also opens up new questions. We have shown that looking at changes in the productivity regime does not resolve the paradox of returns to scale. The demand-based explanations also raise open questions; it remains difficult to predict how far and fast the old industrialized countries can cope with drawbacks in the export position of their manufactured goods. The threat of dualism in consumption splitting up mass markets is another issue; the magnitude of this effect is under debate and therefore also its ability to alter the growth path. These open issues suggest that the present period ought to be considered, as proposed in Chapter 1, as a period of transition. A more decisive assessment of the significance of structural change requires some recognition of the role of new forms of division of labour, investment and demand formation which are emerging. Before attempting this, some consideration needs to be given to the view that the present situation may be the result of erroneous policies.

Inadequate Adjustment Policies?

It has been claimed by some that the so called deindustrialization problem originates from inadequate adjustment policies. While the foregoing view of deindustrialization laid the blame on income effects (import and export demand income elasticities) and 'qualitative' factors such as technological competitiveness and choice of specialization, the opinions set out below, emphasizing the role of policy, principally incriminate price effects. Wage costs in the industrialized economies are seen to encourage international specialization in up-market products, trade in high technology and large-scale domestic development of services (non-tradeable). From this standpoint, the decline in industrial employment and output is not in itself considered a problem. Instead, unemployment and trade deficits are seen to be symptoms of faulty adjustment, attributed to price distortions related to: inadequate exchange rates; excessive public sector spending; and ill monitoring of domestic natural resources.

Some authors have claimed that anomalous exchange rates could explain trade employment imbalances. Lawrence (1984), for instance has stressed that an 'unjustifiable' rise in the dollar in the early 1980s, adversely affected the performance of the US economy in foreign trade, and that once the turbulence of the mid-1980s subsided and the dollar came down again to reasonable rates, the US economy would reassert its competitiveness. This forecast did not come true, since, despite a fall in the value of the dollar of almost 20 per cent against the ECU between 1984 and 1989, the balance of trade deficit in 1989 was still about the same as the \$122 billion deficit in 1984. More disquieting, this stable deficit, since 1984, has included a declining trade balance in high-tech products. This situation has led Krugman (1988) to modify the thesis by apportioning more blame to variability of the exchange rate rather than its actual level. This factor, in being out of the hands of national governments, tends to point towards the greater efficacy of a more structuralist approach questioning the role of exchange within the international monetary system.

Work on the subject of disproportionate government spending, see especially, Bacon and Eltis (1976), emphasizes the crowding out effect of ever growing 'non-market' activities through the diversion (either by fiscal or financial intervention) of resources away from productive investment within the private sector. Two criticisms may be levelled at this approach. First, sectors involved in crowding out could also include the financial sector, which, then, also has to take the blame for industrial decay. Second, assumptions regarding the independence of the dynamics of public spending may be unjustified, in so far as increases in public expenditure after 1973 occurred at a time of declining investment, thus giving rise to a problem of cause and effect in tracing the causes of such expenditure. Here too, the argument tends to favour the role of structural changes over policy effects.

The third adjustment factor held responsible for deindustrialization concerns crowding out related to the discovery of natural resources and its monitoring by the State through control over the pace of investment and taxation. Three European countries provide an illustrative example: the Netherlands (with the tapping of its natural gas reserves in the 1960s), the UK and Norway. The study by Bruno and Sachs (1982) of the 'Dutch disease', after that of Corden and Neary (1978), reveals the substitution effects induced by the development of the energy sector, illustrating how these depended on fiscal policy. Following this logic, it can also be argued that public policy could have counterbalanced the detrimental effects on manufacturing, if more wise long-term strategies had been pursued. The 'Dutch disease' thus could also be interpreted as bad monitoring of two simultaneous structural changes: the discovery of a new non-renewable resource; and a worldwide restructuring of manufacturing activities.

Whether they refer to exchange rates, public spending or disordered foreign trade, the arguments put forward to explain deindustrializtion in terms of inadequate policies suffer from a common flaw. They blame policy errors for effects which are largely the outcome of major structural changes. This reinforces the need for a clearer assessment of the significance of present economic transformations.

NEW COMPLEMENTARITIES BETWEEN MANUFACTURING AND SERVICES

The varying signs of deindustrialization are manifestations of major processes of reorganization in the sphere of production. The question, then, is to identify the main characteristics of the growth pattern which may come out of this reorganization. The discussion below makes a contribution to this endeavour by focusing on changes in the division of labour between firms. Forms of competition, as a major element in the definition of a mode of regulation, are characterized by a nexus of institutions, practices and rules which shape the manner and extent to which production and consumption activities will depend on market mechanisms. We can thus assume that the new growth regime will be marked by some deep changes in the forms of competition accompanying changes in the organization of work within firms. More specifically, our discussion will concentrate on one specific aspect of emerging changes in the inter-firm division of labour, namely the relationship between manufacturing and business (or intermediary) services. Other relevant issues such as the proliferation of agreements between firms, joint ventures or changes in concentration are addressed more fully in the subsequent chapters. Our particular focus follows directly from the deindustrialization debate, which refers to the latter as separate activities.

On this latter point, the debate cannot be boiled down to being simply a matter of classification, as would be the case if all signs of deindustrialization were to disappear and if business services used in manufacturing were 'reintegrated' as tertiary activities of manufacturing firms. In fact, it can be shown that such a 'correction' would not really alter the distinguishing trends of manufacturing industries (for example, decrease in employment, slow-down in output growth, adverse trends in trade), since the order of magnitude of these intermediate activities does not match the structural changes discussed previously.[10] What is at stake is the qualitative dimension of the phenomenon. Let us first consider the nature of some of the new relationships between manufacturing and business services.[11]

The division of labour entered a new era in the 1970s and 1980s. Finance took on a new role, communications services expanded and firms started to contract out a wide range of tertiary activities. Instead of seeing services and manufacturing as, for example, different specializations in export markets, they should be seen as inter-dependent and inter-related activities. Before describing some of the emerging interfaces between goods and services in order to highlight the key features of the new complementarity, let us recall the main characteristics of the business services sector.

On Business Services

The diffusion of information technologies has radically transformed the conditions under which traditional intermediary activities such as transport, communication, finance and trade are organized. This chapter, however, is not primarily concerned with these services. Instead, it seeks to analyse the role of a range of specific services relating to business organization and corporate behaviour and strategy, which can be subsumed under the general heading of 'business services'. Numerous empirical studies have shown how these services (ranging from research activities and marketing to management consultancy) have revived manufacturing activities either in decline or threatened by product or process innovation. Studies by the OECD (1989a), (1989b) on the expansion of engineering, technical and other services to industry highlight some of the main features of recent trends. These include: the relative buoyancy of the sector (accounting for between three and six per cent of total value added in terms of investment and share of value added in each country); the jobs of higher than average grade and quality created by the sector; and an overall activity of the sector which is less sensitive to cyclical changes than other sectors.

The importance which these activities have already acquired is attested by the fact that they can be regarded as a new 'industry'. However, the usefulness of such a classification is limited by the extremely heterogeneous nature of the services involved, their considerable overlap and the sector's very low level of organizational coherence in being characterized by, on one side, a very high degree of concentration (a few multinational consultancy firms – the famous 'big eight') and, on the other side, a vast number of small firms that are difficult to classify.[12]

Business services have also become known for the positive role they play in a firm's production and sales position. First, they improve the quality of the firm's 'interfaces' with the market, via the deployment of advertising and marketing services, while accounting services and more broadly, management consultancy, serve to rationalize management and decision-making. Second, many 'engineering' and architectural, land surveying and quantity surveying services (related mainly to the construction industry and public works) reinforce the firm's productive capacity, both in the course of normal production and when upgrading capacity. Third, business services assist human resource management and allocation. This is a function performed by 'temporary employment services', whose role in relation to labour inputs is similar to that played by engineering services in relation to capital inputs.

Leaving aside temporary employment services, it may be said that a large proportion of business services accompany, in one way or another, investment in the traditional sense, in machinery or buildings. This is particularly true of engineering services, which comprise a set of activities that are dependent on and are linked to: a physical investment (excluding computer services); the desire for better market intelligence; consultancy and training; and computer services and software design. Most of these services impinge on the choice and implementation of investment. Because they have a lasting impact on the firm's assets such services are equivalent to an intangible investment.

Let us now turn to other aspects of the industry–services interface. Four ideal-types of such industry–service links will be described below, stressing:

1. the way in which manufacturing and services are combined to create products ('compacks') in which the use values of goods and services are inseparably linked;
2. the way in which industry continues, particularly where high technology is concerned, to provide the training and know-how needed to enter certain high value-added tertiary markets;
3. some new trends (whether complex services to major firms or co-operative services to network firms) which show a shift towards some kind of 'reintegration' of industrial and tertiary functions;
4. the new and expanded role of communications services to firms resulting from the telematics revolution.

Compacks: A Mixture of Goods and Services

The new industry–services complementarity is reflected in the fact that many manufactured goods embody a growing proportion of intangible 'products'. For example, many products based on the application of information technology in production have an intangible content. Research costs represent 87.3 per cent of total costs of the current generation of read–write computer memory. In many areas the growth of value added, relative to manufacturing, reflects a fairly rapid growth in the embodied 'intangible' content of the manufactured product.

Sometimes the 'tertiary' components of the product are joint or related products. For example, a lot of income is generated by the services that are sold along with computer hardware. In many high value-added activities (for example, computers, telecommunications), after-sales services are supplied along with the equipment proper, not only for maintenance but also to allow the equipment to be used to its full potential.

It is becoming increasingly clear, thus, that the distinction between manufacturing and services is no longer valid for a growing number of major product categories. Both the consumer and the manufacturer perceive the product as a 'compack' (complex products in which basic industrial and service components can be assembled into new products which combine the advantages of mass production and 'customized' production, that is, economies of scale and variety).

In these examples, complementarity results in original products which allow firms both to continue to benefit from the advantages of mass production (for producing the basic components of the 'compack') and to customize products (from being able to assemble the component elements in a multitude of combinations). Products can thus be tailored to markets in which product specification and differentiation have become increasingly important, but without loss of scale advantages.

Industry as a Source of Training and Know-How for Some High Value-Added Services

In the 1960s and 1970s it was widely held that there was a move towards a 'post-industrial' society, dominated by services, and that this was both inevitable and desirable. In the 1980s, however, a very different point of view emerged; one which stressed the continuing importance of manufacturing in the future of the advanced economies. However, arguments regarding the *role* of manufacturing have shifted. It is now argued that manufacturing should be protected and developed because it provides essential training and know-how for particularly high value-added services. This argument has probably found its most systematic expression in the study by Cohen and Zysman (1987), matched more recently by work from the Massachusetts Institute of Technology, see Dertouzos, Lester and Solow (1989).

Two arguments are elicited to underline the role of manufacturing. The first is that complementarities and linkages between industry and services, in most cases, originate in industry. A large body of know-how would be eroded if production were abandoned. The authors, to illustrate their argument, refer to disinvestment in the US steel industry in the 1970s, which led to a situation in which US companies (formerly among the world's leaders) had to import production engineering services to meet orders for some types of specialty steels. In contrast, US aerospace firms, because they have mastered the 'hard' technology of satellites and launchers, earn substantial income from the related meteorological and aerial cartographic services and from satellite telecommunications and observation satellites. On the basis of such evidence, Zysman and Cohen conclude that it would be extremely hazardous for a firm to specialize in services for products in which it no longer possesses manufacturing know-how.

The second argument in support of the importance of manufacturing is based on a comparison between two types of income: that generated by intellectual property (patents, etc,) and that generated by technological rents from mass-manufactured products. In 1986 the US surplus on intellectual property rights was only some $3 billion (against a foreign trade deficit of $170 billion in the same year). Income from the sale of patents and property rights alone is insignificant compared with the income resulting from when a manufacturer 'captures' and incorporates them within a production chain. The authors show that the key to Japan's success in its trade with the US consists precisely in accepting a small deficit on patents in order to be able to flood the US market with manufactures.

This second argument is reinforced on examination of the dynamics of innovation diffusion. Manufacturing know-how, including that related to products embodying imported patents, always generates authentic technical innovations as a product moves through its life cycle. The 'followers' thus become 'innovators', while firms which have made first-generation discoveries but have withdrawn from manufacturing run the risk of being excluded from second-generation innovations and products. The television industry provides an illustrative example. Because US firms stopped investing in this industry (practically from the start of the Japanese offensive into the US market), they were subsequently excluded from the design and production of second-generation products such as video recorders, compact discs and, even more serious (as the authorities are discovering today), high-definition television.

Quasi-integrated Services

Recent studies of the role of business services have stressed two categories of specific linkages: those concerning 'complex' services rendered to large firms; and locally based, 'co-operative' services within 'industrial districts'. Both imply long-term relationships between users and suppliers as well as some mutual involvement in each other's business, resembling some form of quasi integration. Let us briefly review each type of linkage.

A recent survey of services supplied to large firms, ERMES (1988), shows that the supply of services is not 'passive'; consultancy firms are not merely seeking to meet customers' requirements, but are also developing a genuine business strategy in three directions. First, they are increasingly trying to offer services which are tailored to the needs of those who make the strategic decisions in firms, that is, top management. They offer management skills and expertise on many variables (financial, legal and commercial) that form part of strategic decision-making. Second, they are branching out in their own particular areas of competence and developing multi-specialization capability if they do not possess it already. Third, the aim of multi-specialization is to offer an integrated package of products and services.

Following a period during which industrial firms contracted out services to a growing number of specialized firms, it now seems that some specialized services are becoming integrated with services which industrial firms have continued to perform in-house. There seem to be two converging trends. On the one hand, consultancy firms are trying to move closer into the centre of the user firm by offering integrated packages of know-how in the firm's various areas of business. On the other hand, user firms are moving towards a more permanent relationship with consultancy firms and are seeking assistance with sensitive strategic management decisions. Consultancy firms are thus no longer merely providing 'consultancy', but are participating in framing business strategy in a number of areas. From the legal standpoint, however, the user firm and the consultancy firm continue to be entirely separate entities, but their joint-venture, *a priori*, is established on a long-time basis.

Let us now consider the case of smaller service firms with a more local orientation. Localized production complexes, often referred to in the literature by the generic term 'industrial districts', give another example of the new division of labour between industry and services. When analysing the reason for the success of the various types of industrial districts, one is struck by the fact that competitiveness appears to be based less on cost-cutting or microelectronic process innovations than on organizational or product innovations which make it possible to tailor products more precisely to the needs of the market. Business services can thus be used as a means of avoiding the excessive rigidities of pure cost-competitiveness, via 'flexible specialization'.

The Italian clothing firm Benetton (the object of a large number of studies) typifies the new trend to the extent that its success has been built not on process innovation, but, essentially, on organizational and commercial ones. Benetton concentrates on marketing and sales, and manufactures very little itself. Its major organizational innovation lies in marketing. Its shops are run on franchises (that is, it does not commit any capital itself). The head office is kept informed daily of the level and changes in demand for each type of article. By keeping close track of demand and by setting its suppliers very strict standards, the company manages to cut production costs considerably, at the same time as keeping its finger on the 'pulse' of the market. Its innovations are purely organizational, based as they are, on a sophisticated system of communications between the firm and its suppliers, see OECD (1988).

Business services in industrial districts, in the traditional sense, consist in providing access to the interntional market, financing investment or carrying out research and development (R&D) for product or process innovation. They are 'co-operative' in that they are available to firms which may be competitors, but are nevertheless located in the same district (see Becattini, 1989). Such services may develop autonomously or result from a joint venture of local producers.

The New Role of Major Communications Services: the Case of Telematics

In addition to the traditional logistic role played by the telecommunications sector, the current technological revolution is also having an impact at the microeconomic level by increasing the number of ways in which firms can use the communications infrastructure. New services can now be supplied via telematic networks. Telecommunication systems (telephone, telex, radio), increasingly, have become transformed by computers and electronics, and to such an extent that the traditional concept of telecommunications no longer holds. First, information technology and digitization have made it possible to send, via the same medium, data which previously had to be transmitted via separate media.

For example, it is now common for telephone messages, data and images (fixed or moving) to be transmitted via the same medium. As the conventional network becomes digitized, it becomes an integrated services network.

Second, public and private value-added networks have been created. Terminals and various types of equipment – each with their own data bank and information processing capability – connected to the network allow data to be processed and enhanced in the course of transmission. At present, the move is towards 'intelligent' networks which do not merely transfer information from one point to another, as was the case with the traditional telecommunications systems, but are also capable of making qualitative changes to the information transmitted.

The nature and quality of external economies generated by networks are determined to a large extent by the proportion of enhanced services and value-added in the public network compared to those in private networks. For example, France has taken a radically different attitude towards telecommunications from the US or the UK. It has opted deliberately for a strategy to upgrade the public services network as much as possible (for example, by introducing videotex, tranpac and Numeris on the network). In contrast, in the US and the UK, these services are designed and supplied by private operators. Because of such differences, as well as variations in the regulatory framework, the benefits that economic agents will derive from the new telecommunications infrastructure will vary widely. The main impact of the new developments in communications networks is that external economies can now be internalized by firms, although the way in which this may occur will differ in accordance with the national regulatory context and the creativity of the firms themselves. Ultimately, it will mean that some economic agents will enjoy relative advantages over others.

At the microeconomic and practical level, firms use telematic networks in two phases. The first involves the automation of existing functions: complex top-down flows of paper between divisions or departments are replaced by thematic links of various types; users are linked together by microcomputers or data banks which store information. Direct computer links are also established with outside suppliers and partners via private networks which link up the participants involved in a project or in the production of a particular product. Case studies of such systems can be found in work by Antonelli (1989) and Bar and Borrus (1989). One illustrative example is that of General Motors, which, by networking all the activities involved in the design of a new model and allowing each participant to access all the information he or she needs via a common data bank, hopes to shorten the lead time for a new model by several months and to produce better-quality products which meet the customer's requirements.

This phase is usually followed by a second phase of reorganization. Reflecting the growing influence of Japanese just-in-time methods, production is restructured with a view to gearing it more closely to commercial and market requirements. In very many firms (for example, Peugeot in France, Bull in Italy and Nixdorf in Germany), the product mix is decided on the basis of the orders which are keyed into the computer, and orders are then placed with subcontractors.

These changes take time to implement and require know-how that can be acquired only progressively. The concept of a learning cycle is important for two reasons. First, it indicates that the benefits of telematics do not accrue automatically but are realized only after a certain time. Second, it highlights the crucial role played by the regulatory framework, and how the framework determines the opportunities open to firms (for example, by imposing standards on suppliers and users).

The telematic revolution is a further illustration of how new technical developments in services infrastructure can improve overall corporate competitiveness.

Interface Between Industry and Services: an Overview

Let us summarize the key features of the linkages between industry and services. Figure 2.1 presents a simplified, schematic picture of the various ideal-types of dynamic interfaces between industrial activities and services that have been described above.

The first interface, that of supplies of linked goods and services (K1) has been analysed by Bressand and Nicolaides (1988), in their study of the development of compacks. The second refers to the case (K2) in which the manufacturer has the know-how to develop high value-added services (often on a joint basis). Industrial know-how is extended to services, adding, where necessary, specific services know-how. An industrial market (M2.1) thus exists in parallel with a market for services (M2.2). The third case (K3) is the polar opposite of the previous case. Manufacturing is enhanced and revitalized by integrated (or complex) services supplied to major firms, or by co-operative services supplied to networked firms. In consequence, industrial markets (M3.1) are formed alongside the tertiary markets created (M3.2).

The fourth and fifth cases (K4 and K5) illustrate two complementary dimensions of advantage that can result from using telematics networks. In K4, services are used primarily as interfaces between 'producers' (be they partner firms and joint contractors in providing a specific product,

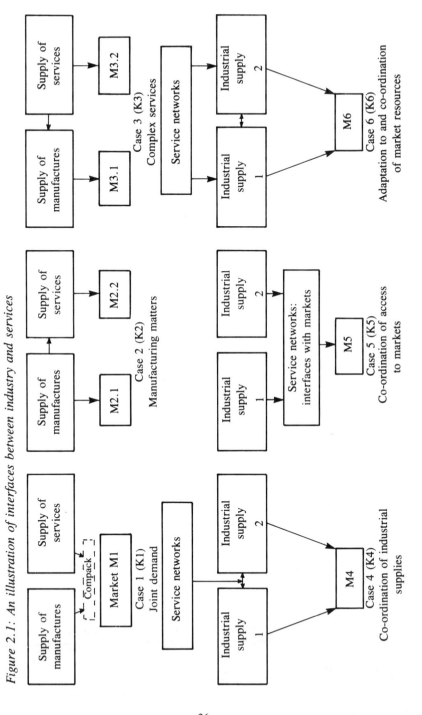

Figure 2.1: An illustration of interfaces between industry and services

or, as in the case of the 'Art to Part' strategy devised by General Motors, co-operation between service provision and divisions in the same firm). In K5, service networks are used as interfaces with the market. The complementary cases of K4 and K5 illustrate what has been called the first phase of the telematics learning cycle.

In contrast, the sixth interface (K6), is a dynamic extension of the two preceding ones. Customers' requests can be accessed, and manufacturers and sub-contractors linked up, via telematics networks, thereby making it easy to adjust manufacturing schedules to the exact specifications and varieties required by the market. This second phase of the learning cycle leads to various forms of internalization of external economies facilitated by the new telematics.

Table 2.3 The dynamic of industry–services interfaces*

	Phase 1	Phase 2
Link 1	K4	K3
	or	or
	K5	K6
	From logistic networks to internal reorganization	
Link 2	K2	K3
	Manufacturing industries develop some know-how in producer services which, in turn, stimulates manufacturing competitiveness	
Link 3	K1	K5
	Joint demand of goods and services which enhances the establishment of customer networks	

* Only linkages identified in the text are illustrated.

Table 2.3 illustrates some of the dynamic links between manufacturing and services. Link 1 refers to the interfaces between manufacturers, or between customers and suppliers, provided by telematic links, giving rise to functional reorganizations within and between firms. Regrouping and recentralization of activities or decentralization, modify the general relationships between clients, sub-contractors, partners and dealers. This leads to new forms of the social division of labour designed to improve the productivity and the competitiveness of the entities concerned.

Link 2 refers to a positive and 'virtuous' circle between manufacturing and services. Manufacturing industry develops tertiary know-how which, in turn, revitalizes manufacturing. Finally, link 3 refers to how the supply of and demand for 'compack' linked goods and services encourages the creation of 'complex' markets consisting of networks aimed at various types of customers.

These are a few examples of the dynamic linkages that are developing between manufacturing activities and services. On the basis of these examples one can examine, as is attempted in the final section of this chapter, whether such new forms of competition or market arrangements are contributing to the establishment of a new growth regime.

TOWARDS A NEW GROWTH REGIME

To assess the contribution of renewed forms of competition to the outcome of a new growth regime we shall begin with listing three of the main challenges to any post- or neo-Fordist growth regime and then go on to see how new forms of division of labour between firms can help to circumvent, counter or meet these challenges.

Features of the Post-Fordist Growth Regime

We shall discuss three major challenges affecting the dynamics of a new growth regime in the 1990s. These include first, the new potential brought about by information technologies, second, the major role of flexible high-volume production and, third, the internationalization of markets and production processes.

Information technologies, led by the development of microprocessors and the means of telecommunication, stand to revolutionize the entire system of industrial techniques. The pervasiveness of this new techno-logical system implies that all activities are affected without delay and that it can also spread to most countries at an unprecedented speed. However, there is a noticeable gap between this first step of diffusion, in which economic agents are aware of the changes before them and may even have acquired new equipment, and the time taken to put fully into use the new techniques.

Indeed, taking full advantage of the potential of these techniques requires some learning, and this, in particular, because their possibilities are not strictly dedicated to one use but are flexible. This raises a great deal of uncertainty about the capability of the users: customization of techniques does not mean that high-volume production is *passé*. On the contrary, a main feature of the post-Fordist growth regime will be, in one way or another, the persistence of high-volume production.

Flexible, high-volume production, which is how the mix of flexibility and high volume can be defined,[13] will remain a key feature of post-Fordism. For authors such as Piore and Sabel (1984), the new flexibility of production systems will greatly reduce the role of high-volume production. We would argue that production processes cannot but reconcile the large economies of scale provided by high-volume production with an increased ability to adjust and differentiate production. As shown in Coriat (1990), new technology has had the precise impact of enabling high-volume production to be more flexible in volume, timing and variety.[14]

The search for technological competitiveness may encourage product differentiation, but this objective need not conflict with achieving high-volume production. This is an organizational issue for firms; a matter of how production and marketing processes are restructured. The critical question is that the success of such restructuring may also require major adjustment of national systems of 'intermediation' (education, communication, trade, finance, etc.) which are not so easy to foster or foresee, especially in the context of the growing international integration of production and markets.

The internationalization of markets and production processes is a basic feature of any future growth regime. This process, in the first place, raises the question of what will remain of national economies as the global economy becomes more and more integrated. Production processes are often designed on a worldwide basis, which, potentially, could bring greater productivity gains. Who benefits from these new gains is not obvious. The productivity gains generated by this enlargement of the division of labour may benefit all parties involved or only that subset with greater control over prices or greater ability to generate positive externalities in the process (via learning-by-doing, technology transfer, incentives to innovate, opportunities for joint ventures, access to new markets and so on). The spread of benefits of this enlargement of markets and production designs on a global level is thus not easy to locate.

These benefits can also be delayed, not only for the usual reasons (for example, lags in adjustments or learning procedures) but also for financial reasons tied with the instability of exchange rates or local political situations. Therefore, the internationalization of markets and production could lead to a severe weakening of the cumulative growth process by depriving the latter of its national basis.

The three characteristics of future growth patterns which we have retained to be central, display some inner contradictions, and this raises some doubts about the consistency of some anticipated scenarios of post-Fordism. The question is to see to what extent the development of industry–services interfaces or how changes in the forms of competition can help to overcome these contradictions.

Contribution of Interfaces Between Industry and Services

On many grounds, business services are dedicated to deal with the tasks, mentioned above, concerning the organization of supply or management of demand. As shown, in looking at the various types of interfaces, business services offer a standard means of vertical inter-firm co-operation but also a mediating function to set up horizontal inter-firm co-operation. It does not follow that services, or changes in the forms of competition, provide the panacea for overcoming the shortcomings of any post-Fordism likely to prevail at the national level. Nevertheless, it is worth exploring precisely to what extent and in which conditions such intermediate activities can help to channel transactions in the post-Fordist economy. To this end, we shall relate the effects of these activities to the three aspects of structural change discussed previously.

With regard to the diffusion of new technologies, the role of hi-tech services is obvious, providing, as they do, information on the choice of equipment, guidance on their use and suggestions for redefining objectives. A strong complementarity exists between the use of such complex services and the IT equipment itself. The services represent a strategic share of the intangible investment required by the diffusion of IT.

The question, however, of whether such services should be provided in-house or not, still remains. Software services, for instance, show a trend towards more outsourcing, which can be explained by the need at both ends to keep in touch with innovations in computers and computing and by the cost advantage of subcontracting routinized jobs. However, a major limit to outsourcing remains the difficulty to set up an efficient relationship between the users and producers of such 'complex' services. We refer here to the intricate issue of the market provision of services. To overcome market imperfections, procedures certifying the quality of services have to be set up. Another limit comes from the fact that the service industries themselves may not really be in a position to co-ordinate the interface between users of IT and producers of IT equipment for the simple reason that these 'industries' are still either too dominated by the producers of equipment or too scattered, in terms of size and country of location, to set up the standards required for full utilization of the potential of IT. The expertise of such newly born activities seems still to be in the making.

In the search for flexible high-volume production, the logistics of business services can be helpful, in mainly two ways. On the supply side, services can contribute to mastering the new technologies of high-volume production and organizing production on a worldwide level. In-house services would not possess the ready expertise to enable significant changes. The increase in services which are externalized by firms in the context of structural adjustment of production processes goes hand in hand with the greater mobility of capital between sectors. The increased flexibility in combining and co-ordinating production capacity worldwide retains all the advantages of high-volume production in terms of static economies of scale at the same time as enlarging the scope for dynamic increasing returns (by enabling innovations, new divisions of labour and so on).

On the demand side, services can help to discover or create market niches. Tying services with the sale and use of durable goods or equipment (as in the case of 'compacks') is one example of such market segmentation. It provides a way of reconciling product differentiation with mass markets through the use of R&D, marketing, advertising or franchised distributors.

To a large extent, the ability of services to adjust production to flexible high-volume stems from their worldwide reach. It is therefore clear that services can play a vital role in the arena of the third structural process discussed earlier, namely the globalization of the world economy. In fact, the process of internationalization of services has been clearly linked with the multinationalization of firms. Firms in accounting, advertising and banking services first set up international operations to follow their clients abroad, and then developed their own international networks. They now stand as landmarks of the 'globalization' of the world economy. Such logistics could be seen as an ideal means of reaping all potential international economies of scale (that is, all productivity gains offered by improved organization at the global level).

The success of services in accompanying the increased internationalization of the economy, however, can also be seen as a process raising the level of competition and risk within national economies as each struggles for its share of productivity gains. This inner contradiction between, *ex ante*, more benefits from internationalization and, *ex post*, less certainty as regards end results at the national level, not only remains but seems to be ever more binding. The footloose nature that services have gained in the process can also be interpreted as a major shortcoming as it is bound to facilitate short-termism. This is a crucial issue to be considered when looking for policies to stimulate economic growth and employment.

Obstacles and Policy Perspectives

We have not ventured to give a full assessment of what will be the new growth regime, as a number of queries still remain. There is a real risk, for instance, that national economies will try to adjust to the new environment by sub-contracting or decentralizing some manufacturing productions towards countries with much lower wages, or that local business services will develop chiefly in order to weaken the bargaining power of the labour force.[15]

Leaving this possibility of regressive adjustment aside, and limiting ourselves to the assessment of the potential for a positive adjustment of productive systems, we are confronted with a dual aspect of structural change. The changes considered above could favour short-termism, globalization and a search for instant flexibility or they could help to set up long-term plans, enter long-term relationships and ensure against the chill wind of market forces or external obstacles. The example of financial services illustrates this dualism: their development could lead to casino capitalism or facilitate entrepreneurial ventures by risking capital on the future of real production and demand requirements.

We do not wish to argue that there is presently a fair balance between the two scenarios,[16] only that policies could try to favour the latter over the former. The means for this are classical: fiscal policy, regulation of the market provision of services and so on. This does not imply strictly protectionist policies. The normalization of most business services, in itself, requires a good deal of regulation. These regulations have to aim strategically in favour of long-term actions. This would help firms to favour long-term strategies and invest accordingly in manpower and equipment.

A strong component of such intervention is that it should take place at a local level. As the integration of national economies tends to reduce the room for manoeuvre of strategic policies, new social compromises could be made at the local, sub-national, level. Central and local funds could be used to set up logistics of semi-private services. Provided that the quality of the services and the jobs that they offer is certified, they could benefit from fiscal advantages or subsidies in proportion to the contribution they make to the development of local economies (as in the case of the celebrated 'industrial districts') or in accordance with their role in monitoring the labour market. Such incentives could contribute towards restoring demand regimes and the cumulative effects of productivity gains. This, effectively, would help to curb the trend towards a regressive flexibility which downgrades jobs in the labour market. A necessary condition for the successful restructuring of production in the direction of fostering a new growth regime is certainly to buttress the creation of good service jobs (see Chapters 8 and 9, especially on the benefits of upgrading). Placing obstacles to trends towards short-termism, through new social compromises at the local or regional level, with support at the national or supranational level (for example, the EEC) is a step in the right direction.

NOTES

1. OECD countries in which the share of industry was more than a third of total employment in the 1960s. This excludes countries such as Greece and Turkey.
2. The only exceptions were Japan and Italy, in which the growth differential reversed only after 1979. In some countries, such as the UK, the reversal occurred before 1973.
3. This cumulative causation pattern of economic growth provides a powerful schematization of the core elements of a Fordist regime of accumulation (see Boyer and Petit, forthcoming).
4. Most are based on international cross-sectional and time-series comparisons. See Cripps and Tarling (1973), Cornwall (1977), Boyer and Petit (1981) and the symposium on Kaldor's Growth Laws in *Journal of Post Keynesian Economics*, **5** (3)(1983).
5. Solow stressed the paradox of slow-down in productivity in times of such obvious diffusion of new technologies.
6. The reasons themselves of such a slow-down of world demand are manifold (dismantling of the international monetary system, oil shocks, Third World debt, etc.).
7. See, for instance, Lafay and Herzog (1989).
8. These include: the workshop economies which are highly dependent on a manufacturing surplus (Germany, Japan and Belgium); the emerging workshop economies, whose dependence on exports of manufacture is increasing (Italy and Sweden); the non-specialized economies, whose balances between manufactures and non-manufactures are changing little as a percentage of GDP (the US and France); and countries specializing in the trade of non-manufactures (Australia, Canada, Norway and the Netherlands).
9. This thesis is not uncontroversial. For Bluestone and Harrison (1986) and Thurow (1980), this decline is already showing in the statistics, while for Lawrence, (1984), the effect is negligible.
10. Rough estimates by Petit (1988) show that value-added in business services, provided by these intermediate uses of manufacturing, averaged to five per cent of the value added in manufacturing in 1980.
11. Hereafter, we shall not consider the role of household services, although their transformation will also play a major role in the future growth regime.
12. A classification used by INSEE in Paris for its surveys distinguishes six categories of services: engineering; architectural, land and quantity surveying; legal and accounting; advertising; temporary employment; and miscellaneous.
13. This expression 'flexible high-volume production', used by Cohen and Zysman, may seem less self-contradictory and therefore preferable to the term 'flexible mass production'.

14. For an assessment of different views on the issue of flexible versus mass production, see Amin and Robins (1990).
15. All the more so, since temporary manpower agencies are counted as business services.
16. One is struck by the fact that these structural changes have mainly affected countries with declining or stagnating manufacturing industries, while booming countries (for example, Japan or the four tigers of Asia) have exhibited patterns of growth which are very much in keeping with the old model of industrial cumulative causation.

REFERENCES

Amin, A. and K. Robins (1990), 'The Re-emergence of Regional Economies? The Mythical Geography of Flexible Accumulation', *Environment and Planning D: Society and Space*, **8**, 7–34.

Antonelli, C. (1989), *New Information Technology and Industrial Change*, CEE, Dordrecht: Kluver Academic Publishers.

Bacon, R. and W. Eltis (1976), *Britain's Economic Problem: Too Few Producers*, London: MacMillan.

Bar, F. and M. Borrus (1989), 'From Public Access to Private Connections: Network Strategy and National Advantage in US Telecommunications', OECD/BRIE Telecommunications User Group Project Seminar on Information Networks and Business Strategies, October, Paris: Organization for Economic Co-operation and Development.

Becattini, G. (ed.) (1989), *Modelli locali di Sviluppo*, Bologna: Il Mulino.

Bluestone, B. and B. Harrison (1982), *The Deindustrialization of America*, New York: Basic Books.

Bluestone, B. and B. Harrison (1986), 'The Great American Jobs Machine: The Proliferation of Low-Wage Employment in the US Economy', report prepared for the Joint Economic Committee, US Congress: Washington D.C.

Boyer, R. and P. Petit (1981), 'Progrès technique, croissance et emploi: Un modèle kaldorien pour six économies europeénnes', *Revue Economique*, **32**, 5.

Boyer, R. and P. Petit (forthcoming), 'Kaldor's Growth Theories: Past, Present and Prospects', in W. Semler and E. Nell (eds) *N. Kaldor and Mainstream Economics*, London: MacMillan.

Bressand, A. and K. Nicolaides (1988), 'Les services au coeur de l'économie relationnelle', *Revue d'Economie Industrielle*, **43**, 141–163.

Bruno, M. and J. Sachs (1982), 'Energy and Resource Allocation: A Dynamic Model of the "Dutch Disease"', *Review of Economic Studies*, **49**, 845–859.

Cohen, S. and J. Zysman (1987), *Manufacturing Matters, The Myth of the Post-Industrial Society*, New York: Basic Books.

Corden, W.M. and J.P. Neary (1978), 'Booming Sector and Deindustrialization in a Small Open Economy', *The Economic Journal*, December, 825–848.

Coriat B. (1990), *L'Atelier et le Robot*, Paris: Christian Bourgeois.

Cornwall, J. (1977), *Modern Capitalism: Its Growth and Transformation*, Oxford: Martin Robertson.

Cripps, F and R. Tarling (1973), 'Cumulative Causation with Growth of Manufacturing', *mimeo*, Department of Applied Economics: University of Cambridge.

Dertouzos, L., Lester, R.K. and R.H. Solow (1989), *Made in America: Regaining the Productive Edge*, MIT Commission on Industrial Productivity, Cambridge, Mass.: MIT Press.

ERMES (1988), 'La Demande de Services Complexes des Firmes Multi-nationales et l'Offre Correspondante', *mimeo*, Groupe de Travail du LAST-CLERSE: University of Lille.

Kaldor, N. (1966), *Causes of the Slow Rate of Economic Growth in the United Kingdom*, Cambridge: Cambridge University Press.

Kaldor, N. (1972), 'The Irrelevance of Equilibrium Economics', *The Economic Journal*, **82**, 1237–1255.

Kaldor, N. (1975), 'Economic Growth and the Verdoorn Law: A Comment on Mr Rowthorn's Article', *The Economic Journal*, December, 891–896.

Krugman, P.R. (1988), 'Deindustrialization, Reindustrialization, and the Real Exchange Rate', *Working Paper No 2586*, Cambridge, Mass.: National Bureau of Economic Research.

Lafay, G. and C. Herzog (1989), *Commerce International: La Fin des Avantages Acquis*, Paris: Economica.

Lawrence, R.Z. (1984), *Can America Compete?* Washington D.C.: The Brookings Institute.

Michl, T. (1985), 'International Comparison of Productivity Growth: Kaldor's Law Revisited', *Journal of Post-Keynesian Economics*, **7**, 4, 474–492.

OECD (1988), *New Technologies in the 1990s: A Socio-Economic Strategy*. Paris: Organization for Economic Co-operation and Development.

OECD (1989a), *Mechanisms for Job Creation: Lessons from the United States*. Paris: Organization for Economic Co-operation and Development.

OECD (1989b), *Information Technology and New Growth Opportunities*. Paris: Organization for Economic Co-operation and Development.

Petit, P. (1988), *La Croissance Tertiaire*, Paris: Economica.

Piore, M. and C.F. Sabel (1984), *The Second Industrial Divide: Possibilities for Prosperity*, New York: Basic Books.

Rowthorn, R.E. and J.R. Wells (1987), *De-industrialization and Foreign Trade*. Cambridge: Cambridge University Press.

Singh, A. (1977), 'UK Industry in the World Economy: A Case of De-industrialization', *Cambridge Journal of Economics*, **1**, 113–116.

Singh, A. (1987), 'Manufacturing and De-industrialization', in J. Eatwell, M. Milgate and P. Newmann (eds) *The New Palgrave Dictionary, Vol 3*, London, MacMillan: 301–308.

Thirwall, A.P. (1982), 'Deindustrialization in the United Kingdom', *Lloyds Bank Review*, **144**, 22–37.

Thurow, L.C. (1980), *The Zero-Sum Society*. New York: Basic Books.

Thurow, L.C. (1987), 'A Surge in Inequality', *Scientific American*, **256**, 5, 26–33.

PART TWO

Organizational Restructuring

3. From Hierarchy to 'Hierarchy': The Dynamics of Contemporary Corporate Restructuring in Europe

Ash Amin and Michael Dietrich

Undoubtedly, manufacturers face a new world. The sound corporation of the future will, for new reasons, resemble the solid corporations of the past.

Kumpe and Balwijn (1988, p. 81)

INTRODUCTION

These are confusing times, when it comes to understanding the organizational dynamics of contemporary industrial change. Old certainties have waned, while new ones are still in the making. The challenge to corporate profitability posed by the long recession of the 1970s, has forced many to rethink long held beliefs concerning the inexorability of trends towards vertical integration, market concentration and the growing power of large corporations. However, more attentive studies by professors of Business Studies, writing for journals such as the *Harvard Business Review*, talk of successful restructuring, by especially the Multinational Corporations (MNCs), in the face of crisis. We are told that MNCs are now 'thinking and acting more globally', see Ohmae (1989), pressing for vertical or systemic integration, with or without direct ownership (Kumpe and Bolwijn, 1988; Drucker, 1990), and remaining big in order to compete globally (Chandler, 1990). Indeed, some political economists now assert that the 'big firms are coming out of the corner' (Harrison, 1989) and that 'oligopoly is alive and well' (Martinelli and Schoenberger, 1991). This thesis, which describes the present period as one of increasing capital concentration, but without any necessary centralization of production[1] (Harrison, *op.cit.*), is not widely accepted. A more fashionable thesis is one which sees an organizational future dominated by the vertical disintegration of production and, by implication,

49

'deconcentration' in terms of questions concerning MNC control and command of the industrial economy. While both theses may agree about the direction of change in the organization of production viewed strictly in operational and technical terms (for example a tendency towards greater division of tasks between firms), there is no consensus with regard to the political economy of such change. For the second thesis, organizational change today is very much about the replacement of the large hierarchically co-ordinated corporation by the flexibly specialized small or large firm.

A third, and equally fashionable thesis as the second one, points to the rise in importance of organizational forms lying in between market and hierarchy. Drawing upon evidence of corporate restructuring in technology or knowledge-intensive as well as craft industries, towards the proliferation of sub-contracting, putting out, strategic alliances and inter-firm partnerships, a new literature has emerged emphasizing the significance of networking as an intermediary or superior form to vertical integration or disintegration. See, for example, Powell (1990), Beije (1988), Hakansson (1987), Johanson and Mattson (1987), di Bernardo (1989), Sako (1988), Miles and Snow (1986). Although much of this literature is careful to stress that networking is very much a contextual outcome rather than a general evolutionary trend in the economy, there is a tendency to imply that networking is becoming more hegemonic than before. More important, in stressing co-operation and mutual benefit as key features of networking, there is a strong suggestion in this thesis that the days of centralized corporate power could be numbered.

These, then, are three major conflicting perspectives on the organizational dynamics of contemporary industrial change. In the European context of, on the one hand, added uncertainty about which kinds of firms and territorial areas are likely to benefit from the creation of the Single European Market (SEM) and, on the other hand, the shift of the Eastern European economies towards market forms of governance, the need for a critical evaluation of these competing visions of change cannot be over emphasized. The new institutional developments will tend to build upon, rather than replace, dominant and emerging patterns of business behaviour, which is why a study of the latter is an essential precondition for deciphering the organizational dynamics of the 'New Europe'.

This chapter examines the corporate changes which have been taking place in the 1980s. It takes issue mainly with the body of thought composing the second thesis, which identifies vertical disintegration and the decentralization of economic power as major organizational tendencies of the future. Since a theoretical critique of this position has been developed elsewhere (Amin, 1989; Amin and Robins, 1990; and, in terms of a more narrowly defined economics, Dietrich, 1991), our objective here is to subject the main conclusions of the thesis to a stylized empirical investigation. Accordingly, following a section which summarizes the arguments of this thesis, the paper explores the direction of change within the EC of corporate activity in the field of mergers and acquisitions, joint-ventures and market concentration. These indicators are used as a crude proxy for examining the validity of the 'deconcentration' argument. In the final section, the chapter returns to the remaining two theses, through an assessment of the significance of more qualitative changes which the large corporations appear to have introduced in their organizational behaviour over the last decade.

VERTICAL DISINTEGRATION THESIS

The strongest case for vertical disintegration comes from a group of theories which describe the present as a period of major structural transformation and transition from one long phase of economic development to another one. Each phase is supposed to be characterized by very distinct organizational, technological and market arrangements. The theory of flexible specialization, pioneered by Michael Piore and Charles Sabel (Piore and Sabel, 1984; Sabel, 1982; Sabel, 1989) and developed further by others, for example, Hirst and Zeitlin (1991), Hirst and Zeitlin (1990), Pyke, Becattini and Sengenberger (1990), is perhaps the one which is most unequivocal about the shape of things to come. The argument is that the enormous increase in market fragmentation, market volatility and consumer sovereignty in recent decades, has terminally challenged the viability of the mass production system, which depended on economics of scale, vertical integration and dedicated machinery, to produce standardized goods for mass markets.

The new market circumstances, it is said, require a new basis for organizing and controlling production; a system of 'flexible specialization'. This is a system characterized by the detailed division of tasks between firms and units, decentralized decision-making and the use of generic technologies and polyvalent labour, in order to respond to rapidly changing market signals with the minimum cost, effort and time. It is argued that such a system of vertically disintegrated and decentralized production, is already a key feature of the most successful examples of industrial restructuring today. Three, now highly familiar, examples tend to be cited: the Marshallian, small-firm, craft industrial districts of the Third Italy regions; high-technology complexes, such as Silicon Valley in California in the US and Route 128 in Massachusetts in the US, which are distinguished by an articulate division of labour between large and small firms; and new experimentations with decentralized divisional structures by leading West German, Italian and Japanese corporations. The appeal is to the cost and flexibility benefits of having loose and locally based co-operation between specialist producers, against the rigidities and inefficiencies of vertical integration. Its narrow reductionism, through which issues concerning corporate power and market strength become a determinant of simply a particular set of production characteristics, has not prevented the spread of the influence of the flexible specialization thesis even into the world of industrial economics. For instance, Keith Cowling, in a recent paper which sets out a new industrial strategy for Europe, reiterates his well-known polemic against the inefficiency of giantism and monopoly, and goes on to appeal for a strategy designed to nurture the formation of small-firm industrial districts. With a sublime disregard for empirical evidence, he argues that flexible specialization has shown itself to be 'superior in performance' to the 'system of mass production operated by giant corporations' (Cowling, 1990, p. 181).

Similar conclusions about the future of industrial organization have been drawn recently by geographers inspired by the ideas of the French Regulation School of political economists. See Scott (1988), Storper (1989), Storper and Scott (1989). Here too, there is the assertion that an old Fordist regime of accumulation and regulation, which derived its strengths from the synergy between mass production, mass consumption and monopolistic regulation of the economy, is giving way to a new and more flexible, 'post-Fordist', phase of capitalist development. As with Piore and Sabel, flexibility in response to changing market structures, and the availability of scale reducing and scope maximizing new technologies, is seen to be the key condition for economic renewal. In organizational terms, the transition from Fordism to 'flexible accumulation', is claimed to encourage 'the tendency for internal economies to give way before a progressive externalization of production under conditions of rising flexibility.' See Scott (1988, p. 175).

Vertical disintegration, then, is counterposed to Fordist 'rigidities' associated with vertical integration and hierarchy, as a means by which economies of scale through task specialization can be combined with external economies of scope and scale. This can then allow producers to 'shift promptly from one process and/or product configuration to another, and to adjust quantities of output rapidly up or down over the short run without any strong deleterious effects on levels of efficiency.' See Storper and Scott (1989, p. 22).

With this theorization, too, the indirect implication is that post-Fordist times signal the end of monopolistic or scale advantages traditionally enjoyed by big firms. It should be stressed, however, that this interpretation of Regulation Theory does not necessarily reflect the position of regulationists based in France. Indeed, for the exponents of the approach based in Grenoble, for example de Bernis (1983), the new developments in production are very much a matter regarding the deepening and extension of monopolistic tendencies, but now on an international scale. For the exponents based in Paris, the organizational tendencies of what is preferred to be called neo-Fordism rather than post-Fordism, continue to remain a melange of old and new forms.

A third, also implicitly anti-monopoly, version of contemporary structural change, draws from the Schumpeterian stress on technology-driven transformation from one long wave of economic development to another. At the simplest level, attention is drawn to Schumpeter's (1939) discussion of the innovation-led 'creative gales of destruction', spearheaded by small entrepreneurs generating new knowledge and new technology to spark-off a new long wave, Rothwell and Zegveld (1982). The proliferation of such firms is noted to be a feature of the years of transition between long waves, before the tendency towards monopolistic behaviour by larger firms sets in, as the technologies of a long wave become widely diffused across the economy. The present period of emergence of a new technological paradigm based upon microelectronics, is interpreted as such a period of greater scope for small firms.

The Schumpeterian schema goes further than simply creating space for the 'boffin' small entrepreneur. In the emerging 'fifth Kondratieff', small firms can also take advantage of the trade-off between flexibility and scale which is permitted by the application of microelectronic technologies and decentralized management structures in production. Recently, this case has been argued by Dosi (1988), who sustains that under the old regime of scale-exploiting and inflexible technologies and management practices, short production runs necessarily implied high unit costs. Now, in contrast, such runs, which meet the greater flexibility demanded by rising market volatility and uncertainty, can be achieved at the same or lower unit costs as before, because new technologies and techniques of production are capable of lowering the scale threshold and the flexibility –output trade-off. Thus, the new long wave, in combining the same efficiency achievements of the previous wave with increased flexibility, implies more successful small firm entrepreneurship. While this argument may appear persuasive if simply the logic of production economies is considered, it fails to recognize other factors which giant firms use to their comparative advantage. It is clear from the work of Prais (1976) that plant-level, or technological, economies fail to fully account for the evolution of giant firms. He identifies marketing, research and development, and especially financial factors as central to explaining their development, see also Hannah (1983). It is consequently difficult to see why technological shifts alone should dictate the evolution of organizational systems, since the rationale for the latter is based largely on non-technological factors.

Almost unwittingly, a peculiar theoretical syncretism based on the theories of flexible specialization, post-Fordism and Schumpeterian long waves, has emerged to presage a period of vertical disintegration and industrial deconcentration. It is interesting to note that such epochal futurology is not, on the whole, to be found among economists developing new theorizations of the firm around contemporary organizational change. The later Williamson (1985), to some extent, is an exception, owing to his eagerness to acknowledge the existence of hybrid forms of organization between market and hierarchy; forms which transcend his earlier theoretical dualism between production and transaction costs as determinants of organizational form, Williamson (1975). In his more recent work (Williamson, 1985, p. 83), he is persuaded that organizational forms such as franchising and joint-ventures are much more common than at first realized. This recognition is based on his greater attentiveness to the economic, legal and organizational literatures. What is not clear, however, is whether Williamson now believes his earlier work to be wrong or obsolete.

'Post-Williamsonitis', in contrast, has produced a more nuanced literature which not only recognizes the co-existence of many organizational forms, but also accepts that these are shaped by contextual differences in the circumstances which confront individual firms. Some writers, for example, draw attention to the multiplicity of 'hierarchy' forms, even within the domain of MNCs, for example, single-product specialists, vertically integrated firms, diversifiers, conglomerates and 'hollow' corporations (Dosi, Teece and Winter, 1989; Buckley, 1988; Hood and Vahlne, 1988; Auerbach, 1988). Others, in contrast, identify the existence of a wide range of new forms of inter-firm co-operation and exchange, implying varying levels of quasi-integration (Monteverde and Teece, 1982), and disintegration (Aoki, 1984). Here too, the existence of different organizational arrangements (for example subcontracting, putting-out, franchising, strategic alliances, small-firm industrial districts, Japanese trading groups) are put down to contextual variations in market circumstances, technology and know-how, corporate and managerial legacies, socio-cultural environments, and so on (Wright, 1988; Powell, 1990; Granovetter, 1985; Dore, 1983; Best, 1990). Put together, this volume of writing on the changing boundaries of the firm, does not anticipate any epochal change from vertical integration, rigidity and monopoly to vertical disintegration, flexibility and deconcentration.

QUANTITATIVE ASSESSMENT OF SELECTED CORPORATE TRENDS IN THE EUROPEAN COMMUNITY

Any empirical, particularly quantitative, evaluation of the thesis predicting epochal change towards a reduced comparative advantage of the largest firms, is clearly fraught with problems. First, it can escape scrutiny by claiming that the latter process is only an emerging tendency, and therefore of limited quantitative significance. Second, and more important, currently available methods of data capture are weak on measuring the significance of many non-ownership based indicators of vertical disintegration and inter-firm collaboration. However, evaluation of measurable characteristics such as market concentration levels and patterns of mergers, acquisitions and joint ventures, does provide some indication of the degree to which giantism is becoming a feature of the past. This section undertakes such an evaluation, concentrating on changes during the 1980s at the level of the European Community as a whole.

Consider, initially, Table 3.1. The data reported in this table, cover operations involving at least one of the 1000 largest firms in the

Table 3.1 National, Community and international mergers (including acquisition of majority holdings) in the European Community

	1982–3		1983–4		1984–5		1985–6		1986–7		1987–8	
	no.	%	no.	%	no.	%	no.	%	no.	%	no.	%
National (Same EC Country)	59	50	101	65	146	70	145	63	211	69	214	55
EC (Different EC Countries)	38	32	29	18	44	21	52	23	75	25	111	29
International (EC+non-EC)	20	17	25	16	18	9	30	13	17	6	58	15
Total	117		155		208		227		303		383	

Note: Percentage totals may not add up to 100 due to rounding.

Source: EC (1987), *Sixteenth Report on Competition Policy*, European Commission, Brussels
EC (1988), *Seventeenth Report on Competition Policy*, European Commission, Brussels
EC (1989), *Eighteenth Report on Competition Policy*, European Commission, Brussels

European Community. Hence any merger activity indicated, especially among the larger of these firms, is likely to increase seller concentration levels (see the theoretical arguments in Hannah and Kay (1977). It is clear from Table 3.1 that total merger activity has increased in each year shown. In terms of annual growth rates of total mergers, these were in the region of one third for 1982/3–1983/4, 1983/4–1984/5 and 1985/6–1986/7. On the other hand growth rates for 1984/5–1985/6 and 1986/7–1987/8 were, respectively, 9 per cent and 26 per cent. Looking at trends that may be evident within the total figures, it appears that during the first half of the 1980s, intra-national mergers increased in importance, but in the second half of the decade, their relative importance declined. The reverse is apparent for mergers between EC countries. In addition, the large absolute size of international mergers in the most recent period should also be noted.

Table 3.2 National (N), *Community* (C), *and international* (I) *mergers by sector* in the European Community*

	1982–3			1983–4			1984–5			1985–6			1986–7			1987–8		
	N	C	I	N	C	I	N	C	I	N	C	I	N	C	I	N	C	I
Food	1	2	0	7	2	2	20	1	1	25	7	2	39	11	2	25	18	8
Chem	10	13	3	21	13	11	25	23	5	23	28	6	38	27	6	32	38	15
Elec	5	3	7	9	2	2	13	5	4	10	0	3	33	6	2	25	4	7
Mech	12	5	2	16	3	4	24	4	3	19	3	7	21	8	2	24	5	9
Comp†	–	–	–	0	0	0	2	0	1	1	0	0	2	0	0	2	1	0
Metal	7	1	2	9	0	0	13	3	1	14	1	2	15	4	0	28	9	3
Trans	2	0	1	5	3	2	8	2	0	6	0	4	15	6	0	3	9	3
Paper	7	1	1	11	1	1	10	5	3	18	4	5	17	7	1	24	6	4
Extra	4	3	2	3	2	2	7	0	0	7	3	0	8	1	0	9	2	1
Text	4	3	2	5	0	0	7	0	0	7	1	1	4	2	0	11	2	1
Cons	6	4	0	13	3	1	14	1	0	12	2	0	13	3	3	21	12	0
Other	1	3	0	1	0	0	3	0	0	3	3	0	6	0	1	10	5	7
Total	59	38	20	100	29	25	146	44	18	145	52	30	211	75	17	214	111	58

* *Key:* Food: food and drink; Chem: chemicals, fibres, glass, ceramic wares, rubber; Elec: electrical and electronic engineering, office machinery; Mech: mechanical and instrument engineering, machine tools; Comp: computers and data-processing equipment; Metal: production and preliminary processing of metals, metal goods; Trans: vehicles and transport equipment; Paper: wood, furniture and paper; Extra: extractive industries; Text: textiles, clothing, leather and footware; Cons: construction; Other: other manufacturing industry.
† For 1982–3 this sector is included under mechanical engineering.

Source: as Table 3.1

A more detailed sectoral breakdown of total merger activity is provided in Table 3.2. It would appear that underlying the aggregate data are three identifiable industrial groupings: sectors which follow the same trend as the overall figures (food, chemicals and transport); sectors which have increased merger activity both domestically and overseas (metals and construction); and industries which appear to have a less obvious trend of internationalization.

Table 3.3 EC mergers by geographical type and economic conditions in industry, 1982–7 (%)

	Strong growth	Moderate growth	Weak growth
National	53.5	70.0	77.1
EC	32.5	19.2	16.8
International	14.0	10.0	6.1

Note: Percentage totals may not add up to 100 due to rounding.

Source: Jacquemin, Buiges and Ilzkovitz (1989).

A possible explanation of this three-way classification is provided in Table 3.3. It is clear that a direct relationship exists between the strength of growth and international orientation of merger activity. The more dynamic industries, which constitute the leading edge of growth in the current phase of economic development in the advanced economies, have a more international focus. Consequently, as these industries increase their relative importance over time, the proportion of purely nationally based mergers will fall.

The picture indicated in Table 3.3 is further complicated by the evidence for motives for mergers and acquisitions, given in Table 3.4. Through the 1980s, there appears to have been a shift in the rationale for merger activity. In parallel with a reduction in the importance of mergers oriented towards rationalization and restructuring, there has been a growth in the importance of those geared towards strengthening of market position. This, together with mergers for expansion purposes, accounted for a growing proportion of the total in the 1980s, rising to 45 per cent in 1987–8, which tends to suggest that there is little evidence for a decline in the importance of scale economies and large size. The insignificance of specialization and the growing importance of complementarity as a motive for mergers, may lend support to the development of scope economies. The reasons, then, tend to suggest that merger

Table 3.4 Main motives for EC mergers and acquisitions (%)*

	1983–4	1984–5	1985–6	1986–7	1987–8
Rationalization, restructuring	38.6	37.8	35.0	29.7	14.8
Expansion	21.9	19.9	18.1	22.1	19.6
Complementarity	—	11.8	14.4	12.4	19.6
Strengthening market position	7.0	9.3	11.3	11.5	25.4
Diversification	9.7	5.6	12.5	5.7	8.3
R&D	4.4	1.9	2.5	5.3	0.7
Specialization	3.5	7.5	1.9	1.3	1.8
Other	14.9	6.2	4.4	11.9	9.8

Note: Percentage totals may not add up to 100 due to rounding.

* Includes only mergers for which precise information about motives is available.

Source: as Table 3.1.

activity in the 1980s sought to exploit both the scale and scope advantages of size.

This conclusion is in line with that drawn recently by Jonquieres (1990a,b), who points to a number of industry specific reasons for merger and acquisition activity in Europe. In the chemicals sector there has been a restructuring towards core business activity, away from conglomerate structures. Thus peripheral activities have been traded across Europe. In other sectors, particulrly those that are high technology intensive, increased internationalization and opening up of domestic markets has led to merger and acquisition activity to exploit scale economies. Characteristically, international mergers have followed consolidation at a national level. Finally, in the food sector the main reason for internationalization has been to establish global brands and distribution networks.

The industries highlighted here have tended to be those that have been most actively involved in merger activity (see Table 3.2). While industry specific characteristics are important they should not, however, obscure the fact, confirmed also by Jonquieres (1990a), that they are an aspect of a general internationalization and integration of economic activity among especially the industrialized countries. This, in turn, suggests that contemporary European merger trends should not be reduced simply to the effects of the 1992 project, since the project is itself part of a wider and earlier trend towards sectoral and corporate integration across Europe.

The data in Table 3.5 add an interesting dimension to this picture, by showing that in each year, at least one half of mergers within the EC are on a giant scale. In terms of trends, although activity in the largest size category declines from being 75 per cent of the total in 1982–83, it then rises again over the decade, to account for 70 per cent of EC mergers in 1987–88.

*Table 3.5 EC mergers by size (combined sales) of firms involved**

	Under 500 m ECU		500–1000 m ECU		Over 1000 m ECU		Total
	no.	%	no.	%	no.	%	no.
1982–3	16	14	13	11	88	75	117
1983–4	29	22	18	14	85	64	132
1984–5	62	34	31	17	92	50	185
1985–6	63	31	33	16	108	53	204
1986–7	101	33	31	10	171	56	303
1987–8	61	16	54	14	268	70	383

Note: Percentage totals may not add up to 100 due to rounding.

* Totals may differ from those in Table 3.1 because the turnover of some firms involved is not available.

Source: as Table 3.1.

To summarize, vertical and horizontal integration through mergers and the principle of giantism, continue to remain an important aspect of corporate strategy, something which the internationalization and liberalization of markets is tending to accentuate. The deployment of such a strategy is one of the ways in which the largest firms continue to exploit their comparative advantage.

If the analysis of mergers suggested here is correct, a tendency for European industry to become more concentrated should be apparent. This is confirmed by the evidence in Table 3.6. During the 1970s and up to 1986, seller concentration levels increased for all size categories shown. Taking the figures at face value, the trend to increasing concentration levels appears to have halted by 1987–8, but this conclusion is suspect. First, examination of the firm size data indicates that throughout the 1980s the same two companies, Shell and BP, featured as the largest in terms of turnover in the EC, and more generally, other oil companies also featured in the top 100. Consequently, oil price changes will have had a disproportionate effect on the data. If the oil companies are excluded

Table 3.6 Evolution of concentration in EC industry: shares of largest firms in total turnover (%)

	1972	1975	1980	1981*	1982*	1983	1984	1985	1986	1987	1988
Top 10	6.3	7.3	8.3	8.7	5.2	6.2	6.5	6.6	7.2	7.0	6.4
Top 20	10.3	11.7	13.1	13.6	7.7	9.0	9.4	9.8	10.9	10.6	9.8
Top 40	15.6	17.3	18.7	19.2	10.5	12.3	13.0	13.6	15.5	15.0	13.9
Top 100	—	24.0	25.0	26.3	14.8	17.2	18.2	19.0	22.2	21.4	20.0

* For 1972–81 the data are based on EUR 10 and NACE 2–4; for 1982–88, on EUR 12 and NACE 1–4. NACE 1–4 covers all industry except building and civil engineering. NACE 1 covers energy and water industries.

Source: EC (1983), *Twelfth Report on Competition Policy*, European Commission, Brussels
EC (1984), *Thirteenth Report on Competition Policy*, European Commission, Brussels
Times 1000 (various dates)
Eurostat (various dates)
Personal communication with EC Directorate A

from the data set, the concentration ratios continue to increase for 1982–86, and then level off. A second reason why the data in Table 3.6 may not accurately track changes in concentration levels, follows from the importance of international mergers in 1987–88, as detailed in Table 3.1. If a previously EC-owned company loses any independent status following merger/acquisition with a non-EC company, the measurement of concentration at the EC-level will be affected. In other words, evidence of declining concentration in the EC in more recent years may be more a statistical accident than a reality.

The above discussion has been restricted to industry qua industry. Table 3.7 describes the experience of the service sector, and shows that this branch of the economy has also experienced a growing number of mergers in the 1980s. For the four time-periods shown, the rate of growth of total mergers has increased by 5 per cent for 1984/5–1985/6, 38 per cent for 1985/6–1986/7 and 56 per cent for 1986/7–1987/8. One interesting difference with the industrial branches of the economy is that there is no obvious internationalization occurring. As far as size considerations are concerned, Table 3.8 shows that over the period shown, mergers in the smallest size category have grown in relative importance, but the absolute size of the 'giant' mergers should still be noted.[2]

Up to now in this section, the question of growing oligopolistic behaviour in the European economy has been examined using merger activity and market concentration ratios as the main measures. Such an

Table 3.7 Service sector mergers in the European Community

	1984–5		1985–6		1986–7		1987–8	
	no.	%	no.	%	no.	%	no.	%
Distribution								
National	30	45	27	39	40	36	40	23
Community	3	4	6	9	5	5	8	5
International	1	2	0	–	4	4	9	5
Banking								
National	10	15	12	17	22	20	53	30
Community	6	9	4	6	3	3	12	7
International	2	3	9	13	10	9	13	7
Insurance								
National	7	10	5	7	17	15	14	8
Community	7	10	3	4	7	6	14	8
International	1	2	4	6	4	4	12	7
Total	67		70		112		175	

Note: Percentage totals may not add up to 100 due to rounding.
Source: as Table 3.1.

Table 3.8 Total EC service sector mergers by size (combined turnover)*
of firms involved†

	Under 500 m ECU		500–1000 m ECU		Over 1000 m ECU		Total
	no.	%	no.	%	no.	%	no.
1984–85	19	28	8	12	40	60	67
1985–86	19	29	12	19	34	52	65
1986–87	54	48	5	5	53	47	112
1987–88	89	51	12	7	74	42	175

* One tenth of assets in the case of banks and premium income in the case of insurance companies.
† Totals in Tables 3.7 and 3.8 may differ because the turnover of some firms involved is not available.
Source: as Table 3.1.

approach, may give undue bias to British and American companies, which accounted for 40 per cent of all cross-border mergers in Europe between 1986 and 1988 (Jonquieres, 1990b). However, Continental European companies may have been more intensively involved in non-

Table 3.9 Joint-ventures in European Community industry

| | 1982–3 | | 1983–4 | | 1984–5 | | 1985–6 | | 1986–7 | | 1987–8 | |
	no.	%	no.	%	no.	%	no.	%	no.	%	no.	%
National	23	50	32	46	40	49	34	42	29	32	45	40
Community	8	17	11	16	15	18	20	25	16	18	31	28
International	15	33	26	38	27	33	27	33	45	50	35	32
Total	46		69		82		81		90		111	

Source: as Table 3.1.

merger based integration, the importance of which is captured by trends concerning joint ventures in the course of the 1980s.

As Table 3.9 shows, total joint-venture activity has increased by almost two and a half times in the six years from 1982 to 1988. The more detailed breakdown shown in Table 3.9 indicates that intra-Community joint-ventures have increased in relative importance, at the expense of joint activity between companies of the same country. The sectoral detail shown in Table 3.10 indicates that, on the whole, the same industries are

Table 3.10 National (N), Community (C), and international (I)
joint-ventures by sector* in the European Community

| | 1982–3 | | | 1983–4 | | | 1984–5 | | | 1985–6 | | | 1986–7 | | | 1987–8 | | |
	N	C	I	N	C	I	N	C	I	N	C	I	N	C	I	N	C	I
Food	1	0	0	2	1	0	1	0	1	2	1	1	0	1	4	6	3	1
Chem	4	1	3	4	2	5	5	0	7	7	7	9	3	1	10	7	5	12
Elec	4	1	5	8	1	10	3	3	7	10	4	5	4	3	14	8	5	7
Mech	3	1	1	5	1	3	8	3	5	5	1	4	9	0	8	4	0	3
Comp†	–	–	–	–	–	–	3	0	0	0	1	1	1	1	3	2	1	2
Metal	2	3	2	6	3	1	8	1	1	5	1	4	1	1	1	2	6	2
Trans	2	0	0	3	1	3	3	1	2	0	3	1	1	3	0	1	4	1
Paper	2	2	0	0	1	3	4	4	2	0	0	0	3	1	2	7	1	1
Extra	2	0	1	2	0	0	3	1	1	2	0	0	0	1	0	3	1	1
Text	0	0	1	0	0	0	0	1	0	0	0	0	0	0	0	0	2	1
Cons	1	0	1	2	1	0	2	1	1	3	2	0	3	2	0	1	2	3
Other	2	0	1	0	0	1	0	0	0	0	0	2	4	2	3	4	1	1
Total	23	8	15	32	11	26	40	15	27	34	20	27	29	16	45	45	31	35

* For definitions of sectors see Table 3.2.
† Before 1984–5 this sector is included under mechanical engineering.

Source: as Table 3.1.

Table 3.11 Main motives for industrial joint-ventures (%)*

	1983–4	1984–5	1985–6	1986–7	1987–8
R&D	34.3	23.6	25.7	18.5	28.7
Production	11.9	14.6	19.4	18.5	20.2
Marketing	29.9	9.1	—	22.2	3.2
Rationalization, restructuring	17.9	25.5	16.1	13.6	13.8
Diversification	—	—	—	1.2	2.1
Expansion	—	7.3	11.3	4.9	5.3
Complementarity	3.0	—	8.1	3.7	5.3
Strengthening market position	—	—	11.3	3.7	3.2
Other	3.0	19.9	8.1	13.6	18.2

* Includes only joint-ventures for which precise information about motives is available.
Source: as Table 3.1.

involved in joint-ventures and mergers, perhaps indicating that to some extent the two are alternative means of organizing large scale activity.

Table 3.11 details the main motives for industrial joint-ventures in the 1980s. The relative unimportance of complementarity is significant. It was suggested earlier that this factor may represent the development of the scope economies which are of central importance to the post-Fordism thesis. It is less important as an explanation of joint-ventures than for mergers. Hence, if scope economies are becoming more central to corporate strategies, it may be that their effects are being internalized rather than being exploited on an inter-firm basis. It is possible, however, that particular scope economies are included under the first three headings in Table 3.11 (R&D, production and marketing). These motives constitute the overwhelming rationale for joint-ventures, but the advantages of large size in these areas are also obvious. In addition, as Table 3.10 shows, in the mid-1980s, roughly two thirds of industrial joint-ventures occurred in four sectors: chemicals, electronic engineering, mechanical engineering and metals production. These sectors cut across both concentrated and relatively unconcentrated industries. Hence any generalizations concerning the comparative advantage of small firms accruing from the development of inter-firm networks would seem to be inappropriate.

'HIERARCHY' WITHOUT HIERARCHY: COMBINING OLIGOPOLY WITH OLIGARCHY

The evidence presented in the preceding section is far from exhaustive, but it does tend to suggest that competition in a new, unfettered, European market is likely to be more oligopolistic than ever before. This does not, however, in any way imply that the organizational aspects of such competition will remain unchanged. On the contrary, there is much evidence to show that the 1980s were a period of major restructuring in terms of qualitative changes in the organizational strategies deployed by different corporations. In some instances, this involved a deepening of old 'Fordist' forms, notably in the mass production or continuous flow industries in which competition is intensely oligopolistic. For instance, in the food, printing, chemicals and mass consumer durables industries, vertical integration and the pursuit of scale economies remains ever present. In certain instances, this has been accompanied by forward integration by the majors in order to gain control over markets and distribution outlets, as well as tighter links between assemblers and suppliers, see Kumpe and Bolwijn (1988).

In other instances, as John Dunning has argued recently (Dunning, 1988), the long recession caused MNCs to review their product strategies and move markedly towards specialization in the high value-added or expanding product markets. The aim appears to have been to focus on areas of greatest technological marketing advantage and sell off interests in secondary or peripheral markets, see also Chandler (1990). Such product divestment has been accompanied also by efforts to achieve greater in-house product differentiation and flexibility, but without loss of central control over operations along the value-added chain. For Dunning (1988), this has been achieved via the deployment of generic and multifaceted technologies, closer co-ordination between product and production strategy and the extensive utilization of advanced information and communications technologies between plants and divisions in different locations.

In strictly functional and operational terms, examples of 'flattened hierarchy' and the decentralized divisional structures so endearing to the theorists of flexible specialization (for example, Sabel's oft-cited companies such as Bosch, Olivetti, Montedison and Xerox), may well have come to the fore. But, even in such numerically limited cases of decentralization, there is little evidence to suggest that centralized control over strategic matters such as research and development, investment and marketing have been relinquished. This is admitted also by Peter Drucker, the California-based business guru so enamoured by decentralized manufacture:

Today's factory is a battleship. The plant of 1999 will be a 'flotilla', consisting of modules centred either around a stage in the production process or around a number of closely related operations . . . [but] overall command and control will still exist.

Drucker (1990, p. 98)

This paradox of simultaneous integration and disintegration also applies to the concept of 'systems organization' beginning to be used in manufacture by the most advanced corporations. Here too, broad functions such as supply, design, manufacture and distribution are run as independent modules, but within an overall framework of an integrated flow system. The more operational and functional disintegration within the corporation, the greater the degree of integrated management and control. The logic of this literature is to suggest that companies should be conceptualized as loci of strategic control, see Dietrich (1990). As will be argued below, this shift away from an ownership-based view of the firm facilitates an understanding of aspects of corporate restructuring which simultaneously involve vertical disintegration in terms of ownership and integration in terms of control.

The most interesting aspect of corporate restructuring which has given the impression of growing decentralizing and anti-monopoly tendencies in the economy, concerns the changing nature of large firms' linkages with suppliers, buyers and competitors. Turning to backward linkages first, at the most extreme pole, the phenomenon which has raised most media and policy attention is that of the 'hollow corporation' (*Business Week*, 1986). On this side of the Atlantic, Benetton, the Italian fashion clothing company, can be cited as an example of this phenomenon. In this company, all but the development, design and distribution of the product is sub-contracted to a myriad of small, specialist, firms. Such extensive production sub-contracting allows least-cost and rapid responses to ever-changing market signals through the externalization of risk, uncertainty and productive capacity. By focusing on activities such as R&D, marketing, distribution and finance, the 'hollow corporation' effectively retains control in all of the strategic areas required for securing profits and market leadership.

Researchers who have studied companies such as Benetton in detail (for example, Belussi, 1987; Brusco and Crestanello, 1990), show that in such cases of 'hollowing-out', key aspects of 'hierarchy' remain intact. Though, for the sake of ensuring reliability of delivery and quality, links with sub-contractors may be stable and negotiated, the latter still have little say over matters such as fluctuations in the size and frequency of orders, delivery schedules, price and liberty to work for other contractors in peak periods. In short, viewed from the perspective of the subcontractor, the problem of centralized control and dependency on one major source of work remains unresolved even in this instance of 'post-Fordist' vertical disintegration. But, this is not the most common form of sub-contracting to have emerged in recent years. Outsourcing by corporations is not, of course, a new phenomenon. It is also an extremely heterogeneous phenomenon which escapes generalization, varying as it does, between firms and sectors, degree of permanence, reasons for deployment and taxonomy of forms (Harrison and Kelley, 1990). However, there is a body of literature which claims to identify significant qualitative changes – in most cases improvements – in the nature of buyer–supplier relations in the big firm sector. For instance, a study of sub-contracting among leading firms in the Welsh economy (Imrie and Morris, 1988) identifies a significant increase in externalization, with buyers stressing greater emphasis on partnership and collaboration rather than on dependence. Similarly, other research, especially voluminous on the motor industry, identifies the shift towards stable and lengthened contracts between firms and their 'privileged status suppliers', involving joint design work, sole-sourcing agreements, purchase of entire systems of sub-assemblies, respect for respective technological strengths and a high premium on total service and quality offered by suppliers (Helper, 1989a, 1989b; Loveridge 1990). Klaus Semlinger in Chapter 5 neatly summarizes the significance of this new development by describing outsourcing as strategic contracting which combines incentives to innovate (provided by the market) with production and communication cost efficiency of asset specificity and the adaptiveness of loosely coupled systems, without additional transaction costs.

To what extent, then, do such new sub-contracting arrangements involving the formation of inter-company production associations, overcome the old dichotomy of market and hierarchy? Or, what amounts to the same thing, how should we conceptualize networking which is not based on dependence and is therefore not part of any one centre of strategic control? At face value, the organizational significance of this trend towards networking cannot be denied. But, against this, should be stressed that 'partnership' is a term applied to only a small number of suppliers of 'preferred status', that is, suppliers of equal strength or sub-contractors who are indispensable. As Powell notes in relation to the outsourcing of highly standardized components,

> there is little concern for collaboration or supplier design work; instead the effort is aimed at finding . . . suppliers that can provide parts at the lowest possible price. Such practices could be a return to earlier times, a part of a

campaign to slash labor costs, reduce employment levels and limit the power of unions even further.

Powell (1990, p. 32)

Even in the case of less hierarchical inter-company associations, it should be noted that their emergence is often related to the profitability of the focal company; a situation in which the old adage of a supplier reaping a disproportionately small share of the profits in relation to its contribution to total value-added, remains unchallenged. Thus, even the flattening of 'hierarchy' between dominant buyers and dominant subcontractors or suppliers need not be interpreted as an example of decentralized corporate control. It is, in effect, an elaboration of hierarchy: a case of quasi-integration between large players along the value-added chain, which potentially can work against the interests of smaller suppliers excluded from the network. See Amin and Smith (1991) for an illustration from the car industry.

Yet another qualitative shift in the organizational behaviour of large firms which has involved a loosening of corporate boundaries, has been the proliferation, especially in the 1980s, of new forms of joint-ventures and strategic alliances. Here too, as argued below, the implications of networking are not at all obvious, in terms of the political economy of corporate power and control. This is particularly the case with regard to the MNCs. There is a growing body of literature which identifies the formation of new global partnerships, between MNCs, of a multi-dimensional nature and on a long-term basis in conjunction with or as a substitute for foreign direct investment. Data related to the trend in joint-ventures in Europe has already been presented in the preceding section. Case study work on strategic alliances has been undertaken mainly in high-technology intensive industries and activities such as research and development (Howells, 1990), semiconductors (Vonortas, 1990), aerospace (Mowery, 1987), computers (Benassi, 1990) and machine tools (Vonortas, 1990). There have also been other, multi-industry, studies of inter-firm alliances and partnerships, for example Zagnoli (1987), Mowery (1988).

Interestingly, all the evidence tends to confirm that the new forms of alliance dominate those industries which are dependent upon large R&D budgets and continual technological innovation for effective competition. They also tend to be industries characterized by growing demand, but often on a stage dominated by major international players. These new 'strategic alliances' between competitors are varied and involve joint R&D, technology transfer and licensing agreements, but also collaborative marketing and co-production in notably new areas of product diversification.

There are a number of reasons explaining the rationale for strategic alliances between the major companies. In an exhaustive review of the relevant literature, Nicholas Vonortas (1990), identifies some of the main reasons. One is the desire of companies dominating the high-tech industries to control the transformation of the market in the context of rising costs and uncertainties attached to constant R&D and product renewal. Another is the use of alliances as a means of rapid access to knowledge, and in a way which allows both partners to secure competitive advantage in their respective areas of strength. Third, the rising importance of selling systems rather than individual products induces cooperation between firms. Alliance formation allows risk reduction, the achievement of scale economies, the gain of quasi-integration advantages by linking up complementary strengths, the sharing of high R&D costs and the co-optation or blockage of competitors. In general, it is a strategy for adjusting to and coping with changing market and technological environments through an organizational flexibility based on synergy between specialists who need each other.

How is this form of blurring of corporate boundaries and greater cooperation between firms to be interpreted? Does the diffusion on a global scale of 'dynamic networks and industry synergy' (Miles and Snow, 1986) imply the end of hierarchy and oligopolistic competition? Or is it, like the new developments in subcontracting, an extension and networking of familiar forms of corporate power and control, a new form of 'flexible integration'? Referring back to Vonortas's analysis, clearly his first type of alliance – to control the transformation of the market –implies the extension of strategic control to encompass the network. But this conclusion is not relevant in other circumstances. When no single centre of strategic power is evident, it is possible to conceptualize networking in one of two ways. On the one hand, as any arena for highly structured and controlled conflict, it is an accentuation of the common economic conception of constrained competition between oligopolists: there are long-run winners and losers from networking, irrespective of the intention of the parties involved. On the other hand, networking can be understood as a form of heightened co-operation. John Dunning describes these alliances as networks of 'multinational galaxies of firms' (Dunning, 1980), dominated by the MNCs, with their 'loose-tight' webs of semi-autonomous subcontractors, partners, financiers and distributors. Seen in these terms, it is difficult to avoid seeing networking as the progressive cartellization of the economy involving rivalry between corporate groupings, on a global scale.

It is wrong, however, to counterpose these conceptualizations of networking as alternatives. Even if networks are structured arenas of conflict and competition, the norms or rules of the game involved facilitate the common strategic objectives of the parties. The fact that in the long-run a sub-group of the network may obtain a disproportionate share of any benefits is irrelevant. At the outset, companies can exist independently of any prepared strategic alliance, thus all networks must reflect a commonality of objectives. To this extent, strategic alliances may represent little more than oligarchic alliances between oligopolists. The existence of hybrid forms between market and hierarchy may not be, then, as far as large firm networks are concerned, as benign a process as is implied in the new vogue set by the networking literature.

CONCLUSION

In this paper we have taken issue with those writers who suggest that the current phase of organizational restructuring involves a decentralization of economic power and control. Our critique does appear to be consistent with recent experience in the EC as detailed in the middle section of this chapter. In proposing that the current phase of restructuring is dominated by continuities and links with the past, we do not wish in any way to deny the enormity of contemporary industrial change as far as the organization of corporate activity is concerned. Our concern is that observations concering operational change should not be juxtaposed simply to issues of market power and control. Corporate power, in our opinion, is becoming increasingly centralized on two levels: first, the locus of strategic control is extending beyond the formal boundaries of the firm; second, a heightened degree of co-operation between oligopolists is occurring. And, this new form of centralization, now across national territorial boundaries, is entirely consistent with new tendencies towards the vertical disintegration of production.

In the emerging Single European Market, the tension between concentration of economic power and a possible decentralization of production will play a critical role in shaping the extent to which growth opportunities are shared. It is by no means obvious that the new phase of 'hierarchy', which we have characterized as a new fusion between oligopolistic competition and oligarchic control on an international scale, will allow an unproblematic resolution of this tension. For the present, it seems that the rules governing the SEM will be subordinate to these simultaneously globalizing and centralizing corporate trends, and that it is these trends, rather than those identified by the vertical disintegration thesis, which will shape the New Europe.

NOTES

1. The distinction between concentration and centralization is based on increases in absolute and relative firm size. The modern economics literature, which underlies much of the empirical material reported in this chapter, conflates this distinction into the more general category of concentration.
2. While there was no obvious and consistent internationalization of mergers and acquisitions in the service sector in the EC in the 1980s, there is some evidence that an internationalization is occurring in terms of the acquisition of minority holdings as detailed in recent EC Competition Reports.

REFERENCES

Amin, A. (1989), 'Flexible Specialisation and Small Firms in Italy: Myths and Realities', *Antipode*, **21**, (1), 13–34.

Amin, A. and K. Robins (1990), 'The Re-emergence of Regional Economies? The Mythical Geography of Flexible Accumulation', *Environment and Planning D: Society and Space*, **8**, 7–34.

Amin, A. and I.J. Smith (1991), 'Vertical Integration or Disintegration? The Case of the UK Car Parts Industry', in C. Law (ed.), *Restructuring the Global Automobile Industry*, London: Routledge.

Aoki, M. (1984), *The Economic Analysis of the Japanese Firm*, Amsterdam: North-Holland.

Auerbach, P. (1988), *Competition*, Oxford: Basil Blackwell.

Beije, P. (1988), 'Markets, Hierarchies and Interorganisational Relations', *Mimeo*, Rotterdam: Department of Economics, Erasmus University.

Belussi, F. (1987), 'Benetton: Information Technology in Production and Distribution. A case Study of the Innovative Potential of Traditional Sectors', *Occasional Paper 25*, Brighton: SPRU, University of Sussex.

Benassi, M. (1990), 'External Growth in the Computer Industry: Organisational Perspectives, *Mimeo*, Milan: IEFE, Bocconi University.

di Bernardo, B. (1989), 'La Rete del Capitalismo Flessibile: Oltre la Dicotomia Gerarchia-mercato', *Economia e Politica Industriale*, **64**, 165–207.

de Bernis, G. (1983), 'De Quelques Questions Concernant la Theorie des Crises', in GRREC, *Crise et Regulation*, Grenoble: DRUG.

Best, M. (1990), *The New Competition*, Oxford: Polity.

Buckley, P.J. (1988), 'Organisational Forms and Multinational Companies', in S. Thompson and M. Wright (eds), *Internal Organisation, Efficiency and Profit*, Oxford: Phillip Allan.

Business Week (1986), 'The Hollow Corporation', *Business Week*, Special Report, 3 March.

Brusco, S. and P. Crestanello (1990), 'Ricerca Comett sul Settore Tessile-Abbigliamento', *Mimeo*, Modena: Department of Economics, University of Modena.

Chandler, A. (1990), 'The Enduring Logic of Industrial Success', *Harvard Business Review*, March–April, 130–140.

Cowling, K. (1990), 'A New Industrial Strategy: Preparing Europe for the Turn of the Century', *International Journal of Industrial Organisation*, **8**, 165–183.

Dietrich, M. (1990), 'Corporate Management and the Economics of the Firm', *British Review of Economic Issues*, **12**, October, 21–36.

Dietrich, M. (1991), 'Firms, Markets and Transaction Cost Economics', *Scottish Journal of Political Economy*, **38**, (1), 41–57.

Dore, R. (1983), 'Goodwill and the Spirit of Market Capitalism', *British Journal of Sociology*, **34**, (4), 459–482.

Dosi, G. (1988), 'Sources, Procedures and Microeconomic Effects of Innovation', *Journal of Economic Literature*, **26**, 1120–1171.

Dosi, G., D. Teece and S. Winter (1989), 'Towards a Theory of Corporate Coherence: Preliminary Remarks', *Mimeo*, Rome: Department of Economics, University of Rome.

Dunning, J. (1988), 'International Business, the Recession and Economic Restructuring', in N. Hood and J.E. Vahlne (eds), *Strategies in Global Competition*, London: Croom Helm.

Drucker, P.E. (1990), 'The Emerging Theory of Manufacturing', *Harvard Business Review*, May-June, 94–102.

Granovetter, M. (1985), 'Economic Action and Social Structure: Theory of Embeddedness', *American Journal of Sociology*, **91**, (3), 481–510.

Hakansson, H. (ed) (1987), *Industrial Technological Development: A Network Approach*, London: Croom Helm.

Hannah, L. and J. A. Kay (1977), *Concentration in Modern Industry*, London: Macmillan.

Hannah, L. (1983), *The Rise of the Corporate Economy*, 2nd edn. London: Methuen.

Harrison, B. (1989), 'The Big Firms are Coming Out of the Corner', *Working Paper 89–39*, Pittsburg: School of Urban and Public Affairs', Carnegie Mellon University.

Harrison, B. and M. Kelley (1990), 'Outsourcing and the Search for Flexibility: the Morphology of Production Subcontracting in US Manufacturing', *Mimeo*, Pittsburg: School of Urban and Public Affairs, Carnegie Mellon University.

Helper, S. (1989a), 'Changing Supplier Relationships in the United States: Results of Survery Research, *Mimeo*, Massachusetts: Center for Technology, Policy and Industrial Development, Massachusetts Institute of Technology.

Helper, S. (1989b), 'Strategy and Irreversibility in Supplier Relations: the Case of the US Automobile Industry, *Mimeo*, Boston: Department of Operations Management, Boston University.

Hirst, P. and J. Zeitlin (1989), 'Flexible Specialisation and the Competitive Failure of UK Manufacturing', *Political Quarterly*, **60**, (3), 164–178.

Hirst, P. and J. Zeitlin (1991), 'Flexible Specialisation vs. Post-Fordism: Theory, Evidence and Policy Implications', *Economy and Society*, **20**, (1), 1–56.

Hood, N. and J-E. Vahlne (eds), (1988), *Strategies in Global Competition*, London: Croom Helm.

Howells, J. (1990), 'The Internationalisation of R&D and the Development of Global Research Networks', *Regional Studies*, **24**, (6), 495–512.

Imrie, R.F. and J. Morris, (1988), 'Buyer–Supplier Relations in the British Economy: an Empirical Study', *Mimeo*, Cardiff: Department of Town Planning, University of Wales.

Jacquemin, A., Buiges, P. and F. Ilzkovitz (1989), 'Horizontal Mergers and Competition Policy in the European Community' *European Economy*, No. 40, May: Commission of the European Communities Directorate-General for Economic and Financial Affairs.

Johanson, J. and L-G. Mattson (1987), 'Inter-Organizational Relations in Industrial Systems: a Network Approach Compared with the Transaction-Cost Approach', *International Studies of Management and Organisation*, **18**, (1), 34–48.

Jonquieres, G. (1990a), 'Wave Reflects Wider Trends', *Financial Times*, 18 October, 34.

Jonquieres, G. (1990b), 'Ventures without Frontiers', *Financial Times*, 18 October, 35.

Kumpe, T. and P.T. Bolwijn (1988), 'Manufacturing: the New Case for Vertical Integration, *Harvard Business Review*, March-April, 75–81.

Loveridge, R. (1990), 'Shifting Boundaries in Subcontracting Relations: the Case of the Automotive Industry', *Mimeo*, Birmingham: Strategic Management and Policy Studies Division, Aston University.

Martinelli, F. and E. Schoenberger (1991), 'Oligopoly Alive and Well: Notes for a Broader Discussion on Flexible Specialisation', in G. Benko and M. Dunford (eds) *Industrial Change and Regional Development*, London: Belhaven.

Miles, R.E. and C.C. Snow (1986), 'Organisations: New Concepts for New Forms', *California Management Review*, **28**, (3), 62–73.

Monteverde, K. and D. Teece (1982), 'Appropriable Rents and Quasi-vertical Integration', *Journal of Law and Economics*, **25**, 321–328.

Mowery, D.C. (1987), *Alliance Politics and Economics*, Cambridge, MA: Ballinger.

Mowery, D.C. (ed.) (1988), *International Collaborative Ventures in US Manufacturing*, Cambridge, MA: Ballinger.

Ohmae, K. (1989), 'Managing in a Borderless World', *Harvard Business Review*, May-June, 152–161.

Piore, M. and C.F. Sabel (1984), *The Second Industrial Divide: Possibilities for Prosperity*, New York: Basic Books.

Powell, W.W. (1990), 'Neither Market nor Hierarchy: Network Forms of Organisation', *Research in Organizational Behaviour*, **12**, 32, 295–336.

Prais, S.J. (1976), *The Evolution of Giant Firms in Britain*, Cambridge: Cambridge University Press.

Pyke, F., G. Becattini and W. Sengenberger (eds) (1990), *Industrial Districts and Inter-firm Co-operation in Italy*, Geneva: International Institute for Labour Studies.

Rothwell, R. and W. Zegveld (1982), *Innovation and the Small and Medium Sized Firm*, London: Frances Pinter.

Sabel, C.F. (1982), *Work and Politics: The Division of Labour in Industry*, Cambridge: Cambridge University Press.

Sabel, C.F. (1989), 'Flexible Specialisation and the Re-emergence of Regional Economies', in P. Hirst and J. Zeitlin (eds), *Reversing Industrial Decline? Industrial Structure and Policies in Britain and her Competitors*, Oxford: Berg.

Sako, M. (1988), 'Competitive Cooperation: How the Japanese Manage Inter-firm Relations', *Mimeo*, London: Industrial Relations Department, London School of Economics.

Scott, A.J. (1988), 'Flexible Production Systems and Regional Development: the Rise of New Industrial Spaces in North America and Western Europe', *International Journal of Urban and Regional Research*, **12**, 171–186.

Schumpeter, J. (1939), *Business Cycles: A Theoretical, Historical and Statistical Analysis of the Capitalist Process*, London: McGraw-Hill.

Storper, M. (1989), 'The Transition to Flexible Specialisation in the US Film Industry: External Economies, the Division of Labour, and the Crossing of Industrial Divides', *Cambridge Journal of Economics*, **13**, 2, 273–305.

Storper, M. and A.J. Scott (1989), 'The Geographical Foundations and Social Regulation of Flexible Production Complexes', in J. Wolch and M. Dear (eds) *The Power of Geography: How Territory Shapes Social Life*, Winchester, MA: Unwin Hyman.

Vonortas, N.S. (1990), 'Emerging Patterns of Multinational Enterprise Operations in Developed Market Ecoonomies: Evidence and Policy', *Review of Political Economy* **2**, (5), 188–220.

Williamson, O.E. (1975), *Markets and Hierarchies: Analysis and Antitrust Implications*, New York: Free Press.

Williamson, O.E. (1985), *The Economic Institutions of Capitalism*, New York: Free Press.

Wright, M. (1988), 'Redrawing the Boundaries of the Firm', in S. Thompson and M. Wright (eds), *Internal Organisation, Efficiency and Profit*, Oxford: Phillip Allan.

Zagnoli, P. (1987), 'Inter-firm Agreements as Bilateral Transactions?', *Mimeo*, Florence: European University Institute.

4. The Japanization of European Industry

Klaus Weiermair

INTRODUCTION

Terms such as 'Japanization', 'Ja-panic' or simply the 'threat from Japanese competition' were throughout the 1980s not only the topic of numerous jokes and small talk among Western businessmen, but at the same time spawned mushrooming literature on the intricacies of the Japanese economy and the peculiarities in the management of her corporations.[1] In this regard the 1980s remind us somehow of the 1960s when such expressions as 'Americanization' and the 'American Challenge' most typified in Servan-Schreiber's book *Le défi Américain* (1967), made their rounds in Western Europe. In both cases large inward flows of Foreign Direct Investment (FDI) coupled with the importation of new technologies and organizational know-how have created an impetus for industrial restructuring and change. Given the US's dominance in business education throughout the post-war period (Locke, 1986) and its emulation in many European institutions, it is probably fair to argue that the Japanese economy, Japanese management and Japanization have today remained far less understood and studied and are still far more stereotyped than the earlier episode of corporate takeover and 'Americanization' in the 1960s. This chapter addresses the question as to the rising importance of Japanese investment and presence in the European Community (EC) and the effect this is likely to have on the structure and performance of the common market economy.

The chapter is organized as follows. We first look at the empirical and quantifiable evidence of Japan's presence in Europe in terms of foreign direct investment and offer some explanations with regard to its location and industrial composition. Following this the qualitative impact of Japanese FDI in terms of new forms of industrial organization and competition is examined. The penultimate section speculates on the likely effects that the 1985 measures to form an integral common market

74

by 1992 will have on the Japanese presence in Europe. Finally, some policy prescriptions and conclusions are offered.

GROWTH OF JAPANESE FOREIGN DIRECT INVESTMENT IN THE EC

The expansion of Japanese involvement in the EC has proceeded in three cycles starting with an initial boom in the late 1960s and early 1970s, followed by a declining period which reached its trough in 1982 and which later gave way to a steady and accelerating rise throughout the latter part of the 1980s. During the two fiscal years from 1987–8 to 1989–90, Japan

Table 4.1 Growth of Japanese foreign direct investment stock in the EC 12

1970–87

	Value (US $m)	Share of Japan's total outward FDI stock (%)
1951–70	628	17.6
1971	712	16.1
1972	1 634	24.1
1973	1 936	18.9
1974	2 099	16.6
1975	2 300	14.4
1976	2 580	13.3
1977	2 794	12.6
1978	3 104	11.6
1979	3 490	11.0
1980	4 033	11.1
1981	4 752	10.5
1982	5 539	10.4
1983	6 483	10.6
1984	8 178	11.4
1985	10 021	12.0
1986	13 370	12.6
1987	19 682	14.1
1988	28 451	15.1
1989	37 127	17.1

Source: Japanese Ministry of Finance, *Zaisei Kinyu tokei Geppo*, various issues.

Table 4.2 Geographical distribution of Japanese foreign direct investment stock in Europe, 1970–89

	1970 Value (US $m)	1970 Share of Japan's outward FDI stock in Europe (%)	1980 Value (US $m)	1980 Share of Japan's outward FDI stock in Europe (%)	1987 Value (US $m)	1987 Share of Japan's outward FDI stock in Europe (%)	1989 Value (US $m)	1989 Share of Japan's outward FDI stock in Europe (%)
Belgium	20	3.1	291	6.5	863	4.1	1 250	3.3
France	22	3.4	354	7.9	1 300	6.2	2 318	6.1
W. Germany	16	2.5	498	11.1	1 955	9.3	3 045	8.0
Ireland	1	0.2	149	3.3	390	1.9	522	1.4
Italy	7	1.1	67	1.5	262	1.2	515	1.4
Luxembourg	8	1.3	105	2.3	4 072	19.3	4 986	13.2
Netherlands	3	0.5	298	6.6	4 166	15.0	8 338	22.0
Spain	4	0.6	173	3.9	883	4.2	1 169	3.1
UK	544	85.1	2 010	44.9	6 598	31.3	12 994	34.3
Other EC	3	0.5	88	2.0	193	0.9	302	0.8
Total EC12	628	98.3	4 033	90.2	19 682	93.5	35 439	93.6
Switzerland	7	1.1	191	4.3	977	4.6	1 687	4.5
USSR	1	0.2	193	4.3	195	0.9	219	0.6
Other Europe	3	0.5	55	1.2	193	0.9	508	1.3
Total Europe	639	100.0	4 472	100.0	21 047	100.0	37 853	100.0

Source: Japanese Ministry of Finance, *Zaisei Kinyu tokei Geppo*, various issues.

Table 4.3 Industrial distribution of Japanese foreign direct investment stock in Europe, 1979–88

	1979		1983		1987		1988	
	Value (US $m)	Share of Japan's outward FDI stock in Europe (%)	Value (US $m)	Share of Japan's outward FDI stock in Europe (%)	Value (US $m)	Share of Japan's outward FDI stock in Europe (%)	Value (US $m)	Share of Japan's outward FDI stock in Europe (%)
Agriculture	0	0.0	0	0.0	5	0.0	7	0.0
Fishing	2	0.1	2	0.0	3	0.0	7	0.0
Mining	859	22.1	859	12.0	890	4.2	1 103	3.8
Total extractive	861	22.1	861	12.1	898	4.3	1 117	3.9
Food	42	1.1	55	0.8	112	0.5	171	0.6
Chemicals	96	2.5	199	2.8	347	1.6	594	2.0
Metals	108	2.8	206	2.9	276	1.3	328	1.1
Machinery	104	2.7	164	2.3	365	1.7	626	2.2
Electrical equip.	72	1.8	294	4.1	704	3.3	1 261	4.3
Transport equip.	53	1.4	149	2.1	797	3.8	913	3.1
Textiles	126	3.2	170	2.4	245	1.2	303	1.0
Paper and wood products	0	0.0	0	0.0	2	0.0	5	0.0
Other manufacturing	82	2.1	191	2.7	462	2.2	656	2.3
Total manufacturing	683	17.5	1 428	20.0	3 310	15.7	4 857	16.8
Construction	11	0.3	40	0.6	57	0.3	59	0.2
Distributive trade	658	16.9	1 660	23.3	3 374	16.0	3 955	13.6
Finance and insurance	704	18.1	1 720	24.1	10 508	49.9	14 853	51.2
Transportation	NSA	NSA	3	0.0	93	0.4	101	0.3
Real estate	NSA	NSA	46	0.6	268	1.3	1 424	4.9
Other services*	878	22.6	1 105	15.5	1 596	7.6	2 626	9.1
Total services*	2 251	57.8	4 574	64.1	15 896	75.5	23 018	79.4
Total†	3 893	100.0	7 136	100.0	21 047	100.0	28 992	100.0

*Other services and total services include an amount which is not possible to allocate between extrative, manufacturing and service sectors.
†The overall total includes an additional unallocated component invested in branch offices or the acquisition of real estate.

Source: Japanese Ministry of Finance, *Zaisei Kinyu tokei Geppo*, various issues.

has invested more in the 12 EC countries than during the entire previous postwar period (see Tables 4.1 and 4.2). In terms of location, the bulk of Japanese FDI originally went to the UK (85 per cent of the total in 1970) whose share by 1989 had, however, gradually declined to 30 per cent of total Japanese FDI in Europe, followed by the Netherlands, Luxembourg, West-Germany and France. By March 1989 more than 85 per cent of Japan's FDI in Europe had been placed in the aforementioned five countries of the EC (Table 4.2). In terms of the industrial distribution of the stock of Japanese FDI in Europe and its evolution from 1979 to 1989 (Table 4.3) we observe the following:

1. Finance and insurance occupy the biggest share (50 per cent); this sector has also shown the quickest growth rate over the past decade. Another 13 per cent is taken up by commerce, making the service sector the single largest area of investment in Europe.
2. Manufacturing which in total only amounts to 16 per cent of all European FDI, is concentrated in transportation equipment, electrical equipment and electronics and general machinery.
3. The only other significant sector has been mining, which after larger investments in the 1960s and 1970s, has, as of late, lost its importance and attraction and in 1989 only amounted to 3.6 per cent of Japanese FDI in Europe (see Table 4.3).

The behaviour of Japanese FDI in Europe differs appreciably from Japanese FDI in North America and Asia, both of which have hosted a much larger amount and percentage share of investment in manufacturing.[2] A large number of scholars in international business and finance have offered explanations regarding the behaviour of the outward flow of Japanese FDI in general and its growth and presence in Western Europe in particular, for example Marsh (1983), Dunning (1986) and Dunning and Webster (1989). The following explanations with respect to the outward movement of Japanese FDI and the organizational form of Japanese involvement are usually provided:

1. Japan has been a relative late comer with respect to FDI and her large corporations have for a long time been reluctant to move operations abroad. Synergies and agglomeration economies from producing at home and pursuing a global export strategy, the inability to shut down plants because of lifetime employment and unfamiliarity with foreign cultures and languages have often been given as reasons for Japan's late entry into international investment and finance, Trevor (1983).

2. Furthermore, and in line with note 1, Japanese MNEs initially concentrated their activities in the sourcing of raw materials in developing regions of Asia and South America, followed by the outsourcing of low value-added manufacturing into South East Asia. This region has also been the least unfamiliar for Japanese management in terms of economic, individual and market behaviour, see Ozawa (1979).

3. From the 1970s there has been a reorientation of Japanese investment towards developed countries, notably the US, Australia, Canada and the UK, involving a shift towards higher value-added manufacturing and services. A combination of factors such as the growing industrial and competitive strength of Japanese manufacturing in certain sectors, the protectionist moves of the US and possibly the EC, the high costs and risks of R&D and the rising value of the yen are often cited as having contributed to these shifts (Dunning and Webster, 1989).

4. In the case of Western Europe much of Japanese investment behaviour over the past decade has been attracted by the size of the EC market as a whole, even though final location may have been decided by factors such as availability of labour, technological and communications infrastructure, familiarity with language, culture and legal systems and/or government incentives.

5. In penetrating European markets, Japanese MNEs have by and large preferred the route of FDI over licensing. The reasons for this are well known from the literature on the transaction costs of international business under market failure which makes it advantageous for Japanese firms to maintain control over various aspects of production and thereby appropriate rents from owner advantages and/or gain economies and synergies from cross-border activities (Dunning, 1981, 1990).

6. With respect to the industrial distribution of Japanese foreign direct investment in the EC, Japanese firms seem to have expanded production mostly in those areas in which they allegedly command a comparative technological advantage over EC and US firms and where the home country equally reveals a comparative advantage in trade (Cantwell, 1989).

7. Most recently Japanese firms have entered into a number of strategic cross-border tie-ups, particularly with European competitors in R&D intensive, high-growth industries. Among the varied motives behind strategic alliances between Japanese and EC firms have been the globalization of research and development activities (*Japan Economic Journal*, 1989), lowered costs from co-operative manu-

Figure 4.1   International tie-ups of the World's leading semiconductor manufacturers

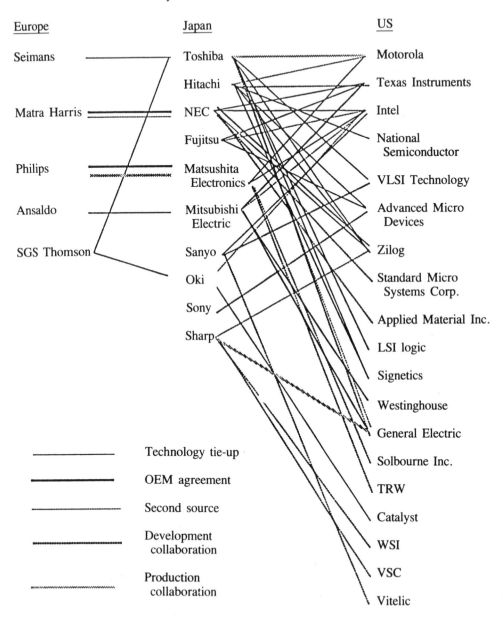

Source: JETRO survey.

facturing and, particularly among auto-parts makers, the ability to develop technologies jointly

> in order to adapt from mass production to small-lot production of customized components caused by the diversification of customers
> JETRO (1990)

A typical example of such tie-ups between Japanese, EC and US firms in the semiconductor industry is shown in Figure 4.1. As is true for many high technology industries, higher levels and more complex forms of networking exist between US and Japanese firms as compared to tie-ups between EC and Japanese corporations (see Figure 4.1).

8. Finally, unlike their American and European counterparts, Japanese firms have not rushed into Eastern Europe which traditionally has only accounted for a small portion of Japan's trade and in this respect neither government offices nor Chief Executive Officers (CEOs) of Japanese corporations foresee major changes (*Japan Economic Journal*, 1990). The opening of Europe's eastern borders will, however, move some of Japan's future FDI further eastward and

Table 4.4 *Joint-ventures in the Soviet Union and Eastern European countries*

	As of fourth quarter, 1987		As of fourth quarter, 1988		As of fourth quarter, 1989	
		Japan		Japan		Japan
Albania	0	0	0	0	0	0
Bulgaria	11	4	14	4	22	3
Czechoslovakia	1	0	8	0	50*	0
East Germany	0	0	0	0	0	0
Hungary	100*	3	180*	4	629	5
Poland	4	0	31	0	450*	0
Rumania	5	0	5	0	5	0
Soviet Union	8	1	105	6	1 020	21
Yugoslavia	250*	2	342	2	632	2
Total	379	10	685	16	2 808	31
Japan's share (%)		2.6		2.3		1.1

*Approximate figures.
Source: JETRO survey.

thereby make such countries as Germany or Austria more desirable locations for Japanese affiliate companies. As can be seen in Table 4.4, over the past three years Japan's share in Soviet and Eastern European joint-ventures even fell.

JAPANIZATION OF EUROPEAN INDUSTRY

As we have seen in the previous section cumulative Japanese FDI in the EC as of March 1990 still amounted to only 17 per cent in comparison to the 41 per cent which had been invested in North America. Also it was shown to be heavily concentrated in only a few industrial sectors such as electrical equipment and electronics, transportation equipment and non-electrical engineering products. Why then the general concern with Japanese greenfield ventures and the rising control and takeover of European corporations by Japanese management as frequently expressed by the EC Commission (1983, 1986, 1988) and as repeatedly portrayed in media headlines and lead articles. There are two or possibly three inter-related reasons which may help explain both the accelerating international investment and takeover activity of Japanese firms as well as the fear of European industrialists and industrial policy makers regarding the increasing *Japanization* of European business. First, the emergence of new forms of competition among firms in many markets which is now much more based on technology, service and quality and which furthermore has become global in nature. It also requires longer-term decision making horizons on the part of economic agents. The new forms of competition have been in sharp contrast with the conventional wisdom of price-based market competition (and the associated activities of market arbitrage and market clearing) conceptualized and executed with short-term decision making models as employed by both Western orthodox economists and practising managers alike. Secondly, in many markets across different European jurisdictions, the new forms of competition have met with strong opposition from vested interest groups among unions, management, educationalists and professionals, as well as bureaucrats in national and provincial governments, who have felt threatened by the combination of an internationalization of markets, accelerated technological change and globalization. At the same time certain corporations, often entire industries, even entire jursidictions have made industrial and organizational restructuring, rapid economic adjustment and management of change their central concern. In conse-quence they were better able to weather the environmental turbulence of the 1970s and 1980s. The third reason why 'Japanization' is perceived a threat is in order to manage and co-ordinate cross-border activities in the

1980s and 1990s, multinational firms now require more innovation and entrepreneurship to help reduce the transaction costs resulting from these activities (Bartlett and Ghoshal, 1989a). There is some evidence available which suggests that home country characteristics may affect and shape differences in the organization, work practices and decision-making procedures of manufacturing affiliates of foreign investors thereby increasing or reducing the above mentioned transaction costs associated with FDI. To the extent that the competitiveness of Japanese MNEs in Europe may be related to the ecostructure of their home country, 'Japanization' may indeed constitute both a cause and consequence of Japanese FDI in the EC.

New Regime of Competition

The evolution of new forms of competition has resulted from both secular changes in economic behaviour as well as from heightened market turbulence in the 1970s and 1980s. It has proceeded much faster in some of the sunrise industries than in the more mature, stable or declining economic sectors and has generally benefited those firms which have either been well equipped to handle the new 'regime' of competition or which otherwise have been quick in adjusting to it. Considerable consensus now exists with respect to the new dimensions or characteristics of 'technology based', global competition and its implications for the structure, conduct and performances of firms and industries (Porter, 1986, 1990; Teece, 1987; Kotler *et al.*, 1985; Piore and Sable, 1984; Hayes and Wheelwright, 1984; Bartlett and Ghoshal, 1989; Vicari, 1989). At the level of the firm the noted changes have entailed a reorientation of strategic management towards:

1. A faster and improved reading (metering) of the environment including a more careful scanning and anticipation of major fracture points in the economic development of industries and markets.
2. A greater emphasis regarding the creation and use of new technologies and new products.
3. A paradigmatic shift away from mass production technologies associated with stable and mature markets, towards more flexible automation technologies. These requirements for more flexibility and adaptability also pose new trade-off questions regarding the degree of specialization of human and physical assets and new forms of integration between production and distribution activities.
4. An intensified search to detect and exploit economies of scope through the extension and segmentation of markets and technologies.

5. A far greater emphasis on entrepreneurship and intrapreneurship in order to resolve major strategic issues and problems raised above in favour of traditional top heavy managerial hierarchies and/or machine bureaucracies.

Hardly anybody in the field of strategic management, neither those writing about it, nor those practising it, disagree about the managerial issues and needs arising out of the aforementioned heightened market turbulence. Rather it is with respect to implementing needed changes, which are foremost at the operational level, where differences exist. For most organizations the problems of adjusting to change today seem to lie much more in the 'doing' and in the 'actions' and not in the 'knowing'. Providing for a dynamic organizational environment of creativity, learning, innovation and 'proactive' management where human resources are cherished as assets rather then being treated as costs appears to be easy for most Japanese organizations, while it is being reserved only for a few of the best managed companies in the case of North America and Europe (Ouchi, 1981; Drucker, 1988; Aoki, 1988; Imai, 1989; Imai *et al.*, 1985; Peters and Waterman, 1982; Peters, 1988).

If Japanese organizations are typically faster and more entrepreneurial in adjusting to the dynamics of social, technological and economic changes in the environment and to the new regimes of competition as some authors have suggested (Kagono, *et al.*, 1983; Imai, 1980; Drucker, 1988), *Japanization* may simply constitute a form of 'barometric' leadership on the part of Japanese companies which will give way eventually to a wider diffusion of these organizational innovations in Europe and elsewhere. In many ways this process should resemble the spread of the M-form organization which originally emanated from the US and has been associated with US's FDI in Europe over the past 20 years (see Wilkins, 1974). Japan and Japanese companies may, however, also have adjusted faster to technological change and to the 'technology race'; or put differently, the technological (and hence also comparative economic) advantage of Japanese relative to European firms may have increased over time. While it is not easy to fully account for and measure technological advantages of enterprises, data on foreign patenting of firms in the US (a close enough proxy) may be used to calculate the revealed technological advantage of large Japanese and European community industrial firms (Cantwell, 1989, p. 118 ff). The empirical evidence provided therein offers some interesting insights into the evolution of technological competition among MNEs across different home countries as well as across time.[3]

It appears that Japanese companies (as well as Japan as a country) have accumulated strong, technological advantages in the electrical equipment, general engineering and motor vehicle industries, exactly those sectors and industries, in which Japanese exports to and investment in the EC have rapidly increased over the past decade. In contrast, in food processing, aircraft production and chemicals and related industries, Japanese firms appear to be lagging far behind their European competitors, thus having resulted in a smaller Japanese presence in Europe. Probably for these very reasons there are attempts at forging strategic alliances with European partners in these sectors (*Japan Economic Journal*, Sept. 24, 1988; *Japan Economic Journal*, July 28, 1990;, *Japan Times*, May 17, 1990) in which 'multi-product firms continually search for technological improvements on their existing operations' where 'new products and processes are not independent of one another' and where 'innovative firms continually attempt to forge their technological trajectories into new environments, including international or global production' (Cantwell, 1989, p. 53 ff). Most important in this regard is the firm specificity in the generation of innovation which requires firm specific investments in organizational and human assets. These may or may not be facilitated (hampered) by market conditions in the FDI sending or receiving jurisdictions. In historical contrast the development of firm specific technological advantages has been far less important during the 'American takeover' period of the 1950s and 1960s when US firms had a technological lead over European firms in many markets, based on more generic and standardized production and organizational technologies and processes. 'Fordist' production and management principles which in the immediate post-war period dominated and were easily transplanted into Europe have, however, been undermined since the mid 1970s by a variety of market developments notably the rise in concern regarding the quality and versatility of products offered, the demobilization of national oligopolistic market structures and processes, and the appearance of new information technologies which negate traditional Fordist principles of production, see Weiermair (1991).

Thus a potential threat of 'Japanization of European businesses' portrays Japanese corporations in specific sectors as fast in adjusting, innovative and technology driven. The opposite is said to have existed at least for some time, in certain firms, in some sectors and in some jurisdictions within the EC. The term 'Eurosclerosis' coined first in the 1970s and banned from the European vocabulary since the appearance of the Cecchini report in 1985 clearly attests to Europe's past difficulties in economic restructuring, needed to correct past developments and to accommodate existing economic and political pressures.

The changed environment of the 1970s and 1980s has required an approach to the allocation and management of resources, that recognizes:

1. A greater flexibility and adaptability of management *vis-à-vis* new market trends, new technologies and new forms of organization, thus the call for more 'entrepreneurship'
2. Greater flexibilities in the deployment and use of labour in enterprises and/or greater flexibilities in the labour market.
3. Increased diffusion and adoption of new technologies particularly those in the fields of information and more importantly the satisfactory implementation of company relevant technologies.
4. New forms of organization that transcend the traditional alternatives of market and hierarchy. Notable is the creation of team management within firms, co-operative supplier and distributor linkages, co-operative manufacturing and/or more generally the development of 'network organizations'.

There is some empirical evidence suggesting that resistance to these needed changes may have been higher among European workers, unions, management and public institutions as compared to their Japanese counterparts.[4] While not always easy to document and even more difficult to quantify, recent work by the OECD (1988, 1989a, 1989b, 1989c) bears this out. In terms of labour and labour market flexibilities, either in terms of wage flexibility or in terms of functional intra-organization labour flexibilities, Japan appears to outperform most other European countries with the UK showing the poorest performance. It is therefore, perhaps, not surprising that in a recent paper Casson (1988) has calculated national scores for entrepreneurship, giving both the US and Japan the highest scores of 18. In comparison the UK, France, Sweden and Italy obtained ratings of 9, 11, 15 and 9, respectively. A number of authors describing Japan's drive towards technological leadership have provided comparative estimates of R&D spending and of Japan's accumulated wealth of technological know-how. Both in terms of (primarily private) resources dedicated to innovation as well as in terms of adjusting and preparing organizations for technical change, Japanese leading corporations show an impressive record comparable to and often superior to industrial leaders elsewhere (Abbeglen and Stalk, 1985; Freeman, 1987). Finally, Japanese corporations have, more than others, advanced new forms of organizations particularly with respect to international business. Japanese corporations were not only among the first truly to globalize industrial production and distribution but have also pioneered a number of new forms of international strategic alliances, and sophisticated cross-border networks (Imai, 1989).

Having given the Japanese an initial competitive edge, all of the aforementioned changes in organizational and industrial structures will eventually become common knowledge and practice and as such will diffuse 'Japanese' elements into the 'European' way of conducting business.

New Competition and Resistance to Change

Many of the changes just described would have occurred throughout the EC during the 1970s and 1980s had it not been for the original (and in some cases continuing) blockage of change through vested interest groups and/or an industrial relations environment which has been hostile to dramatic departures from existing forms of work organizations, supervision and incentive systems associated with the old paradigm of management (Fordism) and with orthodox views regarding the functioning of markets. Much has been written elsewhere about the resistance to the new model of organizational and market functioning and its variation across different industries and jurisdictions (see for example, OECD, 1989c; Boyer, 1988; Weiermair, 1990) and a full discussion would be far beyond the scope of this chapter. At the risk of oversimplification one can draw the following conclusions from the literature dealing with the resistance to, or postponement of, needed organizational and institutional change:

1. A fair amount of organizational and market rigidities has been simply the result of traditional and outdated incentive and reward systems. Life long learning and relearning, retraining and repositioning of skills, desirable because of continued market turbulence, can only be achieved efficiently within a time frame of longer-term job tenure and/or *de facto* job security. Workers or managers would have insufficient incentive for future skill development and information exchange if a firm's planning horizon was dominated by its short-term financial performance (for example, quarterly earnings). Not surprisingly those European jurisdictions which have provided for a longer-term time frame in matters of manpower (Sweden and West Germany) have been relatively more successful in restructuring and moving towards new forms of management (OECD, 1989c, p. 36 ff.).
2. Restructuring tends to be easier with well-trained workers and managers, hence resistance can be expected to be strongest in environments where both ill-trained management (particularly middle management) and unskilled (untrained) workers face the double challenges of new technologies and intensified international competition (see Bartel and Lichtenberg, 1987). On the other hand, firms who set out to develop skills are able to benefit from workers' know-how and competences (Aoki, 1988).

3. Resistance to change is heightened by the power of vested interest groups of long standing and tradition. Britain is often cited as a classical case of a jurisdiction where certain unions and/or business groups have been able to oppose change for a prolonged period of time (Olson, 1982). However, examples abound as well for other European jurisdictions and industries.

4. Restructuring can be impeded by a lack of co-operation among and between firms and education/research institutions as well as between business and government. Unfortunately adversarial, contract- bound and arm's-length relations not only constitute pillars in the neo-classical economic theory of the firm, but they also have been deeply (culturally) ingrained in industrial practice among many Western nations.

5. Industrial relations systems which either explicitly or implicitly cannot incorporate technological or other major environmental changes have created frictions and more resistance to organizational and/or industrial restructuring (OECD, 1988).

Comparative work on any of these five factors would suggest that the Japanese firm (the J-model) is far more adaptable and flexible, both in terms of internationalization and technical change, than typical European or American counterparts.

Market Turbulence and Globalization

A number of authors have suggested that the future multinational firm will be characterized by a 'network-type' organization. Instead of decentralized federations (the M-form organizations) we will see co-ordinated federations, instead of the centralized hub we will find an integrated network of firms emerging, see Bartlett and Ghoshal (1989b). The 'network' organization is greatly facilitated by co-operative market linkages such as those pioneered originally in the sub-contracting system of large Japanese corporations. Network organizations are loosely coupled forums which have both weak and strong ties among constituent markets. The network enables corporations to identify emergent opportunities in order to link specialization across the boundaries of firms and to trigger continuous interactive innovation. Applying the concept to cross-border networks allows a quasi autonomous management in each region along with an interpenetrated global co-ordination of key variables, see Imai (1988, 1989). While the internationalization of 'networks' is in a relatively early stage of development, in their more holistic and systemic approach to management and decision making the Japanese are likely to develop this into an early competitive advantage (or intangible asset) just as they have used their more efficient work organization and quality control systems in international operations to their advantage. Thus when speaking of 'Japanization' we would emphasize here the transfer of 'Japanese-elements' in the governance of firms, which we believe will be far more important in the future than the penetration ratio of Japanese FDI or the import penetration ratio of Japanese products. This is not to suggest that there will be a discrete break in terms of organizational forms across firms in all jurisdictions within the EC. Just as the U-form organization has lived on at varying lengths of time and intensity in different European jurisdictions after the Americans had developed the M-form, the J-form organization and management will similarly diffuse at different strengths and varying speed.

EUROPE 1992 AND THE JAPANESE PRESENCE

The completion of the common market in 1992 will have major effects on the competitiveness of foreign (non-EC) firms locating within the EC. Transaction costs will be reduced because of common technical standards and the elimination of border controls. Economies of specialization and/ or large-scale production will be evident. The development of cross-border horizontal or vertical alliances among firms within the EC market will be easier. Finally, the uncertainties of the EC's future import controls, local content rules and the behaviour of foreign exchange relative to the ECU will be less significant.

Based on the discussion in previous sections the following speculative comments can be made:

1. Given the predicted continuation of trade frictions between Japan and the EC (Ishikawa, 1990; Burton, 1989) and based on the previous experience of rushed Japanese FDI into the US on account of feared protectionism, a dramatic increase in the proportion of Japanese foreign production in the EC prior to January 1, 1993, can be expected.
2. The lowered transaction costs of common governance of enterprises associated with 1992 rules will particularly benefit Japanese firms, whose ownership advantages derive at least in part from their superior capabilities to co-ordinate cross border value-adding activities, see Dunning (1990), Kogut (1983).
3. As a consequence of the increased presence of Japanese companies in the EC, European companies may be forced to close the technological and managerial gaps which have opened in some sectors. A good example is the effect which Japanese management has had upon British industry; many features of Japanese com-

petitiveness have now been successfully incorporated into the arsenal of new industrial practices in the UK, notably just-in-time delivery systems, quality control circles, flexible manufacturing and human resource management practices and work organizations, see Dunning (1986), Dunning and Webster (1989).

4. As a consequence of the narrowing of this management gap, Japanese firms will in the future become more pluralistic in their choice of organizational form. Instead of relying on 100 per cent owned subsidiaries for production in the EC, which has been typical for most Japanese FDI into Europe in the past (on account of internationalization advantages), Japanese corporations will increasingly rely on European partnerships.[5]

5. Finally a large impact on Japanese FDI will come from the completion of the 1992 market which will be sustained, in contrast to the investment response from the fears of Fortress Europe.

IMPLICATIONS OF *'JAPANIZATION'* FOR EUROPEAN INDUSTRIAL, COMPETITION AND LABOUR POLICIES

The evolution of Japan's post-war economy and the international competitiveness of her corporations reveals two aspects of productivity growth which have frequently been misinterpreted and/or ignored by orthodox economists. They are: the importance of *firm specificity* in the investment of human capital and technology, and secondly the gradual and *accumulated* improvement of firm specific technology and skills yielding *dynamic* as opposed to static economies of scale and/or scope. From a theoretical point of view this suggests that analogies with pure market exchange may be inappropriate in understanding firm internal resource allocation processes, and in addition static equilibrium models of competition, based on passive responses to price signals may be inappropriate in analysing what essentially represent a permanent disequilibrium condition. The accumulation of a firm's skills and technology should rather be conceived as a system-on-the-move, centred on a dynamic inter-relationship between the evolution of new and perfection of old skills and technologies in tandem with varied and varying user requirements.[6] Hence, possible policy lessons and/or conclusions from the Japanese experience should centre on measures which strengthen firms' abilities and capabilities to develop firm specific assets and owner advantages, and which in turn render them more competitive internationally.

In the field of labour this means creating functional manpower flexibility within firms. Such flexibility is based on enabling and motivating workers to learn and do a variety of jobs, and encouraging them to do so through the proper human resource policies and organization of work (Cabale and Tapiola, 1989, p. 50). Thus labour market allocation processes and formal education/training systems should be used as complements rather than being considered substitutes for firm internal labour allocation. Governments should provide and subsidize general and generic educational qualifications and let employers organize, sponsor and finance the more job, occupation, and firm-specific skills and qualifications. The results would be a better mix of hierarchy and market forces in shaping and blending marketable and intangible human capital assets. These and related questions are, however, likely to remain among the most difficult issues of labour and education policy harmonization to be resolved for the completion of market integration by 1992.

In the field of industrial and competition policies a number of possible lessons stand out. Although successful in some sectors, the EC needs to move up-market at a faster pace and achieve a higher diffusion of innovation. A good example is the field of robotics, where in 1984 Japan employed four times the aggregate of West Germany, France, Italy and the UK combined (Harrop, 1985). Lack of sufficient R&D efforts to close the technological gap have often been associated with insufficient scale of production due to fragmented national markets (caused among other things, by national purchasing policies), overemphasis on research rather than development (for example, carbon fibres in the UK), inexperience in strategic R&D alliances, where European firms have often been stripped of their technological capabilities by foreign partners and finally over regulation and public financing through national governments.

Therefore, in some sectors, co-ordinated government help in rationalizing production, as has been done in a most admirable way with the Japanese textile industry (Dore, 1986), should be envisaged and encouraged. If organized on a Japanese basis many European MNCs would probably have to reduce the number of plants presently operating within the EC (Turner, 1986).[7] In order to promote such rationalization, cartels and/or strategic tie-ups in R&D, involving a more liberal interpretation of article 85 of the Treaty of Rome (on restrictive agreements and abuse of dominant power) by the Commission and the Courts of Justice, may be required. The same could be said for merger and acquisition activities.

From a more general perspective the successful transformation and restructuring of European industry will depend not so much on the amount of public infrastructure and public policies (of which there is comparative plenty in the EC) but rather on its type and form. Again

Japanese industrial policies may serve as an inspiration. For according to Japanese thinking, the state, state aids and state policies are logical extensions of the market place and added wherever (and only wherever) market forces fail, just as the father figure forms an integral part of the family and directs family affairs, where needed. The thought of Japanese industrial policies being neither firmly rooted in MITI nor in the marketplace (Okimoto, 1989; Komiya *et al.*, 1988) is, to ideology prone economists, just as uncomforting as has been the previously entertained notion of 'network' organizations representing neither a pure market nor a pure hierarchial form of organizing economic activity. Both the micro and macro aspects of Japanese patterns of industrial adjustment, however, will eventually spread to other jurisdictions faced with equal conditions of environmental turbulence and will embrace the countries of the EC. *Japanization* is part of the industrial restructuring because of market turbulence in Europe, just as *Americanization* has been part of European industrial restructuring towards the enlargement of the common market in the 1960s. This will happen while scholars continue to ponder the misplaced question as to where Japanese policy making should be placed in terms of the options of market intervention versus *laissez faire*.

NOTES

1. Given the tremendous and excellent choice of literature regarding the functioning of the Japanese corporation and economy it is somewhat difficult to screen for particular pieces of work, some representative examples are Aoki (1984), Kotler *et al.* (1985), Patrick and Rososky (1976) and Abbeglen and Stalk (1985).
2. In 1988 manufacturing North America attracted over 32 per cent and Asia 38 per cent of all Japanese FDI directed towards these regions.
3. In subscribing to a theory of technological accumulation and economic development Cantwell (1989) shows the inadequacy of neo-classical reasoning and empirical testing with respect to the new forms of technological competition and international activities among large firms. According to his approach, retention and extension of technology has little to do with the well functioning or malfunctioning of markets for technology. Rather innovation is seen as a *firm-specific* process (as opposed to being *product specific*).
4. There are of course appreciable variations among EC countries and these differences must be kept in mind when speaking of Europe and European firms.
5. The diffusion of the J-form organization throughout Europe will lower the transaction cost of joint-ventures and other forms of European–Japanese tie-ups, hence increasing their incidence.
6. For an elaborate treatment see Nelson and Winter (1982).
7. Rationalization should be understood in terms of achieving dynamic efficiencies of scope along with somewhat less important static scale effects.

Thus rationalization should consider a proper balance between scale and scope or scale and flexibility (Weiermair, 1991).

REFERENCES

Abegglen, J.C. and G. Stalk Jr. (1985), *Kaisha. The Japanese Corporation*, New York: Basic Books.

Aoki, (ed.) (1984), *The Economic Analysis of the Japanese Firm*, Amsterdam: North Holland.

Aoki, M. (1988), *Information, Incentive and Bargaining in the Japanese Economy*, Cambridge MA: Cambridge University Press.

Bartel, A.P. and Lichtenberg, F.R. (1987), 'The Comparative Advantage of Educated Workers in Implementing New Technology', *Review of Economics and Statistics*, **LXIX**, 1–11.

Bartlett, C. and S. Ghoshal (1989a), *Managing Across Borders. The Transnational Solution*, Boston, MA: Harvard Business School Press.

Bartlett, C. and S. Ghoshal (1989b), 'The Transnational Company that wins in 1990', *The Economist: The World in 1990*, 97–8.

Boyer, R. (1988), *The Search for Labour Market Flexibility*, Oxford: Clarendon Press.

Burton, F. (1989), Trade Friction between Europe and Japan: The need for a European Consensus, *Mimeo*, School of Management, University of Manchester Institute of Science and Technology.

Cantwell, J.A. (1989), *Technological Innovation and Multinational Corporations*, Oxford: Basil Blackwell.

Casson, M. (1988), 'Entrepreneurial Culture as a Competitive Advantage' *Discussion paper no. 124*, Dept. of Economics, University of Reading, UK.

Dore, R. (1986), *Flexible Rigidities: Industrial Policy and Structural Adjustment in the Japanese Economy 1970–80*, London: Athlone Press.

Dore, R., J.B. Cabale and K. Tapiola (1989), *Japan at Work: Markets, Management and Flexibility*, Paris: OECD.

Drucker, P. (1988), 'Management and the World's Work, *Harvard Business Review*, **88**, 65–76.

Dunning, J.H. (1981), *International Production and the Multinational Enterprise*, London: Allen & Unwin.

Dunning, J.H. (1986), *Japanese Participation in British Industry*, London: Croom Helm.

Dunning, J.H. (1990), 'The Governance of Japanese and U.S. Manufacturing Affiliates in the U.K.: Some Specific Differences' presented at the workshop on the Organization of Work and Technology: Implications for International Competitiveness, Brussels, May 31-June 1.

Dunning, J.H. and A. Webster (eds) (1989), *Structural Change Through the World Economy*, London: Routledge.

EC Commission (1988), *A Comparative Assessment of the European Automotive Industry in the Automotive Industry in the View of 1992*, Brussels: EC.

EC Commission (1986), *EC–Japan Relations*, Commission Communication to the Council, Brussels: EC.

EC Commission (1983), *Japan: Consultations in Train and Envisaged – Working*

Paper of the DGI, on the Agenda for the 509th Meeting of the Commission on 21/03/1979 item III dated March 19, 1979.

Freeman, C. (1987), *Technology Policy and Economic Performance: Lessons from Japan*, London: Francis Pinter.

Harrop J. (1985), 'Crisis in the Machine Tool Industry: A Policy Dilemma for the European Community', *Journal of Common Market Studies*, **XXIV**, (1), September.

Hayes, R.H. and S.C. Wheelwright (1984), *Restoring Our Competitive Edge*, New York: Wiley.

Imai, K. (1980), 'Japan's Industrial Organization', in K. Satoki (ed.), *Industry and Business in Japan*, New York: M.E. Sharpe.

Imai, K. (1988), 'Patterns of Innovation and Entrepreneurship in Japan,' paper presented at the 2nd congress of the International Schumpeter Society, Siena.

Imai, K. (1988), 'Network Industrial Organization in Japan Parts I and II', *Gestion 2000*, **1**, 91–115; **2**, 17–29.

Imai, K. (1989), 'Systematic Innovation and Cross-Border Networks, Transcending Markets and Hierarchies to Create a New Techno-Economic System', paper presented at the International Seminar on the Contributions of Science and Technology to Economic Growth at the OECD, Paris, June 1989.

Imai, K., Nonaka I. and H. Takeuchi (1985), 'Managing the New Product Development Process: How Japanese Companies Learn and Unlearn' in K.B. Clark, R.H. Hayes and C. Lorenz (eds), *The Uneasy Alliance – Managing the Productivity–Technology Dilemma*, Boston: Harvard Business School Press.

Ishikawa K. (1990), *Japan and the Challenge of Europe 1992*, London: Pinter.

Japan Economic Journal (1988), 'Japanese Firms Rapidly Increase Global Research and Development', September 24, 2.

Japan Economic Journal (1990), 'M & A activity slipping to Europe', July 28, 6.

Japan Economic Journal (1990), 'Firms rush into East-Europe', January 20.

Japan Times (1980), 'Technology group to be set up with EC', May 17, 11.

JETRO (1990), *White Paper on Foreign Direct Investment, Expanding Global Investment Exchange and Japan's Responsibilities*, Tokyo: JETRO.

Kangono, T., I. Nonaka, K. Sakakibara and A. Okimura (1983), 'An Evolutionary View of Organizational Adaptation: United States vs. Japanese Firms', *Discussion paper No. 117*, Institute of Business Research, Hitotsubashi University, Kunitachi, Tokyo.

Kogut, B. (1983), 'Foreign Direct Investment as a Sequential Process' in C. Kindleberger and D. Andretsch (eds), *The Multinational Corporation in the 1980s*, Cambridge, MA: MIT Press.

Komiya R. *et al.* (1988), *Industrial Policy of Japan*, Tokyo: Academic Press.

Kotler, P., L. Fahey and S. Jatusripitak (1985), *The New Competition*, Englewood Cliffs: Prentice Hall.

Locke, R. R. (1989), *Management and Higher Education Since 1940. The Influence of America and Japan on West-Germany, Great Britain and France*, Cambridge: Cambridge University Press.

Marsh, F. (1983), *Japanese Overseas Investment*, London: Economist Intelligence Unit.

Nelson, R.R. and Winter, S.G. (1982), *An Evolutionary Theory of Economic Change*, Cambridge, MA: Harvard University Press.

OECD (1988), *New Technology in the 1990s, A Socio-Economic Strategy*, Paris: OECD.

OECD (1989a), International OECD Seminar on: 'Science, Technology and Growth' 5–8 June, Paris, OECD.

OECD (1989b), *'Technological Change as a Social Process – Society, Enterprise and the Individual'*, New Directions in Management Practices and Work Organization, Helsinki Conference Proceedings, December 11–13, Paris: OECD.

OECD (1989c), *Economies in Transition: Structural Significance in OECD Economics*, Paris: OECD.

Okimoto I.D. (1989), *Between MITI and the Market. Japanese Industrial Policy for High Technology*, Stanford, CA: Stanford University Press.

Olson, M. (1982), *The Rise and Decline of Nations*, New Haven: Yale University Press.

Ouchi, W.G. (1981), *Theory Z*, Reading, MA: Addison-Wesley.

Ozawa, T. (1979), *Multinationals, Japanese Style: The Political Economy of Outward Dependency*, Princeton: Princeton University Press.

Patrick, H. and W. Rosovksy (eds) (1976), *Asia's New Giant: How the Japanese Economy Works*, Washington: The Brookings Institution.

Peters, T. (1988), *Thriving on Chaos: Handbook for a Management Revolution*, New York: Perennial Library.

Peters, T. and Waterman R. (1982), *In Search of Excellence*, New York; Warner Books.

Piore, M.J. and C. F. Sabel (1984), *The Second Industrial Divide: Possibilities for Prosperity*, New York: Basic Books.

Porter, M. (1990), *The Competitive Advantage of Nations*, New York: Basic Books.

Porter, M. (ed) (1986), *Competition in Global Industries*, Boston: Harvard Business School Press.

Servan-Schreiber J.J. (1967), *Le Défi Américain*, Paris: edition Denoel.

Teece, D. J. (ed.) (1987), *The Competitive Challenge. Strategies for Industrial Innovation and Renewal*, Cambridge, MA: Sallinger.

Trevor, M. (1983), *Japan's Reluctant Multinationals*, London: Francis Pinter.

Turner, G. (1986), 'Inside Europe's Giant Companies: Cultural Revolution at Phillips', *Long Range Planning* **19/4**, (98), August.

Vicari, S. (1989), *Nuove Dimensioni della Concorrenza. Strategie nei Mercati senza Confini*, Milan: EGEA.

Weiermair, K. (1990), 'Globalization, the diffusion of technology and new forms of work organization', paper presented at the International Ergonomics Association, August, Honolulu.

Weiermair, K. (1991), *The Economics of Industrial Restructuring and Management of Change*, Praeger, forthcoming.

Wilkins, M. (1974), *The Maturing of Multinational Enterprise*, Cambridge, Mass.: Harvard University Press.

5. New Developments in Subcontracting: Mixing Market and Hierarchy

Klaus Semlinger

INTRODUCTION

European industry is facing new challenges. In addition to the competitive power of the Japanese economy and the growing strength of other East-Asian countries, the formation of a real common market in Western Europe increases the pressure to improve the capability of efficient production and flexible supply. However, it might be that the political and economic reform in the Eastern European countries and its impact on the development of new markets will ease this pressure. But this is an open question and, thus, an unknown outcome. Another 'European' solution, of course, is that many companies will try to cope with the increased competition by joining forces with each other. This could happen in two ways which will significantly change the governing modes of economic exchange. The first option is by merger and acquisition which will lead to further economic concentration, and thus substitute market for hierarchy (see, for instance, the chapter by Amin and Dietrich). The second is to reduce in-house production and to increasingly rely on subcontracted supply from (legally) independent firms, an option which, at first sight, appears to replace hierarchy by market forms of governance.

This chapter focuses on the second option. After a short review of the explanation which transaction costs analysis provides for the choice between in-house production and market procurement, the contemporary dynamics of outsourcing and the new features of modern subcontracting will be described in more detail. This will be followed by an analysis of the extent to which these structures and processes of inter-organizational exchange conform to the interpretations of transaction costs theory and more complex sociological models of inter-firm relationships. It will be argued that both miss or at least underrate the strategic intentions and potential of the actors involved. Accordingly, the last section will elaborate on this issue and on questions concerning the distribution of autonomy and risk within the new networks of supply.

'MAKE OR BUY' AS A QUESTION OF ECONOMIZING PRODUCTION AND TRANSACTION COSTS

For a long time economists viewed the firm as a 'black box' optimizing a production function to economize production costs. The idea to regard a firm as a governance structure organizing exchange relations, as an alternative approach to the market-mode of economizing transaction costs (Coase, 1952) had been neglected up to the 1970s when the revival of institutional economics started to make use of this interpretation and productively enlarged the scope of economic analysis, see Williamson (1975).[1] Nevertheless, even then firms (that is hierarchies) and markets were regarded as very distinct patterns, where in the theoretical model of the market only prices regulated exchange, while within firms this was done by rules and directives. Correspondingly, the 'boundaries' of a firm were commonly defined by the line across which only price-mediated transactions took place (Arrow, 1971) and mixed forms were taken as unstable, transitory and not viable (Williamson, 1975).

Early transaction costs analysis proclaimed that there has to be a clear-cut answer to the question, respectively, of 'make or buy' and 'merge or buy'. According to the enlarged view of the task of optimizing, the decision between market procurement and vertical integration depends upon the economies in both production as well as transaction costs, with the extent of asset specificity of transaction-related investments being the decisive factor, see Williamson (1985), p. 90 ff. When asset specificity is low, to purchase goods and services on the market will be more efficient than their in-house provision due to economies of scale and/or scope attainable by an outside supplier who is producing for a larger market and is helped by the avoidance of bureaucratic distortions of hierarchy and by the positive effects of the 'high-powered incentives' of market transactions[2] on cost-control and innovation.

In contrast, when high transaction specific investments are required, in-house production can be equally efficient as market procurement in terms of production costs since there are no scale economies an outside supplier could achieve. Furthermore, with asset specificity in recurrent transactions, hierarchical control will be even more efficient with regard to transaction costs because it is supposed to be more apt to safeguard against opportunism and to overcome the restrictions of bounded rationality.

These advantages are assumed to be especially important if uncertainty is high and, thus, there is need for an extensive adaptability of the items and the terms of the transaction (Williamson, 1985, p. 75 ff.). While outside procurement economizes on steady-state transactions, to effect adaptations across a 'market interface' requires mutual agreement and therefore at least time-consuming and costly negotiations concerning the modifications of the contract. Therefore, the more that asset specificity deepens, and the more likely are recurrent necessities for adaptation, the greater the comparative advantage of in-house procurement where adaptations can be affected by directives.

Obviously, market and hierarchy have their comparative advantages in different settings and neither of them shows its productive features without costs. Accordingly, modern transaction costs analysis admits that there might be reason, if not necessity, for hybrid forms of organization which combine the supposed adaptiveness and security of hierarchical transactions with the potential for production cost economies and the high-powered incentives of market mode exchanges (Williamson, 1985, p. 143 ff.) Nevertheless, such intermediate forms of governance structure are still seen as difficult to obtain, especially since they are unobtainable at zero costs. However, transaction costs theory proclaims that emerging governance structures will only be viable if they are economically efficient, that is, apt to economize on the costs of the entire transaction in question (see Williamson, 1985, p. 92).

ONGOING DEVELOPMENTS IN SUBCONTRACTING

Outsourcing and subcontracting are by no means new ways of organizing the inter-company division of labour. Apart from purchasing raw materials and equipment in different industries there is a more or less developed tradition of buying parts and components from outside suppliers, which, with or without further processing, become integrated into the final, more complex product. Production costs economies of outsourcing have been long recognized and many large companies have been well aware of the possibility of taking outside suppliers as buffers for cyclical fluctuations in capacity utilization, see Schultz-Wild (1978). Nevertheless, the extent and scope of outsourcing had been quite limited up to the mid-1980s and, with regard to the hazards of failing deliveries and unfair pricing, backward vertical integration had been recommended and pursued.

This has changed during the last few years. Outsourcing, that is, the market procurement of formerly in-house produced goods and services from legally independent supplier firms, has increased, and the shaping of new inter-company structures of production networks has become a central management issue. Facing the high competitiveness of Japanese industry on world markets – put down in part to its highly developed system of affiliated subcontractors (see Demes, 1989) – the large automobile manufacturers especially, in Europe and the US have striven for a qualitatively new kind of relationship with their suppliers (Helper, 1990; Loveridge, 1990; Semlinger, 1991).

Modern purchasing policies are heading towards an intensification of inter-company co-operation. The demands made on suppliers are increasing in number and standards. While a competitive price and continuing price decreases are taken for granted, expectations with regard to flexibility have increased. Supply not only has to be carried out within shorter time frames, but also with regard to greater variations in ordered volumes and product design. Furthermore, the deviations tolerated in terms of delivery dates, amounts delivered and product quality are becoming narrower. Finally, the accompanying services now expected from suppliers include more contributions to R&D, better financing arrangements, intensified quality monitoring and document-ation, increased stockpiling and improved communication facilities. At the same time the number of suppliers has been continuously reduced to the extent that today for many parts and components, final assemblers rely on only a single supplier for a part (single-sourcing).

In one of the most developed models of subcontracting in the FRG automobile industry, namely the production of car seats, independent supplier firms have build up entirely new sites close to the final assembly plants of their customers. Each of these supplier plants produces a number of different types of seats which are not only manufactured but also designed by the supplier in accordance with the specific demands of the respective customer. Finally, in being connected via an on-line data-network, the suppliers are expected to deliver the seats with zero-defect quality, just-in-time and in due order, which means that final orders are received shortly after some advance notice, and deliveries are made every hour so that the seats – with shifting specifications and order – can be directly integrated into the work on the final assembly line.[3]

Even in less ambitious cases the new purchasing practices require more transaction specific investments. In general, suppliers are having to take over responsibility for more planning and development tasks, but are still strictly regulated in what they do by the specific requirements of their customers. At the same time, while many contracts are becoming longer (up to three years), they often do not specify a set quantity any more, but simply the quota, a more or less specified overall volume of demand, thus tying the purchase commitment of the buying company to its actual sales prospects.

This intensification of co-operation, however, sometimes referred to as 'integration of suppliers' (Gelder, 1986, p. 35) and 'dissolving the boundaries of the enterprise' (Becker and Weber, 1986, p. 37) does not result in vertical integration. There is no economic and legal merger of the firms involved. On the contrary, a high degree of supplier autonomy is explicitly regarded as being desirable; a number of well-known, large companies have stated that they would like their purchasing volume to not exceed 20–30 per cent of a given supplier's turnover. Sometimes such limitations are even part of the written agreement with subcontractors. To summarize, seen from the perspective of the buying enterprise, outsourcing is a shift from hierarchy to market, but seen from the supplier's perspective, subcontracting is quite the opposite, leading to something like an inter-organizational production association (*Produktionsverbund*) situated between market and hierarchy.

THEORETICAL SHORTFALLS IN EXPLAINING THE NEW SUBCONTRACTING NETWORKS

At first sight the new forms of subcontracting seems to be a specific kind of intermediate structure of exchange between discrete market contracting and hierarchial organization which modern transaction costs analysis concedes may emerge. But under the criteria which transaction costs theory claims to be decisive for the organizational development of exchange relations, one would expect backward integration: single-sourcing, that is, small number contracting, increases the odds for opportunism. The growing demands for flexibility in price and quantity increase uncertainty and call for higher adaptability. Just-in-time delivery pushes frequency of transactions to the extreme. Finally, asset specificity – of every kind[4] – is increased if custom-made products are to be delivered on requests transmitted over on-line data-networks from dedicated sites located in close proximity to the plants of the customer firm. Therefore, at least the most ambitious subcontracting networks (most common for parts and components which are of considerable importance with regard to their size or value[5]) appear to have risen against the predictions of transaction costs analysis.

Furthermore, many new subcontracting relations do not fit with the second proposition of transaction costs theory derived from the assumption of the overall economizing rationale in governance development, that there is no free meal (Williamson, 1985, p. 176). The proposition is that when transaction specific investments yield reasonable cost savings, but vertical integration is rejected and the customer firm is reluctant to produce the part or component on its own, then, to get an independent supplier to substitute for in-house production with efficient technology, would require the buyer to compensate the subcontractor for the adopted risk of the non-redeployable investment.

Currently, despite the enlarged period covered by written contracts, subcontracting links by no means ensure the supplier the amortization of transaction specific investments. In most cases the purchasing companies explicitly refuse to safeguard their suppliers against future cuts in demand. Modern subcontracting schemes barely provide a supplier with any compensation for additional risks apart from the status of remaining a contracted supplier. In fact, oursourcing companies quite often put a squeeze on prices either by proposing cost reductions or, in instances of competitive bids, by dictating a price freeze or a price cut. In addition to this, the shift from guaranteed quantities to quotas confronts the supplier with additional sales and manufacturing risks, as this kind of contract ties up manufacturing capacity without the security of knowing whether it will be utilized as planned.[6]

These risks would be reduced to some extent, if the buyer purchased the specific assets.[7] Indeed, in many cases, buying companies acquire possession of the moulds and dies necessary for the custom-made production of the parts they order by paying for them separately. Many subcontractors, however, hardly regard such an arrangement as a relief, but more as a threat because it makes it easier for the customer to assign follow-up orders to another supplier.[8] In this case, to take the risk of investing in specific assets, serves to reduce the longer-term risk as it creates mutual dependence.

Interdependence, nevertheless, is not guaranteed. Mutuality only exists as far as both the buyer and the subcontractor are dependent on the sales of the final product. However, while the new, quota, contracts stipulate explicit risk-sharing, most outsourcing companies – even when practising single-sourcing – ensure that they could change a supplier if necessary. For subcontractors, in contrast, it is more difficult to get orders from other customers.[9] The buyer is only dependent on a subcontractor to the extent that there is no better alternative in supply. Thus, in order to increase the buyer's dependency, the subcontractor has to improve its competitive performance and to adapt further to the customer's needs.

Outsourcing companies stimulate such efforts with the promise of long term bonds and support them by intensive communication and privileged information. In adapting to this situation, however, the supplier reinforces its dependency on the buyer.[10]

In the end the purchasing firm and its suppliers become tightly interconnected but do not merge. To the extent that the firms involved depend on the sale of the final product they share a common interest. The dependency pattern within the exchange relationship, however, is contingent upon the relative strength of each party within, as well as outside, the distinct relationship. The same applies to the pattern of risk and profit-sharing. There is no clear cut pay-off agreement. The market principle of equivalent exchange is suspended as is the hierarchical regulation of exchange by routines and directives. Thus, while transaction costs analysis provides some insight into the logic of contract development, it insufficiently explains the new subcontracting arrangements.

In the new subcontracting, exchange relations seem to fall back on a more general pattern of reciprocity, that is, contributions are expected to reach balance not in every exchange but over the entire agreement.[11] Relationships of this kind are claimed to be better explained by more complex models of business behaviour in sociology and organizational theory. A short review of such models will show whether they provide a more satisfying description of the new subcontracting systems.

A common feature of these models, which is also one of the major weaknesses of transaction costs analysis (see Francis, Turk and Willman, 1983, p. 3) is the attention they pay to ambiguity[12] in a situation of interdependency, with ambiguity or vagueness being a problem either of performance measurement (Ouchi, 1980, p. 134 ff) or of precise formulation of the overall aim and the expected single contributions within an exchange relation (Butler, 1983, p. 156 ff). Given these circumstances, flexible, coherent and efficient adjustments by the parties involved require, on the one hand, stable relations and feedback processes which render market-mode exchanges inadequate and, on the other hand, non-routine, innovative and risky actions, which are impeded within hierarchial organization.

Obviously, ambiguity in inter-dependent relations leads to a trade-off problem similar to the one transaction costs theory establishes for exchange relations with asset specificity, but, while in transaction costs theory asset specificity only impairs the incentive structure of market-mode exchanges, ambiguity is a problem for both markets and hierarchies. Accordingly, when ambiguity is barely reduceable and transaction specific investments are hard to relinquish, in order to simultaneously allow for creativity, stimulate innovation and ensure reliability of compliance to changing goals, an intermediate structure of incentive and control is necessary which has to be more generic than just a hybrid mixture of market and hierarchy.

Unfortunately, most of the literature about such intermediate forms of exchange is more descriptive than analytical. In all the different approaches, however, it is goal congruence and trust between the parties involved which appear to mediate exchange. The differences between the various models mainly concern the way in which goal congruence and trust are created or emerge, respectively. Within 'clans' it is 'socialization' by which the different actors learn about their inter-dependence and about the traditions of implicit rules which govern their interaction, see Ouchi (1980). In 'communes' this happens through 'indoctrination', with common beliefs and values, among peer groups of 'gregarious' individuals who share a feeling of togetherness, see Butler (1983). The individual actors of 'federations' rely on 'pooled returns' or agreed mutual supervision (Daems, 1983), while mutuality in 'networks' emerges from 'indebtedness' and the repeated experience of reliable standards which no one individual can change, see Powell (1990).

In the new subcontracting systems, however, there is no pooling of returns and no mutual supervision. Although there might be some mutual indebtedness and traditions, and notwithstanding that in many cases there will be mitigation before litigation, these are informal arrangements which are circumscribed by written contracts which lay down explicit prices which are to be paid for the parts and services in question and the duties and rights of each party involved. Some supplier–buyer relationships might in fact be based on mutual trust derived from common values, beliefs and goals, and, as in any real situation, subcontracting systems will diverge from any abstract model of governance. As a rule, however, subcontracting relations are not founded on a trust derived from shared values and beliefs but on trust in the performance and soundness of scrutinized suppliers and buyers. Common values and trust might serve as a smoothing device, t ˅ underpin given agreements, but it is market competition and the threat to terminate the relationship which enforces compliance.

Thus, although the models of clan, commune, federation and network provide a more sophisticated description of modern subcontracting systems than does transaction costs theory on its own, and although all the models hint at the existence of conflict, the picture they portray is much too harmonious to be a satisfying interpretation of the real nature of subcontracting markets. The next section attempts to come to a better understanding by extending the analysis beyond the explanations of transaction costs theory and sociological accounts, to include the elements of strategic contracting.

OUTSOURCING AND STRATEGIC CONTRACTING

The increasing substitution of outside procurement for in-house production and the reshaping of existing subcontracting systems are recent developments within American and European industry. The question which has to be answered then is why such efforts have been intensified or why they are more successful today. The increasing competitive strength of Japanese export industries and the example of their subcontracting systems has already been mentioned as a reason. But the emerging western patterns in outsourcing are different in that, as a rule, there are no (mutual) equity investments and no transfers of personnel, and purchasing companies are eager to ensure that their subcontractors deliver to other customers as well. For a better understanding, closer scrutiny of the rationale behind outsourcing and the prerequisites and limits of its prevalence is necessary.

Manifold Interests behind Outsourcing

Many western manufacturers engaged in mass production today find themselves confronted with both the threat of market saturation and considerable competitive pressure. They can react to these challenges with product differentiation and further product development (increasing product diversity and shorter product life cycles) in order to stimulate and satisfy new markets and evade price competition. At the same time, they can engage in 'systemic rationalization' (Altmann and Sauer, 1986), which includes reducing the numbers of processing phases and cutting back idle time and buffer stocks in manufacturing as well as administrative work. This is achieved, respectively, by means of more manufacturing-oriented product planning and increased utilization of microelectronic technology and greater utilization of modern logistic concepts and electronic data processing.

Thus, while market forces and marketing strategies compel enterprises to achieve greater product differentiation and higher product quality, there is also a need for better integration of the individual manufacturing steps resulting from the new rationalization strategies. In other words, increasing complexity in operational processes has to be matched with greater demands on reliability. This does not leave the inter-company division of labour untouched. On the contrary, reducing in-house production and making increased use of outsourcing is a decisive step in the direction of coping with this demand. Outsourcing in the context of these market and rationalization strategies has five major overlapping functions: to reduce costs; speed up processes; enlarge scope of capability; increase flexibility; and improve the incentive and control structure of hierarchical organization.

First, to engage an outside supplier can reduce costs when the productivity of a specialized subcontractor, owing to learning curve effects, is higher than that of in-house production or when a sub-contractor, in producing for a larger market, can profit from large-scale economies. Lower costs of subcontracted supply, however, are not necessarily derived only from productivity advantages of outside suppliers; small and medium sized supplier firms especially can deliver at a lower price primarily because they pay lower wages and have less non-wage labour costs, see Semlinger (1991), while other subcontractors, quite simply, are forced to accept the squeeze on their profits exerted by the tough stance of buyers on prices (see next section).

Second, with outsourcing, bottlenecks in a company's own production capacity can be avoided, thus increasing the possibility of a parallel execution of different work steps. Additionally, with just-in-time delivery, different work steps can be synchronized (Doleschal, 1989a, p. 177 ff.), which is not only time-saving but also a prerequisite for reducing buffer stocks. Both result in capital costs economies and in a shortening of amortization periods. As these results, however, could also be obtained by in-house production, outsourcing is then primarily a device to improve these options by shortening the time required to build up additional capacity (but see the arguments below related to the fourth and fifth function of outsourcing).

Third, a production process consists of a number of different activities which require different capabilities (knowledge, experience, skills).[13] As a rule firms specialize in activities for which their capabilities offer a comparative advantage and, thus, they tend to concentrate on complementary activities which call for similar capabilities. Problems arise when production requires the co-ordination of complementary but dissimilar activities (Richardson, 1972, p. 891).[14] Because progress in science and technology increasingly is an aspect and result of the division of labour, today, even the biggest enterprise has to fall back on the knowledge and capability of other specialized companies to make use of the most advanced possibilities in production and design.[15]

Fourth, while transaction costs theory accentuates inertia due to the prospect of resistance by exchange partners, the adaptability of an exchange or production system depends also on the extent of physical inertia due to long-term capital commitments. By opting for outsourcing instead of in-house production, fixed costs are turned into variable costs because no capital investments on the part of the subcontracting firm are required. Thereby, physical inertia can be avoided and the risks of capacity utilization and amortization reduced.

Finally, outsourcing is a strategy to overcome behavioural inertia as well. It is a device to improve the innovativeness of an exchange system with regard to goal-related performance and to increases its adaptiveness to changing goals. In accordance with the proposition of transaction costs theory that market-mode transactions employ stronger incentives to innovate, a company can profit from this feature either directly by substituting external procurement for in-house production, or indirectly by threatening internal suppliers with external competitive bids.[16] Therefore, outsourcing – by resorting to the powerful incentives and the free competition of a market-mode exchange – also enforces higher adaptability of the hierarchy-mode of internal exchange, which in bureaucratic organizations is often much lower than conceded by transaction costs theory[17] and the models of many sociological approaches.[18]

The new subcontracting systems briefly described above are designed for more than simply improving efficiency. Their aim is also to increase flexibility and risk-sharing, which are not only merely subgoals of higher efficiency. At the same time, the efficiency of outsourcing as a strategic game itself is not dependent on its economizing effect on production and transaction costs. As already stated, an outsourcing company can profit from lower prices of subcontracted supply which are not derived from higher productivity. Furthermore, increased flexibility does not stem only from the avoidance of in-house capital commitments or better versatility of (smaller) independent supplier units; it can also originate from the enforced higher pliability of the subcontractor.[19] Finally, in order to reduce risk, the outsourcing company need not share it, if it can succeed in shifting some of its risks in sales, manufacturing, control, and R&D to the exchange partners.[20]

It is exactly this potential of shifting risks and enlarging one's own room for manoeuvre by passing down adjustment pressures to subcontractors which makes outsourcing such an interesting strategic option. In contrast to an analogous intra-company division of labour, by which many of the productivity improvements are equally obtainable, external procurement can instrumentalize market competition to put pressure on supplier price and performance and, most important, without purchasing companies having to give much consideration to the working conditions, social structure, profitability or market position of its autonomous suppliers. In summary, outsourcing as strategic contracting is the attempt to combine the high-powered incentives of markets to innovate, with production and communication cost-efficiency of asset specificity and adaptability of loosely coupled systems, without incurring additional transaction costs.[21]

Outsourcing as a Strategic Game

Transaction costs theory does not deny strategic intentions in sub-contracting, but it insists that in the long run, efficiency, that is, the overall efficiency of the entire exchange, will subdue power, that is, unilateral profits extracted from exchange partners by unfair exchange practices (Williamson, 1985, pp. 17, 125 ff.). The flaw is the long-run argument relies on perfect market competition. Perfect competition, however, is only a feature of 'theoretical' markets while real markets are governed by strategic games as well.

Strategic games, in turn, are not only governed by efficiency as the criterion of choice between given options; strategic games also involve the distribution of alternative opportunities. In addition, strategic options and necessities are not defined by a single transaction, and an optimal strategic decision can not be made on just considering the *pros* and *cons* of an isolated exchange or exchange relationship. Thus, while transactions between parties enjoying different sets of opportunities might be unbalanced in terms of a strict *quid pro quo* exchange for the transaction in question or for the entire exchange relation, they could still be perfectly rational for the handicapped party.

Apart from the corresponding goal of strategic purchasing manage-ment, which may shape the relevant supply markets into a buyer's market, see Kraljic (1986), there are many reasons why suppliers will agree to unfavourable contracts. First, a supplier may agree in the hope of a better follow-up contract. Another reason is the attractiveness of being a supplier to a customer who is well known for its quality demands and who orders in big batches. While the value and profitability of expected future contracts might greatly exceed that of the actual contract, being a subcontractor, for example, of a big car manufacturer, improves one's reputation in the market and eases sales and production planning. Third, once a firm has decided on following a strategy of specialization as a supplier, it is with difficulty that it can change course. The smaller the supplier and the more it has adapted itself to the needs of one or a few customers, the more difficult it will find to trade with other outsourcing companies or to penetrate into final demand markets.[22] Apart from this, access to other customers or markets might be barred or all the alternatives might be even less favourable. After all, the management of a supplier firm (due to bounded rationality or specific standards) may be reluctant to shift to other trades or markets just because it subjectively appreciates the discounted future opportunity revenues less than the main contract in hand.[23]

All this is not to maintain that outsourcing, in any case, is a means of exploiting independent subcontractors (or pressurizing internal suppliers). The inter-company division of labour in many cases is not just a zero-sum game but a real improvement in efficiency and flexibility. However, this is not guaranteed. Outsourcing does not inevitably aim at a co-operative partnership like the one described in the different models of consensual exchange. The subcontracting business is built on reciprocity, but sometimes a subcontractor has to be happy just to stay in the game.

It comes as no surprise, that only the Swedish networks approach, which has a business administration and marketing background, emphasizes the strategic quality of 'networking' with actors striving for network control to increase efficiency, security and flexibility for themselves, see Axelsson (1990). Networking, according to the Swedish school, is a strategic answer of management to its limited control over internal resources and activities and the attempt to develop, and to make use of, potential opportunities to influence external actors and their resources, see Hakansson and Snehota (1989, p. 194). Networking activities, thus, are regarded as 'market investments', that is, resource commitments to 'enact a context', to choose a network, and to achieve a favourable position within this network, see also Johanson and Mattson (1985). In any case, even the scholars of strategic networking stress mutuality of knowledge, orientation, dependency and complementarity of interests within networks, for example, Johanson and Mattson (1987, p. 35), Axelsson (1990, p. 21). Although it is admitted that there might be a conflict of interests, it is emphasized that no single actor is able to determine the rules of exchange without approval of the other actors (Hakansson and Snehota, 1989, p. 195 ff.).[24] If there is an 'aggressive' touch in networking, then it is to get into a stronger competitive stance *vis-à-vis* competitors outside the network, see Jarillo (1988, p. 32).

Many scholars of the recent developments in subcontracting acknowledge the strategic character of the process. Some refer to the new inter-company supply systems, which seem to be most advanced in the automobile industry,[25] as 'co-operative manufacturing' (Sabel, Kern and Herrigel, 1991). A recent, thorough study of supplier–buyer relations in US car manufacturing employs Hirschman's dichotomy of 'exit and voice' to conclude that there is a shift from exit-mode relations, through which the powerful US automakers increase transaction costs for their sub-contractors to miminize the suppliers' bargaining power, to relationships which are more 'voice-based', see Helper (forthcoming). The same study, however, shows that intensive communication and mutuality within these networks is rather one sided and mainly to the advantage of the buying firms. It is the suppliers who provide their customers with process control charts, cost accounting figures and technical assistance; and it is the suppliers who adapt to the demands of their customers. Asked for their appraisal of fair treatment under the new regime, the car parts suppliers give, at best, only a 'sceptical affirmative' (Helper, 1990). In Germany, evidence from case studies and expert interviews shows a similar pattern (see Doleschal, 1989b; Semlinger, 1991), as it does also for Japan,[26] where many big manufacturers, known for their almost self-contained supplier 'pyramids', recently have started to encourage their subcontractors to supply other customers as well (Demes, 1989, p. 290 ff.; Ernst, 1989, p. 11).

To sum up, with outsourcing and the intensification of the inter-company division of labour, powerful companies, whose strength might well derive from the weakness of their partners, try to get a focal position within a network of co-operating subcontractors. The buyer–supplier relation striven for is one of 'autonomy and domination', see Bieber and Sauer (1991). That is, the suppliers are formally independent, but can nevertheless be steered by the purchasing company, which defines the 'terms of trade'. Autonomy to supplier units in this kind of relationship is granted in order to mobilize knowledge and creativity by making use of market incentives and competition as a discovery and selection device, see Hayek (1945, p. 520 ff). Autonomy in these relationships, however, achieves a second goal. It absolves the buyer from assuming responsibility for the outcome of the agreed conditions of exchange on the subcontractor – a responsibility the buyer cannot disregard when the supplying unit is an intra-company subsidiary. Thus, autonomy of the supplier under domination of the buyer makes better use of market features also as a disciplinary device.

In as far as an outsourcing company succeeds with these attempts, it, in turn, improves its own autonomy. It gains the flexibility and power of being able to make discrete decisions about whether it or other parties should adapt.[27] In other words, the new developments in outsourcing are a modern emanation of the strategic struggle of management for autonomy, see Bechtle (1980), which now transcends the boundaries of the individual company.

CONCLUSION

The new subcontracting systems, that is, the formation of inter-company production associations, overcome the old dichotomy of market and hierarchy. Their emergence is related to efficiency, yet not necessarily to overall efficiency, but simply the profitability of the focal company. These systems are founded on co-operation and mutual exchange of information, but often the distribution of the yields of co-operation is balanced in favour of the powerful buying company, and communication is simply a device to improve adaptation and compliance of the suppliers to the customer's demands.

To understand the ongoing developments in subcontracting one has to acknowledge the strategic interests and moves of powerful actors. Nevertheless, even for companies which are dominant in their industry, to shape a supplier system of controlled flexibility may remain only an intentional goal, since the characteristics of the actual network will be contingent on more than just the financial power and the market position of the purchasing company. There might be suppliers of equal strength or subcontractors who are indispensable and therefore have to be treated as real or preferential partners. Other potential subcontractors with alternative opportunities at their disposal will be able to refuse or withdraw from unfair contracting. Thus, even for large companies it is not always possible to squeeze suppliers' profits and to exploit their 'passive flexibility', that is, their pliability to external force. Sometimes this is not even necessary because of real advantages offered by the suppliers in terms of productivity and 'active flexibility', that is, versatility with regard to innovative options. Thus, the question of how far and to what extent the ongoing restructuring of the supply markets is a zero-sum game or one offering real gains in efficiency and flexibility, depends on the distribution of strategic opportunities between the parties involved.

The real-world phenomenon of subcontracting cannot be explained by just one theoretical model. In addition, and in contrast to theoretical models, real supply systems are only crude approximations of market, hierarchy or network ideal types. To the extent that traditional procurement from independent subcontractors is no pure market exchange, and to the extent that internal supply from integrated subsidiaries is no pure hierarchial transaction, co-operation within the new inter-company production associations is no pure consensual or reciprocal exchange. Finally, one has to acknowledge that real patterns are not purely intentional but the outcome of the interplay of conflicting or congruent interests and objective opportunities and restrictions. Thus, in order to understand the real phenomenon one has to develop a complex approach which incorporates questions of efficiency and power, but which, even then, does not arrive at unambiguous and generally valid answers.

NOTES

1. In the 1970s scholars at the Institute for Social Science Research (ISF) in Munich – coming from a very different strand of theory – developed a somewhat similar but quite distinct understanding of the 'firm as a strategy' to ensure autonomy (for the invested capital) within the boundaries of market competition and social conflict (Bechtle, 1980). While the Market and Hierarchy debate mainly is about analysing different kinds of governance structures with special concern about the modi and media of exchange, the Munich approach concentrates on the driving moves, combining interests in efficiency and rentability and power and domination. This is not the place for a more detailed discussion, nevertheless, and despite some theoretical reservations, the strategic emphasis of this approach has fertilized the argument here.
2. These are net revenues which can be influenced by performance.
3. See, for example, Zeilinger (1989) for a description of the logistic system of BMW.
4. According to Williamson, these are site specificity, physical asset specificity, human asset specificity, and dedicated specificity (Williamson, 1985, p. 95).
5. For example, in the automobile industry this applies to car seats, fuel tanks and dashboards.
6. This risk is very different from the uncertainty about receiving a follow-up contract, which could be regarded as a normal market risk that could be counteracted through appropriate marketing efforts.
7. As a rule there is no explicit compensation for increasing unit costs when the finally ordered quantity falls below the announced one.
8. Williamson would not see any problem in this risk, if the first supplier gets its variable costs paid (Williamson, 1985, p. 172). However, coverage of costs only partially describes the contractual choice situation, as is discussed later in this chapter.
9. This might be the case due to the overall increasing importance of transaction specific investments. In any case, a change by the customer indicates that a competitive supplier has the edge on the old subcontractor who, without improving its performance, would hardly make headway with tenders to other buyers.
10. Accordingly, in contrast to Williamson (1985), it is also arguable that it is the subcontractor investing in specific assets who becomes the 'hostage'.
11. See the stimulating discussion of the differences between market, hierarchy and network in a recent paper by Powell (1990).
12. Although in transaction costs analysis uncertainty is one of the three factors defining the situational setting of a transaction, and ambiguity is acknowledged as a severe problem of measurement and control, their impact on the development of governance structure is barely elaborated and also somewhat contradictory, see Williamson (1985).
13. This argument draws upon the highly imaginative and stimulating interpretation of the institutional organization of industry by Richardson (1972), whose functional and situational approach, in this author's opinion, is more comprehensive than the transaction cost approach and worthy of further exploration.
14. In relation to increasing uncertainty, Loveridge (1990), laying more

15. Note that this is not a problem of efficiency but of availability and feasibility.
16. For empirical evidence see Loveridge (1990), Helper (forthcoming) and Jürgens and Reutter (1989, p. 136 ff.).
17. This proposition comes as a surprise because Williamson explicitly refers to the work of Simon as one of the intellectual roots of his theory, while Simon is an early and prominent sceptic of the actual power of hierarchical control. See for example, Simon (1976, p. 15).
18. For a discussion of the simultaneous usage of market and hierarchy for a mutual improvement of each mode in intra-company regulation, see Häusler (1990).
19. For a more detailed explanation of this distinction, see Semlinger (1990) pp. 9 ff.
20. For a more detailed discussion of the associated risks, see Semlinger (1989), (1991).
21. Thus, the cake is even bigger than the one Williamson is denying (1985, p. 176); one can have it and eat it too!
22. Changing or mixing strategies is not only a problem of efficiency, see Porter (1980) but of feasibility as well. While large companies have the opportunity to follow different strategies at the same time, smaller firms will have problems to meet the financial, organizational, capacity and other requirements needed for mixed strategies and strategic change.
23. Worth mentioning too, is the impact of modern information and communication technologies which improve the options of intensive and up-to-date data exchange, and thus increase the opportunities of control and communication at low costs.
24. In this assumption, this school of networking finds itself in agreement with the more sociological approaches to the network phenomenon and transaction costs theory.
25. There is some evidence, however, that in the West German furniture industry the phonomenon is even more advanced, Döhl (1989).
26. Due to the very hierarchial structure of Japanese supplier–buyer relationships and the gap of technological competence between the final assemblers and their first rank suppliers on the one hand and the lower ranking suppliers on the other, buyers provide technological assistance to their subcontractors. With a more detailed comparison of the structure and development of subcontracting networks in the US, Europe and Japan one would be able to reveal the many factors which explain the historical, dynamic and contemporary differences in the inter-company division of labour.
27. This does not correspond with the common definition of power but with that of Deutsch (1966) p. 111, who refers to it as the ability to refuse learning, which is more to the point in relation to the problem in question.

REFERENCES

Altmann, N. and D. Sauer (eds) (1986), *Systemische Rationalisierung und Zulieferindustrie*, Frankfurt a.M.: Campus.

Arrow, K.J. (1971), *Essays in the Theory of Risk-Bearing*, Chicago: Markham.

Axelsson, B. (1990), 'Researching Industrial Networks – Some Strategic Issues.' Paper presented to an international workshop on 'The Socio-Economics of Inter-Firm Cooperation', Berlin: Social Science Center Berlin (WZB), 11–13 June.

Bechtle, G. (1980), *Betrieb als Strategie. Theoretische Vorarbeiten zu einem Industriesoziologischen Konzept*, Frankfurt a.M/New York: Campus.

Becker, W. and J. Weber (1986), 'Strategische Beschaffung als Schlüssel zum Einkäufermarkt', *Beschaffung aktuell*, **43**, 36–38.

Bieber, D. and D. Sauer (1991), 'Kontrolle ist gut! Ist Vertrauen besser?' In H.G. Mendius and U. Wendeling-Schröder (eds) *Zulieferer im Netz. Neustrukturierung der Logistik am Beispiel der Automobilzulieferung*, Köln. Bund-Verlag.

Butler, R.J. (1983), 'Control through Markets, Hierarchies and Communes: a Transactional Approach to Organisational Analysis', in A. Francis, J. Turk and P. Willman (eds), *Power, Efficiency and Institutions*, London: Heinemann, 137–158.

Coase, R.H. (1952), 'The Nature of the Firm', *Economica* (New Series), **4**, 386–405.

Daems, H. (1983), 'The Determinants of the Hierarchical Organisation of Industry', in A. Francis, J. Turk and P. Willman (eds), *Power Efficiency and Institutions*, London: Heinemann, 35–53.

Demes, H. (1989), 'Die pyramidenförmige Struktur der japanischen Automobilindustrie und die Zusammenarbeit zwischen Endherstellern und Zulieferern', in N. Altmann and D. Sauer (eds), *Systemische Rationalisierung und Zulieferindustrie*, Frankfurt a.M: Campus, 251–297.

Deutsch, K.W. (1966), *The Nerves of Government: Models of Political Communication and Control*, 2nd edn, New York: Free Press.

Döhl, V. (1989), 'Rationalisierungsstrategien von Abnehmerbetrieben und Anforderungen an die Zulieferer – das Beispiel Möbelindustrie', in N. Altmann and D. Sauer (eds), *Systemische Rationalisierung und Zulieferindustrie*, Frankfurt a.M: Campus, 29–52.

Doleschal, R. (1989a), 'Just-in-time-Strategien und betriebliche Interessenvertretung in Automobil-Zulieferbetrieben', in N. Altmann and D. Sauer (eds), *Systemische Rationalisierung und Zulieferindustrie*, Frankfurt a.M: Campus, 155–205.

Dolsechal, R. (1989b), 'Die Automobil-Zulieferindustrie im Umbruch', Graue Reihe der Hans-Böckler-Stiftung, *NF 15*: Düsseldorf.

Ernst, A. (1989), 'Subcontraktbeziehungen in der industriellen Zulieferung in Japan', *ifo-Schnelldienst*, **42**, (5–6), 9–24,

Francis, A., J. Turk and P. Willman (eds), (1983), *Power, Efficiency and Institutions*, London: Heinemann.

Gelder, E. (1986), 'Innovative Endprodukte erfordern neuartige Zusammenarbeit mit den Vorlieferaten – nicht nur in der Technik', *Beschaffung aktuell*, **8**, 34–35.

Hakansson, H. and I. Snehota (1989), 'No Business is an Island: The Network Concept of Business Strategy', *Scandinavian Journal of Management*, **5**, (3), 187–200.

Häusler, J. (1990), 'Steuerungsmechanismen und Beziehungsmuster in divisionalisierten Großunternehmen', *Mimeo*, Max-Planck-Institut für Gesellschaftsforschung: Köln.

Hayek, F.A. (1945), 'The Use of Knowledge in Society', *American Economic Review*, **35**, (4), 519–530.

Helper, S. (1990), 'Supplier Relations at a Crossroads: Results of Survey Research in the US Automobile Industry', *Mimeo*, Department of Operations Management, Boston University.

Helper, S. (forthcoming), 'Strategy and Irreversibility in Supplier Relations: The case of the US Automobile Industry', *Business History Review*.

Jarillo, J.C. (1988), 'On Strategic Networks', *Strategic Management Journal*, **9**; 31–41.

Johanson, J. and L-G. Mattson (1985), 'Marketing Investments and Market Investments in Industrial Networks', *International Journal of Research in Marketing*, **2**, 185–195.

Johanson, J. and L-G. Mattson (1987), 'Interorganizational Relations in Industrial Systems: A Network Approach Compared with the Transaction Cost Approach', *International Studies of Management & Organisations*, **17**, (1), 49–63.

Jürgens, U. and W. Reutter (1989), 'Verringerung der Fertigungstiefe und, betriebliche Interessenvertretung in der deutschen Automobilindustrie', in N. Altmann and D. Sauer (eds), *Systemische Rationalisierung und Zuliefer-industrie*, Frankfurt a.M: Campus, 119–153.

Kraljic, P. (1986), 'Gedanken zur Entwicklung einer zukunftsorientierten Beschaffungs- und Versorgungsstrategie', in G. Theuer, W. Schibel and R. Schäfer (eds), *Beschaffung – ein Schwerpunkt der Unternehmensführung*, Landsbert/Lech, 72–93.

Loveridge, R. (1990), 'Shifting Boundaries in Subcontracting Relations: The Case of the Automotive Industry'. Paper presented to an international workshop on 'The Socio-Economics of Inter-Firm Cooperation', Berlin: Social Science Center Berlin (WZB), 11–13 June.

Ouchi, W.G. (1980), 'Markets, Bureaucracies, and Clans', *Administrative Science Quarterly*, **25**, 129–141.

Porter, M.E. (1980), *Competitive Strategy: Techniques for Analyzing Industries and Competitors*, New York: Free Press.

Powell, W.W. (1990), Neither Market nor Hierarchy: Network Forms of Organization', *Research in Organizational Behavior*, **12**, 295-336.

Richardson, G.B. (1972), 'The Organisation of Industry', *The Economic Journal*, **82**, 882–896.

Sabel, C.F., H. Kern and G. Herrigel (1991), 'Kooperative Produktion. Neue formen der Zusammenarbeit zwischen Endfertigern und Zulieferen in der Automobilindustrie und die Neuordung der Firma', in H.G. Mendius, U. Wendeling-Schröder (eds), *Zulieferer im Netz. Neustrukturierung der Logistik am Beispiel der Automobilzulieferung*, Köln: Bund-Verlag.

Schultz-Wild, R. (1978), *Betriebliche Beschäftigungspolitik in der Krise*, Frankfurt a.M.: Campus.

Semlinger, K. (1989), 'Fremdleistungsbezug als Flexibilitätsreservoir. Unter-nehmenspolitische und arbeitspolitische Risiken in der Zulieferindustrie', *WSI-Mitteilungen*, **42**, (9), 517–525.

Semlinger, K. (1990), 'Small Firms and Outsourcing as a Flexibility Reservoir for Large Companies'. Paper presented to an international workshop on 'The Socio-Economics of Inter-Firm Cooperation', Berlin: Social Science Center Berlin (WZB), 11–13 June.

Semlinger. K. (1991), 'Small Firms in Big Subcontracting', in N. Altmann, C. Köhler and P. Meil (eds), *Technology and Work in German Industry*, Frankfurt a.M/New York: Campus.

Simon, H.A., (1976), *Administrative Behavior*, 3rd edn., New York: Free Press

Williamson, O.E. (1975), *Markets and Hierarchies: Analysis and Antitrust Implications*, New York: Free Press.

Williamson, O.E. (1985), *The Economic Institutions of Capitalism*, New York: Free Press.

Zeilinger, P. (1989), 'Just-in-Time bei einem Automobilhersteller', *CIM-Management*, **3**, 15–20.

6. Inter-firm Technological Alliances: A Transient Phenomenon or New Structures in Capitalist Economies?

Vivien Walsh

INTRODUCTION

The last two decades of the twentieth century are seeing profound changes in the economic and social systems of Europe. The generation and commercial exploitation of technology has played, and will continue to play, a fundamentally important role in shaping its economic, institutional and social development. At the same time, economic and social institutions will decisively determine the efficiency with which technology will be generated and adopted or commercially exploited. However, conventional economic theory in the neo-classical tradition, with its focus on short-term analyses of fluctuations in supply and demand for goods and services, has difficulty in dealing with long-term, dynamic processes.

Similarly, the neo-classical concern with market forces and profit maximization tends to neglect the effect of strategic plans of companies and the policy initiatives of governments. Privately owned, business firms are not the only actors making decisions that decisively affect economic growth or quality of life; neither are their decisions the optimal choices based on perfect knowledge of production alternatives, factor prices and market demands, that conventional economic theory suggests. The innovation literature has long since demonstrated (for example, Pavitt, 1980; Nelson and Winter, 1977) that knowledge of alternatives is imperfect, obtaining it has a cost, and market conditions and technologies are continuously changing. Satisfactory analysis combines ideas from disciplines such as sociology, psychology and political science as well as economics. Neo-Schumpeterian and other evolutionary approaches to technological change start from a broader perspective of this type, see for example, Dosi, *et al.* (1988).

This chapter will use such perspectives to explore the emergence and commercial exploitation of biotechnology: a new technology which has the potential to make an important contribution to economic growth in the future. An important feature of the commercialization of bio-technology has been the establishment of new innovative firms as well as the move by established firms into the new field; and the growth of collaborative agreements between the new and the established firms, in which technological and other knowledge is shared.

The phenomenon of inter-firm co-operation raises an important general question: why, in market economies where firms are expected to compete, should they co-operate? Why not produce the new techno-logical knowledge by themselves or buy it? More specifically this chapter addresses the question: how should the forms of collaboration observed in an emerging techno-economic field, in particular the agreements between new small firms and large established firms, be characterized and explained?

This chapter will not only examine these issues in the light of recent work on evolutionary theories of economics and technological change. It will also refer to some empirical findings of collaboration in bio-technology from a recent study of new biotechnology firms conducted by the author in collaboration with a group of researchers in Edinburgh, see Walsh (1988), Oakey, *et al.* (1990). The purpose of that study was to examine the fate of new firms established to exploit commercially the largely academic discoveries in genetic engineering in the early 1970s, rather than focus specifically on co-operative alliances between those firms and other institutions.[1] However, the number and variety of linkages established by the biotechnology firms was a striking observation made during the study.

INTER-FIRM COLLABORATIVE AGREEMENTS

Co-operative ventures and joint agreements between business firms have received increasing attention in recent years, in the form of conferences on the subject,[2] the establishment of data bases[3] and a variety of publications.[4] National programmes like the Alvey programme in Britain, and International ones like the EC's ESPRIT programme, have stimulated further attention to the phenomenon as well as encouraged more agreements. Chesnais (1988), for example, identified nine types of inter-firm agreement – and six types of study of inter-firm agreements.

The data bases mentioned above are likely to be incomplete, especially for earlier years, smaller firms and certain countries (Chesnais, 1986), and may not have been amended to take into account all the agreements that have been dissolved or have led to mergers and acquisitions (Sharpe, 1989b). Nevertheless these data bases, together with the increasing number of industry studies and case studies[4] all indicate a real and substantial growth in the number of co-operative agreements between firms over the past decade.

Certain forms of linkage between firms have been known for a long time, like the cross-licensing agreements characteristic of industries with a high propensity to patent (Telesio, 1979), the trusts of the late nineteenth century, the cartels of the 1930s and various customer–supplier arrangements involving joint development or technological assistance, for example in synthetic materials (Walsh *et al.*, 1980), and computers (Freeman, 1982). What is new is the considerable increase in numbers of agreements, different types of collaboration (Chesnais, 1988), increased range of industrial sectors involved (Mowery, 1989) and numbers of agreements between firms in different countries (*ibid*). Particularly significant is the increase in co-operative agreements involving the production of new scientific and technological knowledge, not just joint-ventures in marketing and/or production. For example, Morris and Hergert (1987) report that 64 per cent of alliances in their data base involve new product development. This chapter will focus on agreements involving technological co-operation.

An economic analysis of inter-firm agreements is of particular importance to a discussion on the future of Europe, since co-operation between firms within the EC is a major objective of the latter's 1992 programme (CEC, 1985; Cecchini, *et al.*, 1988). The liberalization of trade within a common European space and with the countries of Eastern Europe will certainly affect industrial collaboration, but Kay (1990) argues that the completion of the internal market will encourage firms to substitute other strategies for joint-ventures. This issue will be discussed later.

MARKETS AND HIERARCHIES

Firms which have invented a new or improved product or process can, by patenting and copyright, establish property rights over the relevant technological information. Use of tacit knowledge and trade secrets, and developing lead times and learning curve advantages, also establish the information as private property in practice, if not in law. Teece (1986) points out that these practices may actually be more efficient than patents, especially in some industries. The firms which have produced advances in technology can then issue licences to other firms to use that information in exchange for royalties. This is essentially a market-place transaction in existing technology or a sale of intellectual property rights (subject to certain restrictions). Contract research involves a different form of arms-length transaction, in which the technological assets do not yet exist but are developed for a fee (Teece, 1988).

Both types of market-place transaction are an alternative to the generation of new technological knowledge within the firm by means of in-house research and development (R & D). An innovating firm and its technological capabilities may also be acquired as a whole by take-over or merger and the innovative activities absorbed and managed by the acquiring firm. In both of these cases the innovative activity is, or becomes, organized hierarchically within the firm. Inter-firm alliances involve neither complete intra-firm control of the product development and production process, nor purchase of the necessary technology and other capabilities through 'normal' market transactions.

Williamson (1975) proposed that, in general, transactions take place more efficiently via the market unless special circumstances exist. A substantial body of literature has emerged from the ensuing 15 years' research into the nature of these circumstances, how they arise, their institutional implications and so on, for example Williamson (1985). Pisano (1990) has summarized some of this work, pointing out that few of the resulting publications have been concerned with in-house versus external sources of R & D (compared with studies of production and supply activities). Those that have, for example, Kay (1979) and Teece (1988), concluded that, in the case of R & D, hierarchies are usually more efficient forms of organization than markets. Clearly, however, there are occasions when neither markets nor hierarchies are entirely satisfactory.

CHANGES IN THE STRUCTURES OF FIRMS AND MARKETS

The institutionalization of R & D, as the in-house R & D laboratory, was one of the most important organizational innovations of the past century, according to Freeman (1982). It revolutionized the way in which firms competed and changed their technological bases. By internalizing R & D, it increased the firm's control over the rate and direction of technical change, made appropriation of new areas of knowledge easier and reduced to some extent at least the uncertainties inherent in innovation. It therefore enabled a firm more easily to negotiate and control some aspects of its environment rather than simply respond to it (Coombs, Saviotti and Walsh, 1987).

Capitalist economies in the twentieth century have been characterized by, among other things, increased market concentration and increased vertical and horizontal integration, with the evolution of large multi divisional corporations (Chandler, 1962; Kay, 1982) and increasing multinational operation (Caves, 1982; Michalet, 1985), including world-wide sourcing strategies by the MNEs. Kay (1979) argues that the take-off of R & D as a specialist, integrated function in the firm was complementary to the widespread adoption of the highly structured and functionally differentiated M-form of company organization.

Nelson and Winter (1982) have demonstrated that both market structure and technological performance are generated endogenously, and that causal connections between increasing firm size and industrial concentration, on the one hand, and innovative success, on the other, go both ways. Levin *et al.* (1990) argued that both of these are determined by the structure of demand; technological opportunity; and the ability of firms to appropriate the returns from private investment in R & D.

The increased tendency to co-operation between firms, in R & D and new product development as well as production and marketing, would seem to be a trend counter to concentration, integration and in-house production of technology. The author will argue that co-operation agreements are very closely related to firms' attempts to appropriate the returns from investment in both private *and* public R & D.

REASONS FOR INTER-FIRM CO-OPERATIVE ALLIANCES

The firm's environment has become increasingly competitive and rapidly changing. Internationalization of markets has increased, competition has become more intense and product cycles have become shorter in a range of industries, notably the more high technology ones (Coombs and Littler, 1987).

Science, including quite fundamental advances in scientific knowledge, has become increasingly important in providing or contributing to new technological opportunities. In many cases breakthroughs have resulted from the cross-fertilization of different disciplines. This underlines the increasing importance of multidisciplinary research and the need to keep up with advances in *many* areas to achieve a *single* commercially exploitable breakthrough. Technology has become increasingly con-vergent, for example computer technology and communications have become more and more important to each other, machine vision technology has become increasingly important to robotics (Mowery,

1989), and biotechnology to pharmaceuticals, food processing and other technologies.

In this environment firms are faced with pressures to become more research intensive, to develop a wider and wider range of competences, to produce higher value-added products and to get them onto the market more quickly. All of this increases the cost and risks to the individual firm; the need to enter more and more markets (both geographically and in terms of end-use applications and types of user), overcoming a variety of non-tariff barriers to entry; and the need to get access to new areas of technology, and/or production and marketing expertise. Entering into a co-operative agreement with another firm may thus be seen as a good method of:

1. Sharing the costs and risks of R & D.
2. Gaining access to new areas of technology.
3. Gaining access to new markets.
4. Gaining access to skills.

This said inter-firm agreements are not without their problems as many authors have pointed out, for example, Mowery (1989), Pisano (1990).

The commercial exploitation of genetic engineering to produce innovations in a variety of industrial sectors depended on an ability to master and co-ordinate a large number of complementary fragments of knowledge and learning procedures. Sharp (1989b) has listed some eight disciplines needed for genetic engineering, never mind the commercial production of goods as a result of applications of that knowledge. I shall argue that the way in which different institutions were involved in the realization of these innovations induced firms to specialize in a particular aspect of the innovation process. Commercial success then required that they form links with firms with other specialisms.

BIOTECHNOLOGY

Biotechnology is 'the processing of materials by biological agents' (Bull *et al.*, 1982), the agents in question being micro-organisms, plant and animal cells and enzymes, and the processes being fermentations, cell cultures and bio-catalytic processes, respectively. This definition includes some of the earliest, pre-capitalist activities such as brewing; the large-scale industrial capability developed for microbial production of anti-biotics during and after World War II; and recent developments including most notably genetic engineering, introduced in the 1970s and often taken to be synonymous with 'biotechnology'. This third-generation biotechnology involves the transfer of genetic information between strains and species so that cells or micro-organisms can be induced to synthesize products or perform reactions which would otherwise be unnatural to them (Sherwood and Atkinson, 1981).

These latter developments have grown out of the discipline of molecular biology – which developed almost exclusively in universities and other public research institutions, rather than in industrial research organizations. Technical change in biotechnology is still heavily dependent on quite fundamental advances in science and hence on the public research system. Nevertheless, the development of products and processes based on genetic engineering also depend on the industrial capability which grew as a result of the second generation of biotechnology mentioned above, based in turn on the less exclusively academic disciplines of microbiology, biochemistry and chemical engineering (Faulkner, 1989).

Many of the most important and well-publicized breakthroughs of third-generation biotechnology, such as recombinant DNA techniques (1973) and cell fusion techniques for producing monoclonal antibodies (1975), were made well over a decade ago. Yet it is still difficult to forecast the eventual output, and its value, of all the commercial applications of these breakthroughs. Sharp (1985) has collated some estimates and the OECD (1989) some others. Indeed, many of the small biotechnology firms we visited have yet to produce a product or generate any profits.

Biotechnology is a series of technologies, and cannot be said to be located in a single industrial sector. Indeed, that is one of the reasons why it is often cited as having considerable potential for fuelling a new period of economic upswing. The analogy is drawn with microelectronics and information technology. Developments in biotechnology are, however, nowhere near as far advanced. It was estimated in 1987, for example, that there were only 30 000 people employed worldwide in biotechnology, a smaller number than the number just of professional workers employed in the semiconductor industry, see Pearson (1987). Sharp (1989a) suggests that biotechnology is currently in a phase roughly equivalent to the period in the 1950s when the semiconductor was beginning to take over in microelectronics. The potential is based on the large number of products and processes which involve (or could involve) biological substances and phenomena and may be (or are already known to be) subject to genetic engineering. This spans the health care, chemicals, food, energy and extraction industries, which together represent a major portion of the international economy (Dunhill and Rudd, 1984).

An important contribution to evolutionary economic theory has been the work of Freeman and others. See for example the collection edited by Dosi *et al*. (1988). At the heart of the approach by Freeman and Perez (1988), for example, is the idea that 'some new technologies, after a prolonged period of incubation and crystallization, offer such a wide range of opportunities for new markets and profitable new investment that, when social and institutional conditions are favourable, entrepreneurs have sufficient confidence to embark on a prolonged wave of expansionary investment'. Their analysis is based on the idea of a 'techno-economic paradigm' or cluster of inter-related technical, organizational and managerial innovations.

Genetic engineering provided a paradigm change in biotechnology, in the narrower sense of 'technological trajectory' put forward by Dosi (1982) (a new 'natural trajectory' in Nelson and Winter's (1977) terms). It changed the whole set of basic ground rules, opening up new approaches to old problems and new fields of development (Sharp, 1989b). Third-generation biotechnology has, in turn, provided a paradigm change in the technological bases of a whole range of industrial sectors, the most advanced of which is pharmaceuticals, by providing new approaches to the search for therapeutic compounds ('designer drugs' rather than 'molecular roulette') and new processes for making them. (The OTA (1984) reported that 62 per cent of biotechnology applications were in pharmaceuticals.) Whether it will form the basis of a new 'techno-economic' paradigm (like electric power or synthetic materials) with effects in most branches of the economy, remains an open question (OECD, 1989).

COMMERCIALIZATION OF BIOTECHNOLOGY

In America, despite great uncertainty about the potential of the new technology, attempts to exploit it commercially quickly followed the scientific discoveries. Indeed, given the hype surrounding the launch of new biotechnology firms, followed by disappointment at the time taken to get from scientific potential to commercial product, many would say 'too quickly'. A rash of new firms were established, often by the academic discoverers going into business themselves after the Schumpeterian (Mark I) model (Schumpeter, 1912). The peak year for start-ups was 1981, with 43 established (OTA, 1984). The main source of funds was the venture capital market. Venture capitalists in fact initiated the whole process, by identifying commercial opportunities, scientists, premises, etc., and orchestrating relationships with other necessa y organizations (Florida and Kenney, 1988).

A significant slice of finance came from established manufacturing companies in the form of venture capital, research funding or equity investment. Equity investment of $119 million was made by established firms in 1982, see OTA (1984). Exchanges of technological knowledge were usually part of the deal. Japanese firms began to catch up by the end of the 1970s and a key strategy for them was to establish collaborative links with American start-up companies. European firms have lagged behind somewhat. In Europe, the new biotechnology start-up firm has been much less common than in the US, the result of a number of institutional and cultural factors: the venture capital market is less well established and academics and other public sector researchers are less inclined to become entrepreneurs, for all manner of reasons (Sharp, 1989b). Biotechnology followed the US pattern most closely in Britain, with about 50 new independent firms established 1975–87 (Walsh, 1988). The peak year for start-ups was 1982, a year later than the US, with 10 formed.

Dosi and Soete (1988) stress the importance (to national economic competitiveness) of innovative advantages, which are firm specific and cumulative (built on previous technological advances within the firm). They are also both the result and cause of technological specialization in certain areas (Cantwell, 1989). At the same time, Nelson and Winter (1982) find industry performance strongly related to *exogenous* knowledge: 'the innovative R & D efforts of firms. . . take advantage. . . of new technological opportunities that have been created elsewhere.'

Technological progress proceeds cumulatively along trajectories defined by the technological paradigm, but technological discontinuities occur when new technological paradigms emerge, offering new clusters of innovative opportunities (Orsenigo, 1989). New paradigms make obsolete the skills and competences accumulated by established firms – Schumpeter's (1942) 'gales of creative destruction'. At times like these new innovators – who are not 'locked into' the old established procedures and research perspectives – can most easily appear.

LARGE FIRM–SMALL FIRM COLLABORATION

Although the internalization and organization of R & D by large established corporations meant that they were able to remain at the forefront of new technology and generate successive waves of innovation, they have not always been the ones to introduce whole new technological paradigms. Some large firms, like drug companies ICI, Glaxo and Wellcome in Britain, were involved in biotechnology research from the beginning. Outside the drug area, ICI was responsible for the innovation of Pruteen, a single cell protein used as an animal feed additive.

In general, however, the pharmaceutical industry, although probably the most research intensive and innovative of all the sectors which have been affected by the new developments in biotechnology, and one doing an unusually high proportion of basic research, nevertheless continued for years to concentrate on the old paradigm they had established – a rather hit or miss approach to synthesizing as wide a range of new chemicals as possible ('Molecular roulette') and large-scale screening of natural and synthetic compounds for potential biological or therapeutic effects. They did this in the face of well-established declining returns to effort and rising costs. The new paradigm, genetic engineering, came from outside the drug industry, developed in university and government funded laboratories and first commercialized by new start-up firms.

Large corporations, especially multinationals, have opportunities and market power not available to single product/market firms. This includes their ability to act as centres of finance capital and to cross-subsidize activities in one market with profits from another. Chesnais (1986) has reviewed work by economists in Italy and France on these advantages, concluding that such firms act as nets, in two senses of the word: networks of horizontal and vertical flows of inputs, intermediates, finished products and information (a capability enhanced enormously by the adoption of information technology); and 'nets' in which to 'catch', appropriate and exploit all kinds of productive resources, inputs and information.

In the case of biotechnology, the large firms were able to appropriate some of the new areas of knowledge, even though they had not (on the whole) produced it. As Teece (1986) has pointed out, under certain circumstances 'profits from innovation may accrue to the owners of certain complementary assets rather than to the developers of the intellectual property.' Teece was referring to cases where inventions are easy to copy or patents can be 'invented round'. In the case of biotechnology, the large firms used their possession of the 'complementary assets' needed for commercialization to negotiate collaborative agreements with the new entrants, and in that way not only to maintain their advantages, but to gain access to new areas of knowledge and expertise.

The 'complementary assets' in the case of the large established pharmaceutical firms, and which the new entrants did not have, were their national and international product distribution system; their teams of representatives who promote branded drugs to the doctors who prescribe them and the chemists who sell them; their experience, resources and networks of medical consultants for clinical trials to establish safety; their capabilities in formulating a therapeutic compound into a pill, liquid, suppository, etc.; and the long-term relationships established with government representatives and health authorities who give the firms licences to carry out clinical trials and then market their drugs, and who negotiate the conditions of the licences, and in some countries the prices that can be charged. And the contribution of these assets represents something like 90 per cent of the cost of bringing a new drug onto the market.

When they were first established, the small US firms had easy access to venture capital, and subsequently to investments *via* stock market flotation. Nevertheless, because they did not usually have the complementary assets for producing and marketing products, they were obliged to enter agreements with the larger firms, especially in pharmaceuticals. Some of the new entrants were able to become manufacturers, for example in producing diagnostics kits where entry barriers were low. Others supply reagents and equipment for genetic engineering research to industrial and public sector laboratories. However, most of the small companies have only been able to produce products in co-operation with larger established firms.

In the case of more recent US start-ups and many of the British firms we visited, there was not even easy access to finance. The stock exchange crash of 1987, and its weakness for some time afterwards, prevented many firms which had found capital to start up but counted on flotation for raising the necessary further funds. Lunzer (1988) reported 'visions of an independent biotechnology industry are fading fast as companies scramble for the cash needed to stay alive'. Only 21 per cent of the British firms received start-up capital from venture capitalists. A majority (56 per cent) used personal savings as their main means of funding the launch of their firms. Furthermore, 21 per cent of firms claimed that shortages of capital had *directly* inhibited their introduction of new innovations.

Many of these firms therefore had an additional incentive to collaborate with large established firms: the desperate need for funds (Walsh, 1988). The over-riding concern of most of them was to build or maintain their technological bases. For this reason many of them were reluctant to do contract research for the larger companies, or to enter into agreements with them which involved giving away too much of the know-how and inventions that represent their 'seed corn' for the future. However, often there was not much choice. The more adept and experienced small firms were able to secure more benefits from their agreements with established companies, for example by acquiring production capability through joint-ventures with plant contractors, or through opening up marketing opportunities via the granting of limited, as opposed to exclusive, licences (Faulkner, 1989). Many of them have made real gains from their agreements. But the chances are limited of most of them developing into manufacturing companies, independent of larger companies.

Some small firms act essentially as external laboratories for large firms, by doing contract research: 40 per cent of the firms we visited did contract research. Services (rather than products) represented more than 50 per cent of turnover for 35 per cent of firms. One case is perhaps an extreme example: the firm is essentially the research activity of a university department, incorporated as a business in order to exploit its commercial potential more effectively. The establishment of these researchers as a firm was initiated by a chemical/pharmaceutical multinational based in Britain. One of the founders of the business came from the large firm, and the venture capitalist who arranged start-up finance, had only recently left the same large firm. The chemical company is still an important customer of the small business, together with two foreign-owned pharmaceutical companies.

Despite the general feeling among the biotechnology firms that finance was difficult to obtain, the venture capital firms have a different point of view. Rothschild's Biotechnology Investments Ltd. is not generally short of money to invest, only in good projects to invest in. BP Venture Research has underspent its budget in every one of the last 10 years, see Cookson (1990). Biotechnology firms are typically weak in a variety of business skills, such as strategic management, financial planning and market orientation. Several firms which received venture capital were required by the investors to recruit directors with management skills. In all, 58 per cent of firms we visited were founded by people with no management (only technological) qualifications or experience. Access to such skill is one more reason for entering into an agreement with an established firm.

The benefit to the large firms in entering partnerships with small biotechnology firms were:

1. Minimizing risks and costs associated with biotechnology R&D. Contracts with small firms can be used as feasibility studies. If exploitable results are not obtained, or if it turns out to be an area of research the large firm wants to pursue no further, and the agreement is cancelled, the large company will not have committed itself to investment in highly skilled in-house staff and new facilities. Contracts with several small firms spreads the risk of not immediately finding relevant results.

2. Although patents normally remain the property of the small firm, established corporations often obtain an exclusive licence to the technology developed through the contract, and keep most of the earnings. In this way the large firm is able to appropriate returns not only from private investment in R & D (its own), but also public investment in R & D in universities, hospitals and research institutes. Many small firms were established as spin-offs from public sector research, and many continue to have strong links with public research institutions. Two managing directors were still (officially) full-time academics. Among the British biotechnology firms, for example, 45 per cent maintained links with their founders' former organization. In addition, 30 per cent used universities as a major source of technological information while another 30 per cent used research institutes, Medical Research Council, National Health Service and government laboratories for the same purpose.
3. Equity investments not only allow the established firm to have a 'window on the new technology', but if the small firm is successful, it will provide a large return on investment when it goes public.

CONCLUSION

Small firms are at the centre of a complex web of inter-linkages between a multiplicity of organizations. The general view of biotechnology that emerges from most surveys is of a collection of generally small, highly scientifically and technologically advanced firms, with a variety of linkages both to public sector research and to large established enterprises, acting to some extent also as a channel for the transfer of know-how to the large enterprises, not only from their own R & D but also from publicly funded R & D. The British firms were probably rather less well established as businesses and less technologically sophisticated than their US counterparts. Although some of them were in the world leading class (notably Celltech – see Dodgson, 1990), it was difficult to see how some of the smallest survived. Only 25 per cent were developing products in collaboration with large firms, and although 80 per cent produced some products, many of these were intermediates, reagents and equipment rather than final products, and/or the products represented only a minority of their business activities. Services, such as information, consultancy and contract R & D were the mainstay of a majority of these firms, in some cases their major output.

Independent biotechnology firms are therefore vulnerable to domination by established enterprises for a number of reasons: most important is their lack of experience in production, marketing and national and international distribution of final products, and compliance with certain kinds of regulatory requirement; in addition some firms and firms in some countries have difficulty getting finance, while some firms are still deficient in business expertise. The large firms offer the expertise and the funds that they lack, but often attached to the 'strings' of rights to the technological know-how which represents the small firms' major asset. As Amin and Dietrich have suggested in Chapter 3, since the established firms are in the dominant position, the inter-firm alliances in biotechnology would appear to be a new form of hierarchy, rather than an intermediate stage between Williamson's market and hierarchy.

Nevertheless, the trend of new biotechnology firms carrying out contract R & D for established firms, or entering collaborative R & D agreements with them, represents a new pattern in the institutionalization of R & D, which over most of the past century has been towards increased internalization. This trend has more in common with the design function, which has increasingly been sub-contracted to independent firms over the past 30 or more years (much longer in Scandinavia) (Walsh *et al.*, 1991), and other functions of manufacturing firms (Gershuny and Miles, 1985).

Whereas sub-contracting represents an increase in transactions via the market place (as examined in detail in the previous chapter), in this case in technological know-how, collaborative agreements represent something of a blurring or dislocation of the institutional boundaries within which the R & D function is located, even though hierarchical relationships of a different kind may be dominant. There is thus some separation between the institutions within which production of goods and services takes place, and the institutional structures within which technologies are developed and taken to the point of innovation.

Given the trends in technological complexity, international competition and shortening product cycles mentioned earlier, co-operative ventures are likely to be used as a strategy by firms for some time to come, especially where resources are limited and governments are encouraging co-operation. However, in any individual case, they may not be so long-lasting.

The biotechnology firms' alliances, for example, depend on the needs of the partners – the small biotechnology firms for access to production, marketing and distribution competence and other complementary assets, for finance and for management skills; the large firm for technological capability. If either partner becomes independent of the other the reason for the collaboration disappears.

Large firms have for some time been investing increasing sums in their own biotechnology R & D. Du Pont for example, was spending $ 120 million on this in 1982, four times the amount spent by the largest of the independent biotechnology firms (OTA 1984). A number of bio-technology firms have been brought up by large established companies in their end-use industries – for example, Genentech bought by Hoffmann La Roche, Hybritech bought by Eli Lilly and Genetic Systems bought by Bristol Myers. Six of the British firms had been taken over (three by overseas firms) or merged by the time we visited them – all for financial reasons on the small firms' part and to move into, or vertically integrate, existing interests in biotechnology on the buyers' part.

Although the largest number of independent biotechnology firms are American, and only two European firms (Celltech [UK] and Transgene [France]) are in the same league as the top US firms in terms of turnover, the same is not true for the established firms. The chemical industry, for example, is the third largest manufacturing sector in Europe, and it is EC and Swiss firms that dominate the industry worldwide, with 11 firms in the top 20, including the four largest. The strategies adopted by the world's large established chemical firms (towards biotechnology and in other spheres) clearly has profound implications for the future of Europe. At the same time EC and individual European countries' industrial and technological policies will have to take into account the fact that success will be decisively determined by the behaviour of these multinationals.

Once the established firms can see more clearly which areas of biotechnology, if any, are going to be vital to their future business activities, they are likely to build up in-house R & D capability, possibly by buying a biotechnology firm or by recruiting staff with whom they already have established links via collaborative agreements. Kay (1990) has shown that the degree of market completion is an additional factor stimulating the growth of mergers relative to agreements. The trend thus appears to be going in the direction of the established firms generating more concentrated market structures, maintaining their dominant role and precluding the autonomous development of the independent bio-technology firms. They may then move on to establish joint agreements in new areas of uncertainty.

NOTES

1. We visited 43 out of the 49 biotechnology firms established in the UK from 1975 onwards (after the third generation breakthroughs), which were independent companies at formation rather than subsidiaries of larger groups, and which were listed in the Association for the Advancement of

British Biotechnology's *Directory* (1988). The largest of these firms employed under 500 people.

2. For example, The Strategic Bridging Conference, Stockholm, Sept 1990 (Strategic Management Society); Networking in Biotechnology, Copenhagen Business School, Jan 1990; The Co-operation Phenomenon, EOLAS, Dublin, Nov 1989; EEC/FAST Workshop on Technological Co-operation Agreements Between Firms, Université de Paris X, Nanterre, Nov 1988; Montreal International Workshop on Networks of Innovators, Université du Québec à Montréal, May 1990.

3. For example:
TASC at TNO and CATI at MERIT (Netherlands) (Hagedoorn and Schot, 1988; Hagedoorn and Schakenraad, 1988, 1990).
INSEAD Business School, Fontainbleau (France) (Morris and Hergert, 1987).
FOR (Italy), Ricotta (1987); CNEL database, Politecnico di Milano (Mariotti and Colombo, 1991).
LAREA-CEREM, Nanterre, Paris (Delapierre and Zimmermann, 1986; Zimmermann, 1988)

4. For example:
Theoretical papers and literature surveys such as Chesnais (1988), Teece (1986), Mowery (1989), Katz and Ordover (1990).
Case Studies and Industry Studies such as Chesnais (1986), von Hippel (1987), Coombs and Richards (1989), Mariti (1989), Sharp (1989b), Pisano (1990).

REFERENCES

Bull, A., G. Holt, and M. Lilly (1982), *International Trends and Perspectives in Biotechnology*, Paris: Organisation for Economic Co-operation and Development.

Cantwell, J. (1989), *Technological Innovation & Multinational Corporations*, Oxford: Blackwell.

Caves, R. (1982), *Multinational Enterprise and Economic Analysis*, Cambridge: Cambridge University Press.

Cecchini, P., *et al.* (1988), *The European Challenge: 1992*, Aldershot: Wildwood House.

CEC (1985), *Completing the Internal Market*. White paper from the Commission to the European Council, Commission of the European Communities, Luxembourg.

Chandler, A. (1962), *Strategy & Structure*, Cambridge MA: MIT Press.

Chesnais, F. (1986), 'Some Notes of Technical Cumulativeness, the Appropriation of Technology and Technical Progressiveness in Concentrated Market Structures', *Paper presented to the conference on Innovation Diffusion*, Venice, March.

Chesnais, F. (1988), 'Technological Co-operation Agreements between Firms', *STI Review*, December, 52–119.

Cookson, C. (1990), 'A Reward Worth the Gamble', *Financial Times*, London, 27 June.

Coombs, R. and D. Littler (1987), 'Trends in Funding & Conduct of Research & Development', Report to EEC/FAST Programme, Brussels.

Coombs, R. and A. Richards (1989), 'The Technological and Business Strategies of Innovating Firms', *Paper presented to the British Academy of Management conference*, Manchester, Sept.

Coombs, R., P. Saviotti and V. Walsh (1987), *Economics & Technological Change*, Basingstoke: Macmillan.

Delapierre, M. and J-B. Zimmermann (1986), 'Les strategies d'accords des groupes européens: entre la cohesion et l'éclatement', *mimeo*, LAREA/CEREM, Univ. Paris X Nanterre.

Dodgson, M. (1990), *Celltech: the First 10 Years of a Biotechnology Company*. Discussion Paper Series, Brighton: Science Policy Research Unit, Sussex University.

Dosi, G. (1982), 'Technological Paradigms and Technological Trajectories', *Research Policy* 11, 147–162.

Dosi, G., C. Freeman, R. Nelson, G. Silverberg and L. Soete (eds) (1988), *Technical Change & Economic Theory*, London and New York: Frances Pinter.

Dosi, G. and L. Soete (1988), 'Technical Change and International Trade' in G. Dosi *et al* (1988).

Dunhill, P. and M. Rudd (1984), *Biotechnology and British Industry*. Biotechnology Directorate, Science and Engineering Research Council, Swindon.

Faulkner, W. (1989), 'The New Firm Phenomenon in Biotechnology', in P. Rosa, S. Burley, T. Cannon and K. O'Neil (eds), *The Role and Contribution of Small Business Research*, Aldershot: Gower.

Florida, R. and M. Kenney (1988), 'Venture Capital Financial Innovation and Technological Change in the USA', *Research Policy*, 17, 119–137

Freeman, C. (1982), *The Economics of Industrial Innovation*, London and New York: Francis Pinter.

Freeman, C and C. Perez (1988), 'Structural Crises of Adjustment: Business Cycles and Investment Behaviour', in G. Dosi *et al.* (1988).

Gershuny, J. and I Miles (1985), 'Towards a New Social Economics', in B. Roberts, R. Finnegan and D. Gallie (eds) *New Approaches to Economic Life*, Manchester: Manchester University Press.

Hagedoorn, J. and J. Schakenraad (1988), 'Note for the EEC/FAST Seminar for European research groups on Inter-Firm Technological Co-operation Agreements', Université de Paris X Nanterre, November.

Hagedoorn, J. and J. Schakenraad (1990), 'Inter-firm Partnerships and Co-operative Strategies in Core Technologies', in C. Freeman and L. Soete (eds), *New Explorations in the Economics of Technological Change*, London and New York: Frances Pinter.

Hagedoorn, J. and J. Schot (1988), 'Co-operation Between Companies and Technological Development', *Mimeo*, Delft: TNO.

Katz, M. and J. Ordover (1990), 'R & D Co-operation and Competition', in *Brookings Papers on Economic Activity*, 137–203.

Kay, N. (1979), *The Innovating Firm*, Basingstoke: Macmillan.

Kay, N. (1982), *The Evolving Firm*, Basingstoke: Macmillan.

Kay, N. (1990), 'Industrial Collaborative Activity and the Completion of the Internal Market', *Mimeo*, Department of Economics, University of Strathclyde, November.

Levin, R., A. Klevorick, R. Nelson and S. Winter (1990), 'Survey Research on R & D Appropriability and Technological Opportunities', *Mimeo*, New Haven: Yale University, Economics Dept.

Lunzer, F. (1988), 'Cash Crisis Creates Biotech Alliances', in *High Technology Business*, April, p. 18.

Mariotti, S. and M. Colombo (1991), 'Mergers and Acquisitions – Italian Case Study,' unpublished interim report to EEC/FAST-MONITOR Programme on Globalisation of Economy and Technology, *Mimeo*, Politecnico di Milano.

Mariti, P. (1989), 'Constructive Co-operation Between Smaller Firms', Paper presented to EOLAS Conference, The Co-operation Phenomenon, Dublin, November.

Michalet, C-A. (1985), *Le Capitalisme Mondial*, Paris: Presses Universitaires de France, 2nd edn.

Morris, D. and M. Hergert (1987), 'Trends in International Collaborative Agreements', *Columbia Journal of World Business*, Summer p. 15.

Mowery, D. (1989) 'Collaborative Ventures Between US & Foreign Manufacturing Firms', *Research Policy*, **18**, 19–32.

Nelson, R. and S. Winter (1977), 'In Search of Useful Theory of Innovation', *Research Policy*, **6**, 36–76.

Nelson, R. and S. Winter (1982), *An Evolutionary Theory of Economic Change*. Cambridge, MA: Harvard University Press.

Oakey, R., W. Faulkner, S. Cooper, and V. Walsh (1990), *New Firms in the Biotechnology Industry – Their Contribution to Innovation and Growth*, London and New York: Frances Pinter.

OECD (1989), *Biotechnology: Economic and Wider Impacts*, Organisation for Economic Co-operation and Development, Paris.

Orsenigo, L. (1989), *The Emergence of Biotechnology*, London and New York: Francis Pinter.

OTA (Office of Technology Assessment) (1984), *Commercial Biotechnology*, Washington DC: Government Printing Office.

Pavitt, K. (1980), *Technical Innovation and British Economic Performance*, Basingstoke: Macmillan.

Pearson, R. (1987), 'Key Skills for Biotechnology', Institute for Manpower Studies, *Mimeo*, University of Sussex, Brighton.

Pisano, G. (1990), 'The R & D Boundaries of the Firm: an Empirical Analysis', *Administrative Science Quarterly*, **35**, 153–176.

Ricotta, E. (1987), 'Accordi di Collaborazione: Strumenti Flessibili per Strategie Globali', *Mimeo*, FOR-START, Rome.

Schumpeter, J. (1912), *Theorie der Wirtschaftlichen Entwicklung*, Dunker and Humblot, Leipzig; English translation (1934) *The Theory of Economic Development*, Cambridge, MA: Harvard University Press.

Schumpeter, J. (1942), *Capitalism, Socialism and Democracy*, New York: Harper and Row.

Sharp, M. (1985), 'Biotechnology: Watching and Waiting', in M. Sharp (ed.) *Europe and the New Technologies* London and New York: Frances Pinter.

Sharp, M. (1989a), 'Biotechnology in Britain & France – the Evolution of Policy' in M. Sharp and P. Holmes (eds), *Strategies for New Technology*, London: Philip Allen.

Sharp, M. (1989b), 'Collaboration in the Pharmaceutical Industry – Is it the Way Forward?' DRC Discussion Paper, Science Policy Research Unit, *Mimeo*, Sussex University, Brighton.

Sherwood, R. and T. Atkinson (1981), 'Genetic Manipulation in Biotechnology', *Chemistry and Industry*, April.

Teece, D. (1986), 'Profiting from Technological Innovation: Implications for International Collaboration, Licensing and Public Policy', *Research Policy*, **15**, 285–305.

Teece, D. (1988), 'Technological Change and the Nature of the Firm', in G. Dosi *et al.* (1988).

Telesio, P. (1979), *Technological Licensing and Multinational Enterprises*, New York: Praeger.

von Hippel, E. (1987), 'Co-operation Between Rivals: Informal Know-How Trading', *Research Policy*, **16**, 291–302.

Walsh, V. (1988), 'Desperately Seeking Solvency: External Linkages of UK Biotechnology Firms', *EEC/FAST Seminar on Inter Firm Technological Co-operation Agreements*, Univ. Paris X Nanterre, November.

Walsh, V., R. Roy, M. Bruce and S. Potter (1991), *Winning By Design*, Oxford: Basil Blackwell.

Walsh, V., J. Townsend, P. Senker, and C. Huggett. (1980), 'Technical Change and Skilled Manpower Needs in the Plastics Processing Industry', *Occasional Paper No 11*, Science Policy Research Unit, University of Sussex, Brighton.

Williamson, O. (1975), *Markets and Hierarchies*, New York: Free Press.

Williamson, O. (1985), *The Economic Institutions of Capitalism*. New York: Free Press.

Zimmermann, J-B. (1988), 'Towards a General Framework for Inter-firm Agreements Data Bases', *EEC/FAST Seminar on InterFirm Technological Co-operation Agreements*, Univ. Paris X Nanterre, November.

PART THREE

Implications for Labour

7. Flexibility and Fragmentation in the Labour Market

Thomas P. Boje

INTRODUCTION

The aim of this chapter is to analyse the main traits of development in the labour market of the 1980s and explain this development in terms of institutional labour market theory. In particular, attention will be focused on the relation between segmentation and flexibility. Under which circumstances do the two concepts supplement or counteract each other? In the 1980s the reorganization of production processes and the firm has forced the labour market to become more flexible at the same time as appearing to be still more segmented. In this context, segmentation has to be understood in a much more complex and differentiated manner than it was in the labour market theories of the 1970s.

The labour market of the 1960s and 1970s was characterized by, first, an industrial dualism and a stable labour market structure, second, job segmentation based on discrimination and closed employment relations, third, internal labour markets defining the entrance threshold to work and the career pattern of employed workers and, finally, an institutionalized bargaining system for negotiation of wages and work conditions.

This labour market structure has changed dramatically during the 1980s. Internationalization of the economy, an increasingly fragmented market structure and growing labour costs have led to growing pressure for a reduction of labour costs and an increasing demand for flexibility in the use of labour; a demand which has changed the traditional organizational structure of firms by causing them to establish smaller units and dismantle hierarchical governance structures. Furthermore, the demand for flexibility has introduced several contingent forms of employment in the labour market, with growing fragmentation of the labour force and increasing income inequality arising as consequences of this new development.

In this chapter, I wish to extend the analysis of organizational restructuring in earlier chapters, by focusing on the relationship between labour market flexibility and fragmentation of work organization, and to examine how it has influenced the employment conditions of workers and industrial relations. More specifically, attention will be focused on the different forms of contingent employment, namely part-time work, different types of temporary work and forms of externalization of work by the contracting out of specific parts of the business organization. My conclusion is that flexibility and fragmentation have dismantled internal labour markets, polarized the job market, weakened the bargaining power of the organized labour and created a growing inequality in the conditions of employment.

THEORY OF SEGMENTATION AND THE INDUSTRIAL LABOUR MARKET

In the beginning of the 1970s researchers developed, under the heading 'Labour Market Segmentation', a complex of institutional theories to explain the structure and functioning of the labour market in North America and Western Europe (Doeringer and Piore, 1971; Gordon, 1972; and Bluestone, 1970). These theories conceptualized the labour market as being divided into distinct segments acting differently and with restricted inter-segment mobility. The theories developed as a critique of the neo-classical labour market approach. One of their main achievements was the attempt to explain why specific groups in the labour market were not able to stabilize their employment relations, despite high levels of economic growth and low unemployment during the 1960s, see Kalleberg and Sørensen (1979), Attewell (1984), and Boje and Toft (1989).

In its original and most simple form, the theory of segmentation described the labour market as divided into primary and secondary sectors; a division which emerged out of an economic structure divided into a core and a peripheral sector. The primary sectors of the labour market are characterized by high wages, good working conditions, employment stability and favourable opportunities for advancement, while the secondary sectors are characterized by low wages, instability in employment, high labour turnover and lack of career possibilities (Bluestone, 1970; Doeringer and Piore, 1971). Initially, the distribution of workers in the two labour market segments was explained by individual and behavioural variables, for example, social background, instability and lack of work skills, Piore (1970). In the course of time the theories have been refined, and the earlier description of the labour market has been succeeded by more dynamic explanations. Today, labour markets are still seen as being segmented, but the nature of segmentation is related to variations in the business cycle and to changes in the strategies of employers and unions (Sengenberger, 1981).

The economic and organizational basis of the segmentation theories was the concept of 'Fordist' production, characterized by mass production, a highly developed technical division of labour and homogeneous market conditions (Gordon, 1972). According to Edwards (1979), the large, core firms sought to control labour and the production process by internalization of all production functions. The big monopolies, typically, controlled all parts of the production process in a vertically integrated production chain and they controlled markets by developing internal labour markets and establishing long-term employment relations. Only in the peripheral firms was to be found unstable and diversified production for highly competitive markets. Here, employment relations were short-term, and the governance structures of firms that of simple control, see Edwards (1979).

The emergence of internal labour markets and big firms in the core sector has played an important role in the theories of segmentation. The internal markets are characterized by a preference for allocating vacant positions to those already in employment, promotion by seniority following well-defined job ladders and entrance to the firm at the bottom of the job hierarchy (port of entry). A stable and highly complex firm-level organization is a precondition for the appearance and functioning of internal markets.

During the last two decades the hypotheses of the segmentation theories have been tested in a large number of empirical studies. The results have led to several modifications of the early theories. The dualist approach to segmentation, for instance, has been dropped and instead sensitivity to a more multi-segmented structure has been developed. Despite the many adaptations, however, the theories must still be regarded as a conceptualization of the labour market which is closely attached to developments concerning manufacturing industry, the male labour force, 'Fordist' production concepts, a dichotomous economic structure, and, in the labour market, a distinction between skilled and unskilled workers and between long-term and short-term employment.

These descriptions of the industrial labour markets of the 1960s are inadequate to explain the emerging labour market structures of the 1980s. Several of the segmentation researchers have also suggested that the labour market structures of the 1980s cannot be described coherently, by the 'classical' dualistic model. Gordon, Edwards and Reich conclude their analysis of the American labour market with the observation that 'the structure of segmentation has begun to decay and . . . explanations are underway that will significantly alter existing institutions in each of the three principal labour segments'. See Gordon, Edwards and Reich (1982), p. 226.

Into the 1990s it is obvious that the structure of the labour market has changed. Today's much more diversified and variable labour market has changed the focus of the segmentation researchers 'from discussing the existence of labour market segmentation to analysing the restructuring occurring in the labour market' (Rosenberg, 1989a, p. 329). The labour market has become more 'flexible' but not necessarily less segmented – indeed, the contrary. Following other segmentation researchers such as Wilkinson (1987), Sengenberger (1988) and Rosenberg (1989b), the argument in this chapter will be that the search for flexibility has increased the division and the segmentation of the labour market and caused more inequality and instability within the labour force. Before discussing in detail the consequences of the search for flexibility, the next section specifies the characteristics of the new labour market.

NEW LABOUR MARKET OF THE 1980s

Numerous analyses of the production process, the organization of the firm and of the labour markets have clearly indicated several fundamental changes in the functioning of the labour market and in the use of labour. One of the most prominent descriptions of the new conditions operating in production and the labour market has been formulated by the 'flexible specialization' thesis of Piore and Sabel (1984). It is the argument of Piore and Sabel that in an ever more unpredictable and fragmented commodity market, conditions for successful competition require that firms combine small-batch production and the use of broadly qualified workers, instead of the 'Fordist' combination of mass production* and narrowly qualified workers. This thesis has been extended and more or less successfully documented in several empirical studies. See for example, Christopherson and Storper (1989), Tarling (1987), Noyelle (1987). Noyelle, for instance, talks about the rise of a new economy characterized by the development of information technology and the rise of a service economy. Both tendencies demand increasing qualification of the workers. This upskilling of the labour force is concurrent with polarization in the conditions of employment of workers. One consequence of this is a growing number of contingent workers and a loss of protection from competition suffered by many workers in the internal labour markets (Noyelle, 1987, p. 117).

The most significant changes in market conditions and the organization of production, in terms of their consequences for the development of the labour market into the 1990s, will be discussed below.

Instability and Unpredictability in the Production Process

The present market conditions are characterized by instability and unpredictability. First, we have seen a considerable internationalization of product markets during the last two decades. The development towards one single market in Europe and the emergence of the Newly Industrialized Countries (NICs) with an abundance of cheap, mass-produced goods, indicate the presence of intensified competition. Many national industries, which previously have been protected by import regulation and custom rules, are in serious trouble today. This growing international competition creates difficulties for a large number of the traditional manufacturing industries (for example, clothing, textiles shipbuilding and automobiles). They have been forced either to move from high wage industrial regions to low wage regions or to close down business completely and surrender the market to products from the NICs. Secondly, there has been a change in consumer patterns and tastes – changes which have forced firms to make quick adaptations to meet the demand for new specific products and to introduce sudden transform-ations of the production process. This flexibility in the production processes has been made possible by computer-based technology, and it has meant that the traditional mass production firms have become an obsolete mode of organization. Through the introduction of computer-based technology it has become possible to produce in small batches, adjusted to consumer demands. A more appropriate place for such production is the highly specialized firm, rather than the traditional mass-producing firm.

Shift from Manufacturing to Service Industries.

In the last two decades there has been a shift in the economy away from manufacturing industry to service industry and, in the labour force, from goods-producing jobs to administrative and service jobs and from blue-collar to white-collar work.

As shown in Table 7.1, employment in agriculture and industry (manufacturing industry, construction and mining) has been falling during the last decade, while employment in the service industries has grown in all three countries. During the 1980s, this development has been interpreted by some, as shown in Chapter 2, as a trend towards

Table 7.1 Sectoral employment trends in the US and Europe (1973 and 1986)

	Agriculture			Industry			Services		
	1973 %	1986 %	1973–86 % change	1973 %	1986 %	1973–86 % change	1973 %	1986 %	1973–86 % change
US	4.2	3.1	−1.1	32.0	26.6	−5.4	63.8	70.4	+6.6
Sweden	7.1	4.2	−2.9	36.3	30.1	−6.2	56.6	65.6	+9.0
Denmark*	8.1	5.8	−2.3	33.1	27.9	−5.2	58.2	66.3	+8.1

*Denmark: 1976 and 1986.

Source: OECD (1988) *Employment Outlook*, Paris, September.

deindustrialization (Bluestone and Harrison, 1982; Cornetz, 1988). In the analysis of Bluestone and Harrison, deindustrialization indicates the closure of manufacturing firms, dismissal of blue-collar workers and lack of investment in the manufacturing industries. It has meant a dismantling of many of the strongholds of male, blue-collar workers. Instead a growth in employment has taken place in the service industries and among white-collar workers.

Today, more than two-thirds of the labour force in all three countries are employed in the service industries and as white-collar employees. This development is a result of three different tendencies: a sharp fall in the proportion of blue-collar workers; growth in the service industries (especially among white-collar workers); and a change in the composition of the labour force in manufacturing industries towards more jobs for managers, technicians and sales and clerical workers. See, Bluestone and Harrison (1982), Noyelle (1987), Rosenberg (1989a). Many of the new jobs in the service industries have been filled by female workers, who entered the labour market in large numbers precisely during the 1970s and the beginning of the 1980s. The consequences of the changes in the industrial structure and in the employment patterns of the workers have been a growth in the number of small firms, a weakening of internal labour markets in relation to recruitment, training and career development and, finally, the introduction of several new forms of employment – part-time, contract and temporary.

Changing Firm

In the segmentation theories, the firm has been seen as consisting of stable and homogeneous units, with the big firm characterized as having a hierarchical organization. Today firms have taken on a much more differentiated appearance. Bluestone and Stevenson (1981) have described the firm as a hybrid including both highly-qualified, high-waged and stable jobs in a primary segment and low-qualified, low-waged and unstable jobs in secondary segments. Atkinson (1987) uses the term 'the flexible firm', with its labour force composed of subgroups of workers, each with a very different employment relation to the firm. He distinguishes between three different subgroups. The first is a core group of workers who perform what the firms consider to be the most important job functions. They have long-term employment, they are well paid, and they are mainly male. The second subgroup is composed of several peripheral groups of workers who perform the more routine and mechanical jobs in the firm. They have part-time or temporary jobs, they receive a lower pay than the core workers and they are mainly women. The third consists of external groups of workers who are agency temps, self-employed workers, or subcontractors. They work on very different kinds of jobs ranging from the highly specialized to the very simple tasks. They are not considered by the firm as a part of its labour force but 'as a second group of numerically flexible workers', see Atkinson (1987, p. 94).

This transformation of the firm and its labour market can be explained by three principal technology-related tendencies. First, the implement-ation of computer-based machinery and communications technology has loosened the organization and control of production from its narrow operational context. Computer technology has made it possible to organize the separate parts of the production process (conception and execution) independently and, at the same time, control each part of the process very closely. The single parts of the production process can be placed in dispersed sites while still being controlled from a central position. This makes it possible for a company to locate parts of the production in regions with, for instance, a cheap and relevantly qualified labour force. In numerous cases big firms have been divided up – in the manufacturing industries, into main production and subcontractor sites and, in the business service industries, into front- and back-office sites.

Second, a dissolution of the vertically integrated production process has taken place. The new technology has enabled the big and complex firms to reorganize. Under the mass production and mass consumption system, a number of production processes were housed under the same roof. This kind of organization has turned out to be inefficient in coping with rapidly changing product markets. To increase flexibility, multi-product and multitask firms have been divided into minor units. The 'Fordist' mass-production concept has been succeeded by flexible, 'just-in-time' production in small batches within small-scale production units.

Third, the new technology and the changed organizational structure of the firm has reduced the importance of the internal labour market in the allocation and qualification of the labour force. The responsibility for training has been taken over by public institutions or the individual worker. The growing number of educated workers and the increased capacity of higher educational systems has made it more advantageous and easier to hire workers from the external labour market, instead of the firm providing internal promotion and on-the-job training. This is especially the case for the growing number of job positions in the administrative, professional, and managerial occupations. The reduced importance of internal markets has, on the one hand, meant increasing opportunities, especially for women and minority groups, to get some of the jobs formerly monopolized by men. On the other hand, the dismantling of internal markets has reduced the job protection traditionally enjoyed by a great number of non-professional male workers.

More Differentiated Labour Force

This complex segmentation of the labour market has meant the emergence of a more differentiated labour force. There are several reasons for this development: the appearance of the flexible firm and its different subgroups of workers each with specific links to the firm; the reduced importance of internal labour markets for the recruitment and promotion of workers; the provision of vocational training for a fast-growing number of young workers by a highly developed and strongly differentiated formal educational system, with training within the firm restricted to shorter courses; and the increased heterogenization of the labour force, caused by the entrance, in great number, of women, minority groups and so on. From having been previously dominated by men, today the labour force is almost equally composed of men and women. Simultaneously many new forms of non-standard employment have been introduced, which fulfil the need of firms for increased variation in the size and composition of the labour force.

This development in the labour market has, in general, represented an up-skilling of the labour force, but, at the same time, there has been a polarization in the employment conditions of the labour force. This apparently contradictory process has occurred for three main reasons. First, the need for workers with professional and technical qualifications has been growing fast in the private as well as the public service industries, and furthermore, many well-educated women have entered the labour force. Second, there has been a widespread growth in the volume of service workers employed temporarily, or part-time on a low wage and without any vocational training or work experience. Third, the dismantling of the internal labour market has weakened job security for many blue-collar workers, as a result of which many have been dismissed or laid off. A further indication of polarization in the labour force is the huge number of workers such as the long-term unemployed who have lost any connection to the labour market.

Weakening of the Organized Working Class

The comprehensive reorganization of the production process, but more importantly, high and sustained unemployment, has, as a consequence, produced several significant changes in the institutional structure of the labour market. Most importantly, unemployment has, in many respects, weakened the negotiating position of the trade unions, and companies have acquired greater freedom to determine the wage and working conditions of employed workers. High unemployment has also forced many unemployed workers to accept a part-time or temporary job or work for which they are over-qualified. High unemployment and the weakening of the trade unions has changed the functioning of labour market institutions. Competition between different groups of workers has become more widespread, the traditional labour relation based on a full-time and long-term labour contract has been partially dissolved and growing wage and employment differentiation has occurred in the single firm as well as the whole labour market. Of course, we can find big variations in the degree to which this weakening of the working-class has affected different European countries. The process has been most dramatic in the UK, Holland and, to some extent France, while it has hardly begun to unfold in Denmark and Sweden – countries with a high level of organization among workers and with a well-developed institutional network in the labour market (Scheuer, 1989).

Today's labour market, shaped by the above mentioned trends of development in the macro-economic structure and in the firm, is very different from the labour market of the 1960s, upon which the segmentation theories were based. The labour market is still segmented but in a much more complex manner than described in the dual labour market model. Today, the labour market is a service labour market with many small firms and with about 70 per cent of the labour force employed in private and public service industries. Manufacturing industry is stagnating, and many of the strongholds of organized labour in the vehicle, steel, and print industries have been gradually liquidated. The theory of a two or three partition-based labour market is no longer sustainable. The labour market has become a complex determination of a lot of different variables. Summarizing the discussion above, there are several reasons for this complexity. First, and perhaps most important, the high and sustained unemployment and the weakening of the trade unions has been followed by a deregulation of the labour market and growing competition among groups of workers. Next, there has been the growing reluctance of employers to establish long-term employment contracts. With the flexible firm, there have also emerged several forms of non-standard employment (part-time, temporary, fixed-term) and a growing number of self-employed individuals attached to the bigger firms by subcontracts. In addition, the labour market has changed from being male-dominated to a gender- and ethnically-mixed phenonemon that is more hetero-geneous than before. Finally, the increased differentiation of educational patterns has led to a substitution of craft workers by officially trained workers with a career trajectory that is more attached to the profession than to the firm.

FLEXIBILITY – DEFINITION OF THE CONCEPT

The increasing demand for flexibility in the firm and in the labour market has received a great deal of attention from researchers as well as politicians, in their attempt to solve structural problems in the labour market and renew economic growth. The need for flexibility can be seen as a consequence of increased product market competition, continually changing technology and changes in consumer tastes (Rosenberg, 1989a, p. 394). These changes require a greater variety of products in the market and the production system must be able to produce economically smaller quantities of more products (Piore and Sabel, 1984). The complex set of relations between workers and firms has, in the theoretical literature in many cases, been reformulated with a focus on the application on the concept of *flexibility*.

The concept of flexibility in general can be defined as 'the capacity to adapt to change', and that means the ability and readiness of the firm or the individual worker to make changes both on the macro- and micro-level, see Meulders and Wilkin (1987, p. 5). Flexibility has often been taken as being good for both employers and employees. But this position is by no means always correct. Labour market flexibility is two-sided for workers as well as for firms/employers. For workers, a high flexibility on the one hand means increased possibilities of moving around in the labour market and better utilization of the workers' qualification in their actual jobs. On the other hand, a high flexibility also means more precarious employment conditions and lack of protection from dismissal or alteration in wage- and work-conditions. In the discussion of flexibility it has been argued that comprehensive dismissal regulations increase unemployment and that a high flexibility will reduce the level of unemployment. So far, this argument has not been proven empirically in the debate on flexibility. For firms, high flexibility makes it easier to adjust the employment level to changes in product demand and in the organization of production. However, too high a level of flexibility will increase the firm's cost of training and recruitment and perhaps also make work organization more inefficient. For both workers and firms it is important to find an equilibrium between flexibility and stability in the labour market and in the relations between employers and employees.

- In analyses of flexibility it is important to separate the different forms and dimensions of flexibility. Flexibility has a completely different meaning seen from the respective point of view of employers and employees; the introduction of a certain kind of flexibility will favour one side but hurt the other side. Also within the labour force, flexibility has different consequences for individual groups of workers. In some cases a higher flexibility may cause marginalization of one group of workers, while another group becomes more integrated into the labour market.

From the perspective of firms it is possible to differentiate between four dimensions of flexibility:

1. External numerical flexibility, which means the adjustment of the number of employees to the needs of the firm/company. This kind of flexibility includes 'any measures which free employers from a lengthy employment relationship with their employees' (Meulders and Wilkin, 1987, p. 7), achieved through more flexible redundancy procedures, the introduction of contracts or temporary work and/or the expansion of various forms of part-time work (OECD, 1989b, p. 14).

2. Internal numerical flexibility, which concerns 'the scope that the employers have for modifying the number of working hours without modifying the number of employees' (OECD, 1989b, p 14). Here we are talking about flexible working time which can take several forms – shift work of various kinds, annual leave, varying daily number of working hours, and so on.

Both these forms of numerical flexibility concern the freedom of the employers to fire and hire employees according to the requirements of the production technology, the methods of work organization and the demand for products. Often an increased numerical flexibility can only be accomplished if a deregulation of rules concerning dismissal and job security has taken place. In that case an increased flexibility indicates that several rights achieved by the workers through trade unions and political activity will be abrogated.

3. Functional flexibility which means that workers' job assignments are modified to accommodate the needs of the firm. To be achieved, workers must have several skills and be able to switch job functions when the production requirements change. Functional flexibility takes place inside the firm without changing the total number of working hours (OECD, 1989b, p. 15).
4. Wage flexibility, which means labour cost reduction and the firms' attempts 'to replace across-the-board pay structures by some form of performance-linked system' (OECD, 1989b, p.16). Wage flexibility can be seen as a means by which employers raise productivity, and as a mechanism to initiate the other types of flexibility such as increased mobility and adaptation to technological changes.

Analyses of the labour market indicate that different forms of flexibility are applied to specific groups of workers. Numerical flexibility normally applies to the peripheral and external groups of workers in the flexible firm. Through numerical flexibility the firms' labour force can be regulated. Functional flexibility is used primarily on the core groups of workers in the firm. These workers have a stable and long-term employment contract and flexibility is attained by requalification and re-placement within the firm.

From the employees' point of view flexibility primarily is concerned with *educational adaptation* to structural changes in the firm and in the labour market. In this context, flexibility can be defined as the ability and possibility of educational groups or individual workers to change job functions, Jensen (1990). According to this definition, a worker is flexible when he/she is able to and has a chance to use the acquired qualification in different sectors and industries, Vejrup Hansen (1985) p.247. Here the crucial problem for the workers will be the possibility of finding a job in which they will be able to utilize their acquired qualifications. If not, workers can be forced to take a job which draws on only a restricted part of their qualifications. This implies, in a longer-term perspective, a de-qualification of the workers concerned. Thus, for the individual worker flexibility very often is two-sided. On one side it is positive: the worker is able to find a new job more easily and use the acquired qualifications in many different job functions and industries. On the other side flexibility can be negative to the extent of representing a down-grading of the worker's job function followed by a permanent de-qualification and reduction in wages. Which aspect may be dominant in a specific context, depends on market conditions, the size of unemployment, and the institutional or organizational power of the working class.

FLEXIBLE LABOUR MARKET – SOME EMPIRICAL EVIDENCE

The need for more flexible employment forms has been implemented in the labour market by the introduction of a variety of different kinds of non-standard forms of employment, and by a demand for higher mobility among the employees. In this section I shall review the empirical evidence, focusing in particular, on how the demand for more flexibility has been implemented in the Danish labour market. This demand for flexibility is an international trend, see OECD (1986, 1989b), and in the evaluation of its impact I shall compare developments in the Danish labour market with those in Sweden, the US and other EC countries. Sweden has a labour market which is very similar to the Danish one, while that in the US is essentially less organized and regulated than the Danish one. Evidence for other EC countries taken as a whole is considered in order to provide a yardstick against which firms such as those in the Danish labour market will have to measure themselves in the years to come. The empirical analysis refers to three different aspects influencing the demand for increased flexibility in the labour market: the extent of non-standard forms of employment; the development of part-time work (voluntary and involuntary); and the mobility between employment and unemployment.

Non-standard Forms of Employment

Seen from the point of view of firms, the demand for increased flexibility has been obtained by the employment of workers on a more temporary basis. This has made it easier for the firm to adjust the number of workers/working-hours to the changing cycle of production. During the last decades strong growth in the number of workers employed as self-employed, temporary, and part-time workers, has taken place in all principal labour markets (see Table 7.2).

Denmark, compared with the other EC countries, has a bigger share of the working force employed as temporary and part-time workers (Table 7.2). Temporary workers here are defined as contract, fixed-term or casual employees. This kind of employment has a larger share in Denmark in all industries and for both men and women than in other

Table 7.2 Share (%) of non-standard forms of employment in EC countries (1985–6)

	Denmark		EC average	
	Men	Women	Men	Women
Share of self-employment in total employment				
All sectors	10.6	9.6	12.2	8.7
Agriculture	59.3	66.3	67.2	70.2
Industry	7.9	12.3	7.3	7.8
Services	11.6	7.7	15.9	9.4
Public administration	0.0	0.0	0.2	0.1
Share of temporary workers (other than self-employed) in total employment				
All sectors	10.2	10.7	6.3	8.6
Agriculture	6.6	7.9	3.5	5.4
Industry	8.8	8.8	5.0	6.9
Services	10.6	11.5	6.8	9.3
Public administration	13.1	11.9	8.4	10.1
Share of part-time workers (other than self-employed and temporary) in total employment				
All sectors	8.1	33.7	4.1	26.8
Agriculture	5.0	13.1	2.2	11.2
Industry	3.4	24.5	1.8	20.4
Services	11.4	39.0	5.7	31.0
Public administration	1.9	31.1	1.9	24.4
Total share of non-standard forms of working: self-employment, temporary workers and part-time workers				
All sectors	28.9	54.0	22.6	44.1
Agriculture	70.9	87.3	72.9	86.8
Industry	20.1	45.6	14.1	35.1
Services	33.6	58.2	28.4	49.7
Public administration	15.0	43.0	10.5	34.6

Source: OECD (1989a).

EC countries. This can be explained in several ways. First, the legal regulations of employment protection in Denmark are extremely liberal. It is possible to hire and fire most workers from day to day without any restrictions, while the salaried workers have a higher degree of protection in their jobs. An illustration of the unstable employment conditions of many workers is the extensive use of temporary lay-offs in the Danish labour market. The number of temporary lay-offs is equivalent to about one-third of workers who have experienced unemployment (Jensen and Westergaard-Nielsen, 1988; Anker, 1990). Second, the high number of temporary lay-offs can be explained by the specificity of the Danish unemployment benefit system. The benefits offer high wage compensation and are paid from the first day of unemployment. Unemployment benefit is often used, in relation to temporary lay-off of employers and workers, as a supplement to ordinary income (Ministries of Labour, Finance, Social Affairs and Education, 1989).

The unemployment benefit system is also one of several reasons why the proportion of part-time workers in Denmark is higher than in most other OECD countries – Netherlands and Sweden have a slightly higher proportion (OECD, 1988, p. 149). The share of part-time workers in Denmark is higher than the EC average for both industries and gender – the difference is especially pronounced for male workers (see Table 7.2). Again there are several possible explanations. One is, as mentioned, the Danish unemployment benefit rules which allow part-time workers to receive benefits for the hours which would add up to full-time work if they are searching for full-time work. The present high level of unemployment in Denmark implies that most part-time workers get supplementary unemployment benefits. Another explanation is a very high female labour market participation rate compared to the other EC countries, combined with the fact that female workers want part-time work more often than do male workers (OECD, 1989b). Finally, a third explanation can be found in the size of the public sector which is much bigger in Denmark than in the other EC countries and typically, as with the service sector in general, employs far more part-time and temporary workers than do other industrial sectors.

Self-employment, in contrast, is more widespread in the other EC countries than in Denmark. This is especially the case in agriculture and services while self-employment in industry (owing to the greater preponderance of smaller firms) is more widespread in Denmark than the other EC countries for both men and women.

The extension of non-standard forms of employment can be taken as a manifestation of flexibility and a high level of adaptability to changes in production requirements, firm structure and labour market conditions. With its high share of part-time and temporary work, the Danish labour market appears to be more flexible than the other EC countries as a whole. But this is not necessarily the case in reality. The extension of non-standard forms of employment is by no means a sufficient condition for flexibility. Part-time work does not always have a temporary form. In Denmark nearly 90 per cent of the part timers are permanently employed (see Table 7.3).

Table 7.3 Proportion of wage and salary workers in Denmark in permanent and temporary jobs by full- and part-time status (1985)

	Part time (%)	Full time (%)	Total (%)	Total ('000)
Permanent employment	22.7	65.0	87.7	1 937.5
Temporary employment	2.9	9.4	12.3	272.8
Total (%)	25.6	74.4	100	
Total ('000)	564.8	1 645.5		2 210.3

Source: OECD (1987).

Among the permanently employed workers, more than 25 per cent in 1985 were employed as part timers. Thus for many part-time workers this employment form is a permanent situation. This is especially the case in the public sector and in commerce and retail. See Nätti (1990), Anker (1990). Although not all non-standard forms of employment are precarious, generally speaking 'the work is "precarious" because temporary workers and those working part time generally do not, in practice, have the same basic rights or access to the same social benefits as full-time long-term workers' (Rosenberg, 1989a, p. 398).

Composition of Part-time Employment

Working part-time, especially in the service industries – retail, restaurants, health service and social services – has a permanent character and is an employment form which is widespread among female workers. The proportion of part-time work among women is particularly high in

Denmark and Sweden (Table 7.4), which also have the two highest labour market participation rates for women in the world, see OECD (1988, p.131).

Table 7.4 Size and composition of part-time employment in Denmark, Sweden and the US (%)

	Part-time employment as a proportion of:								Women's share in part-time work			
	Total employment				Female employment							
	1973	1979	1983	1986–7	1973	1979	1983	1986–7	1973	1979	1983	1986
Denmark	21.2	22.7	23.7	23.7	45.1	46.3	44.7	41.9	86.8	86.9	84.7	80.1
Sweden	18.0	23.6	24.8	25.2	38.8	46.0	45.9	45.1	88.0	87.5	86.6	85.9
US		16.4	18.4	17.3		26.7	28.1	26.1		67.1	66.8	67.6

Source: OECD (1988).

In Denmark and Sweden, more than 80 per cent of part-time workers are women. During the 1980s, women's share of part-time work was stagnating, but despite this, women still constitute the majority of part timers. In the US women constitute 'only' two-thirds of the part-time workers, and only one-fourth of employed women work part-time, compared with 45 per cent in the Scandinavian countries.

Table 7.5 Proportion of part-time employment in Denmark*, Sweden and US† by age and gender

Age (years)	Males			Females		
	DK	S	US	DK	S	US
15–19	47.6	28.4	59.6	62.1	51.5	66.6
20–24	9.0	7.3	16.8	21.6	27.7	25.6
25–54	2.7	3.9	4.0	40.2	45.2	21.0
55–59	2.9	5.1	6.1	55.4	51.3	24.3
60–64	10.5	24.7	12.1	64.8	63.1	32.2
65+	30.6	–	46.2	66.5	–	59.4
All persons	8.7	6.7	10.2	41.9	45.1	26.1

* 1986 for Denmark.
† 1987 for Sweden and the US.

Source: OECD (1988).

The pattern of labour market participation differs widely in the US and Denmark. In the US a large number of women leave the labour market due to marriage and child-birth – part-time work is concentrated among young women and women without children (see Table 7.5). In Denmark women stay in the labour market even when they are married and have small children, as part-time workers utilizing the provision of child-care by the public day-care centres. In this period women work permanently on part-time and they supplement their income with unemployment benefits. The different employment pattern of Danish and American women with small children seems, broadly speaking, to be determined by different regulations concerning unemployment benefit and admission to public day-care.

In all three countries the large majority of the part-time workers are women. This is most significant in the Scandinavian countries where part-time employment is typically permanent and voluntary, while part-time employment in the US is more a temporary and involuntary working form. See OECD (1990) p. 181. Furthermore, part-time employment is closely connected to the service industries and most widespread in the public sector: this sector includes nearly 40 per cent of the labour force in Denmark and Sweden and only 16 per cent in the US.

Working part-time has several negative consequences for career possibilities. The OECD has calculated a dissimilarity index showing the connection between gender segregation by occupational group and the female share of employment (OECD, 1988, p. 148). The OECD finds the Danish labour market to be more segregated and career possibilities more closed to Danish women if compared to the American labour market. The American labour market seems more open because of its less institutionalized industrial relations and its heterogeneous educational system, see OECD (1988) and Boje (1990).

Flows into and out of Employment

Another aspect in the evaluation of labour market flexibility concerns the pattern of flow into and out of employment and the mobility between different positions (industries and occupations) in the labour market. The Danish labour market is characterized by a considerable level of employee mobility. More than 50 per cent of the labour force changes position in the labour market in a year. This may occur as a result of entry into and exit from employment, flow into and out of the labour force and by change of job and occupation in the employed labour force.

The entry into employment from unemployment and the exit from employment to unemployment is, in Denmark, higher than in the other EC countries (see Table 7.6).

Table 7.6 Entry into and exit from employment in the EC (1985–6)

	Denmark		EC average	
	Men	Women	Men	Women
Persons not in employment in the preceding year as a percentage of current employment				
All sectors	8.4	10.7	6.5	9.1
Agriculture	14.8	22.6	10.2	15.2
Industry	7.7	12.0	5.7	8.8
Services	8.9	10.2	7.3	9.5
Public administration	5.3	7.3	4.6	6.9
Persons employed in the preceding year and not currently employed as a percentage of current employment				
All sectors	8.1	12.7	6.1	7.8
Agriculture	15.7	49.5	8.8	17.4
Industry	9.3	12.9	6.5	8.2
Services	7.8	11.8	5.7	7.7
Public administration	5.4	8.6	6.1	5.4

Source: OECD (1989a).

The higher level of mobility in Denmark holds for all the industrial sectors and for both men and women. Table 7.6 shows that this higher mobility is especially characteristic of the agricultural and industrial sectors in Denmark. Here the use of temporary employment and lay-off is especially widespread as part of the adaptation to seasonal and conjunctural fluctuations in the demand for labour. Otherwise in the service industries the use of non-standard forms of employment has typically a more permanent form. Finally, the higher mobility level in Denmark can also be found among employees in the public sector, but here it is primarily among women.

When compared to Sweden or the US, we do not find that the level of mobility in Denmark is notably high (see Table 7.7). Both the flow into the employed population and the outflow are much higher in the US than in Denmark. This is a clear indication of an open labour market characterized by high government growth but also a significantly high risk of unemployment and greater possibility for re-employment (Kutscher

Table 7.7 Monthly flows into and out of unemployment in Denmark, Sweden and the US (1979–88)

	Inflow as a percentage of the employed population (15–64)			Outflow as a percentage of total unemployment		
	DK	S	US	DK	S	US
1979	0.76	0.58	2.07	15.0	34.5	43.5
1983	0.40	0.77	2.46	6.9	27.1	37.8
1988	0.44	0.40	1.98	8.3	30.4	45.7

Source: OECD (1990).

and Sorrentino, 1989). Sweden too has a markedly higher level of flow out of unemployment than Denmark, probably due to its very active labour market policy in which re-employment programmes play a major part (Furåker *et al.*, 1990). Danish workers clearly have greater difficulties getting out of the unemployment situation. The Danish labour market policy gives a low priority to active programmes, and more than three-fourths of the expenditure on labour market programmes goes to passive measures, whereas in Sweden the ratio is the opposite.

The difficulties experienced in Denmark by workers seeking release from unemployment have been documented in many analyses of Danish unemployment. These analyses show clearly that Danish unemployment is highly concentrated. A minority group of workers – 20 per cent of the labour force – experiences more than 50 per cent of the total unemployment, see Ploug (1990, p. 88). The unemployment pattern differs very much from the pattern in Sweden and the US, in which the burden of unemployment is considerably more spread out among workers and the incidence of long-term unemployment smaller than in Denmark (see Table 7.8).

The category of workers unemployed for more than six months covers more than half of the total unemployment among male workers in Denmark and nearly two-thirds among female workers. In Sweden this group of workers accounts for 20–25 per cent of the total unemployment, while in the US its share is 'only' 10–15 per cent of the total unemployment. In Denmark long-term unemployment is most serious among women, whereas in the US it is most widespread among men. American women who lose their jobs typically leave the labour market and return

Table 7.8 Incidence (%) of long-term unemployment in Denmark, Sweden and the US

	Men*			Women*		
	D	S	US	D	S	US
6 months and over						
1980		19.0	12.5		15.1	8.5
1983	54.3	25.9	28.2	67.5	23.8	17.9
1985	61.5	24.8	18.4	68.2	29.5	11.9
1987	46.7	22.2	17.1	60.6	24.4	10.2
1988	48.2	22.7	14.6	54.9	19.7	9.0
1989		20.6	12.5		16.1	6.9
12 months and over						
1980		6.8	5.2		4.4	3.1
1983	27.8	10.8	16.0	38.6	9.7	9.6
1985	36.7	10.9	11.7	41.3	11.9	6.8
1987	24.2	7.5	10.0	36.0	8.5	5.7
1988	28.2	8.3	9.4	29.2	8.1	5.1
1989		7.6	7.4		5.4	3.7

* Percentage of total male and female unemployment.

Source: OECD (1987), (1990).

during more favourable employment conditions, while men stay in the labour market and become registered as unemployed. In Denmark (and Sweden), with its more generous unemployment benefits system, both men and women tend to remain in the labour market and become registered as unemployed during periods of unemployment.

Flexibility and Emerging Employment Patterns.

Compared with other OECD countries, the extension of 'flexible' forms of work, composed of temporary work, the number of part-time workers and the level of mobility, has been significant in the Danish labour market. This may lead to the conclusion that Denmark has a more flexible labour market than other countries. This, however, is a conclusion which must be modified in several aspects. First a large proportion of part-time work is not synonymous with high flexibility. In the Danish labour market the majority of part-time workers are employed permanently on a part-time basis and, accordingly, not more flexibly than most full-time workers. Especially for female workers part-time employment has acted as a career trap. The greater difficulties faced by Danish (and Swedish) women in pursuing a career in the labour market have been caused mainly by their extensive dependence on part-time employment and, it has to be said, the negative attitude of trade unions towards part-time jobs. Second, the high level of mobility and labour turn-over in the Danish labour market too, as a whole, does not indicate high flexibility, see Anker (1990, pp. 122–124). The two phenomena tend to be concentrated among the group of permanently employed workers, and concern intra-occupational rather than inter-occupational mobility. Third, the division of the Danish labour market in groups of employed and unemployed workers is much more pronounced than in the Swedish and American labour markets. Long-term unemployment covers a higher proportion of total unemployment and the entrance to the labour market for young workers and for the unemployed seems more restricted in Denmark than in most other OECD countries.

In conclusion to this section, the employment pattern of the Danish labour market shows a high nominal flexibility among employed workers but a distinct division of the labour force by occupation and industry. Furthermore, the Danish labour force is characterized by a pronounced division into groups of employed and marginalized workers.

EXTERNALIZATION AND DIVERSIFICATION

There are two significant tendencies to be noted as outcomes of the demand for higher flexibility in the labour market. One is the development from internalization to externalization of work and employment through the separation of the firm from its workers and through the introduction of contingent forms of employment. The other is the development towards a more diversified labour market characterized by a multi-segmented labour force and a growing polarization in the employment condition of different groups of workers.

From Internalization to Externalization

The increased externalization of work and employment is a result of the vertical disintegration of the firm organization. As Noyelle has argued.

Under old-fashioned vertical integration large firms sought to establish control over both a large scope of activities in the production process and a large scale of the production of specific outputs. Under vertical disintegration, firms tend to specialize in types or classes of production rather than in the production of large quantities of specific outputs as in mass production. The essence of the firm becomes flexible production

Noyelle (1987, p. 101)

The 'old-fashioned' large firms tend to internalize job functions and workers, while the 'new-look' firms tend to externalize both job functions and workers.

In a recent article, Pfeffer and Baron (1988) have analysed the externalization of work in the American labour market in the last decade. Despite big variations in labour market structure and participation, in the impact of trade unions on industrial relations and in the legal regulation of the labour market from country to country, the same tendency towards greater externalization is taking place in the European labour markets. The externalization has assumed four main forms:

1. Externalization by separation of the firm from the workers. Different kinds of self-employment, such as, for example, long-distance work, 'home-work' and 'telecommuting', have been growing as the development of information technology and data communication has made it possible for work to be decentralized, while it is controlled from a central place. This kind of externalization has been especially pronounced in financial services and commerce, but it has also grown in the last decade in more traditional industries such as textiles and clothing.

2. Externalization by the use of temporary or contingent employment. Here we find two different forms of employment arrangements: casual employment by hiring temporary workers; and part-time employment. As indicated earlier, the number of part-time jobs has grown dramatically since the beginning of the 1970s. Since 1982 however, the number of part-time jobs has stagnated or fallen, but this has been more than compensated by a growth in other forms of non-standard employment such as temporary work, contract work or self-employment. In its earliest form, temporary employment was used in clerical work, but today it is also widespread among technicians and on all occupational levels in the service sector – health, education and so on. Altogether there has been a restructuring of employment conditions from stable, long-term employment to temporary and part-time employment; a situation in which workers

do not have the same rights and protection in the labour market as the permanently employed workers (Appelbaum, 1986).

3. Externalization of specific parts of the production process. This kind of externalization takes on several variants. First, a parcelling-up of the whole production process and a contracting out of tasks to other firms – subcontractors and independent companies. Second, workers employed through temporary staffing agencies on a temporary or contractual basis. This means being on the payroll of the agency, but being directed in work by the host firm. In most highly industrialized countries we have seen a drastic increase in the amount of workers employed via agencies (see Pfeffer and Baron, 1988, pp. 266–70). The parcelling-up of the production process or the contracting out of specific forms of production is one of the forms the tendency to vertical disintegration has taken. The big production units have been split up and parts of the production process organized outside the main firm.

4. Externalization of vocational education. In all industrialized countries we have seen an explosion in education in the last two decades. Most of the growth in education has been related to the third level of the educational system – college or university education. In many countries this level has replaced traditional craft or on-the-job training. Despite its substantially higher level of education among young workers, one-fourth of the youth generation does not get any kind of vocational training in Denmark. After receiving a basic education for 9–11 years, many embark on a vocational education but never complete it. The public and formalized system of qualification has taken over the educational obligations of companies, but it has not fundamentally changed conditions for unskilled groups of workers. For them the result has been an increase in problems of managing the new technologies and adjusting to the flexible labour market.

Diversification of the Labour Force

These different kinds of externalization have been companies' answer to a more unstable and competitive product market, new computer-based technology, and a more educationally differentiated labour force. Flexibility introduced by externalization has intensified competition between different groups of workers, increased differentiation in the labour force, and promoted an even greater division of the labour force (Nielsen, 1988). The *diversification* of the labour force and a *marginalization* of specifically vulnerable groups of workers have been two of the most significant consequences of the demand for flexibility. This development has taken three main visible tendencies.

The first is a multi-segmented labour market structure. The segmentation of jobs has penetrated all parts of the labour market – even the single firm is divided into several sub-markets. Compared with 'classical' segmentation theory, the division of today's labour market has taken place along with other dimensions both in the firm and in the labour market as a whole. As described earlier, the 'flexible firm' is composed of three different sub-groups of workers, and employers have adopted different strategies of flexibility towards each of these sub-groups. The core groups of workers confront a demand for functional flexibility. These workers are employed on a long-term basis to accomplish those activities which firms regard as the most important and unique. Their qualifications are important for the firms to retain, and they are requalified with changes in technology and the organization of the firm. The peripheral workers confront a demand for numerical flexibility. These workers carry out the most routine and mechanical jobs in the firms. They are often employed on a part-time or temporary basis and on a shorter job tenure. Furthermore, their qualifications are available in the external market and are therefore easy to replace. Outside the 'flexible firm' it is the external workers – the third group – who are employed by firms, which lease-out or sub-contract specific and restricted tasks to them. Through this differentiation of the employment strategies of firms, a core/periphery structure has developed at the level of both the single firm and the total labour market. See Atkinson (1987, p. 91) and Rosenberg (1989a, p. 394).

The division of the labour market into primary and secondary segments must be seen more as an ideal type than a real description of labour market structure. Industries, firms and jobs can, according to the core/periphery model, be placed between two extremes of the labour market, each of which are represented in both the primary and secondary segments, see Nätti (1990), and Boje and Toft (1989).

The second major tendency has been the dismantling of internal labour markets. The impact of internal labour markets in the areas of recruitment, advancement and training of workers has been reduced. Two aspects of externalization in the labour market are of special importance in this process. One is that the externalization of tasks has reduced the number of long-term employed workers and the size of most firms. Large, vertically integrated firms with bureaucratic forms of control have declined in number, and consequently, so has the importance of internal labour markets. The other is that there has been an externalization of education and, during the last decade, a general up-skilling of the new generation of workers. This has made it possible to recruit workers from an external pool of well-educated young workers, with qualifications matching the requirements of firms at specific levels.

The externalization of tasks and education and the associated loss in importance of internal labour markets has removed protection for workers in many firms. Semi-skilled male workers in particular have lost their traditional protection through the dismantling of internal markets as new groups of workers have taken over their jobs. This development appears to be more widespread in the US than in the Scandinavian countries. But in Denmark too, many women have taken over occupations previously dominated by men. The resistance to changes in the labour market has, in Scandinavia, been very fierce because of the 'obligation' of individual trade unions to protect specific groups of usually male workers.

The third major tendency has been the polarization of employment conditions. The labour market of the 1980s was characterized by both an up-skilling of the labour force and a polarization of employment conditions. As described earlier the labour force has experienced marked up-skilling for two reasons: the need of new technology for more qualified workers in order to be handled efficiently; and the incorporation of a lot of unskilled work by computer-based processing functions, which has left workers with problem-solving functions (Noyelle, 1987, p. 16). But the demand for flexibility and the resulting externalization of work has not meant a simultaneous up-grading of employment conditions. On the contrary, a polarization has occurred. The well-qualified workers have secured better conditions and more secure jobs, while a deterioration has taken place in the work conditions of large groups of un-skilled workers. The latter only too often have become temporary workers and their earnings have been reduced. This contradictory development can be explained by 'the weakening attachment of the employees to the firms and the relative loss of sheltering from competition which workers attained in the past' (Noyelle, 1987, p. 117) and by the reduction in the power of trade unions to negotiate wage settlements incorporating the interests of the weakest groups in the labour force. The weakening of these groups has been a consequence of 'the decline in importance of collective labour standards and a renewed emphasis on the individual employment contract' (Rosenberg, 1989a, p. 398).

In many aspects polarization has been gender-specific. While men have retained the majority of permanent and well-qualified jobs in the core group, women have come to be employed in large numbers in the peripheral groups or among the external groups of workers. Thus women make up the overwhelming majority of the part-time, temporary and self-employed workers.

CONCLUSION

The theories of segmentation or dualism in the labour market were based on a stable labour market; dominated by strong internal labour markets and an institutionalized system of industrial relations protecting the skilled, male workers. Furthermore, the labour market and its organizations were dominated by workers in manufacturing. This situation has changed dramatically and, consequently, made a reformulation of the labour market theories a necessity. The labour market has grown more unstable and diversified. In this chapter I have tried to outline the reasons for this development. The role of the firm as the principal focus for long-term employment, upward mobility and qualification is weakening. Instead, less permanent forms of employment have taken over – part-time work, temporary work, self-employment, home-working and so on. The process of training is now taking place in an external form. Firms are tending to externalize both production processes and workers, in order to reduce production costs and increase organizational adaptability as much as possible. The result has been the appearance of the flexible firm, with its demand for labour flexibility.

For workers, this development has led to better and more general qualifications. But, at the same time, the stability of employment has been under attack. The trade unions have been weakened because of high and sustained unemployment and also because of the dismantling of their traditional strongholds within male-dominated manufacturing industries and by the appearance of new groups of workers – women, minority groups and so on. As a consequence, the need by firms for flexibility, a more differentiated labour force and changing employment conditions have, together, created a situation of increasing marginalization of specific groups, polarization, and inequality within the labour force.

REFERENCES

Anker, N. (1990), *Flexibilitet på arbejdsmarkedet – mobilitet, hjemsendelse og midlertidig ansættelse i Danmark og Sverige*, Copenhagen: Danish National Institute of Social Research.
Appelbaum, E. (1986), 'Restructuring Work: Temporary, Part-time, and at-home Employment', in H. Hartmann (ed.) *Computer Chips and Paper Clips*, Washington D.C.: National Academy Press, 268–310.

Atkinson, J (1987), 'Flexibility or Fragmentation?, The United Kingdom Labour Market in the Eighties', *Labour and Society*, **12**, (1), 87–105.

Attewell, P. A. (1984), *Radical Political Economy Since the Sixties*, New Jersey: Rutgers University Press.

Baron, J. and W.T. Bielby (1984), 'The Organization of Work in a Segmented Economy', *American Sociological Review*, **49**, 454–473.

Bluestone, B. (1970), 'The Tripartite Economy: Labour Market and the Working Poor', *Poverty and Human Resource*, Abstract no.5: 15–35.

Bluestone, B. and B. Harrison (1982), *The Deindustralization of America*, New York: Basic Books.

Bluestone, B. and M. H. Stevenson (1981), 'Industrial Transformation and the Evolution of Dual Labor Market', in F. Wilkinson (ed.), *The Dynamics of Labor Market Segmentation*, New York: Academic Press, 23–46.

Boje, T. P. and C. Toft (1989), *Arbejdsmarkedets og Segmenteringsteorier*, Åbenrå: Institut for Grænseregionsforskning.

Boje, T. P. (1990), 'Arbejdsmarkedets Institutionalisering – sociologiske tilgange til forståelse af arbejdsmarkedet', in P. Gundelach, N. Mortensen and J. C. Tonboe (eds), *Sociologi under Forandring* Copenhagen: Gyldendal, 291–349.

Christopherson, S. and M. Storper (1989), 'The Effects of Flexible Specialization on Industrial Politics and the Labor Market: The Motion Picture Industry', *Industrial and Labor Relations Review*, **42**, (3), 331–347.

Cornetz, W. (1988), 'The Dark Side of the "Employment Miracle" in the USA', *Intereconomies*, January/February, 39–48.

Doeringer, P. and M.J. Piore (1971), *Internal Labour Markets and Manpower Analysis*, Lexington, Mass: Lexington Books.

Edwards, R. C. (1979), *Contested Terrain: The Transformation of the Workplace in the Twentieth Century*, New York: Basic Books.

Furåker, B., L. Johansson and J. Lind (1990), 'Unemployment and Labour Market Policies in the Scandinavian Countries', *Acta Sociologica*, **33**, (2), 141–164.

Gordon, D. M. (1972), *Theories of Poverty and Underemployment*, Lexington, Mass: Lexington Books.

Gordon, D. M., R. Edwards and M. Reich (1982), *Segmented Work, Divided Workers. The Historical Transformation of Labour in the United States*, London: Cambridge University Press.

Jensen, P. and N. Westergaard-Nielsen (1988), *Temporary Layoffs. Studies in Labour Market Dynamics*, Aarhus University.

Jensen, V. (1990), 'Arbejdskraftens Flexibilitet', *Mimeo*, Dept of Political Science, Aarhus University.

Kalleberg, A. L. and A. B. Sørensen (1979), 'The Sociology of Labour Markets' *Annual Review of Sociology*, **5**, 351–379.

Kutscher, R. E. and C. E. Sorrentino (1989), 'Employment and Unemployment patterns in the U.S. and Europe, 1973–1987', *Journal of Labor Research*, **10**, (1), 5–22.

Meulders, D. and L. Wilken (1987), 'Labour Market Flexibility: Critical introduction to the analysis of a concept', *Labour and Society*, **12**, (1) 3–17.

The Ministries of Labour, Finance, Social Affairs & Education (1989), *Hvidbog om Arbejdsmarkedets Strukturproblemer,* Copenhagen.

Nätti, J. (1990), 'Flexibility, Segmentation and Use of Labour in Finnish Retail Trade', *Acta Sociologica*, **33**, (4), 373–382.

Nielsen, L. D. (1988), 'Flexibility – between Economy and Local Labour Markets', Copenhagen: Business School Institute for Transport, Tourism & Regional Economics.

Noyelle, T. (1987), *Beyond Industrial Dualism*, London: Westview Press.

OECD (1986), *Flexibility in the Labour Market: The Current Debate*, Paris: Organisation for Economic Cooperation and Development.

OECD (1987), *Employment Outlook*, September, Paris: Organisation for Economic Cooperation and Development.

OECD (1988), *Employment Outlook*, September, Paris: Organisation for Economic Cooperation and Development.

OECD (1989a), *Employment Outlook*, July, Paris: Organisation for Economic Cooperation and Development.

OECD (1989b), *Labour Market Flexibility: Trends in Enterprises*, Paris: Organisation for Economic Cooperation and Development.

OECD (1990), *Employment Outlook*, July, Paris: Organisation for Economic Cooperation and Development.

Pfeffer, J. and J.N. Baron (1988), 'Taking The Workers Back Out: Recent Trends in the Structuring of Employment', *Research in Organizational Behavior*, **10**, 257–303.

Piore, M.J. (1970), 'Jobs and Training', in S.H. Baar and R.E. Barringer (eds), *The State and the Poor*, Cambridge, Mass: Winthrop Publishers.

Piore, M.J. and C.F. Sabel (1984), *The Second Industrial Divide*, New York: Basic Books.

Ploug, N. (1990), *Arbejdsløshedsrisiko og beskæftigelseschance*, Copenhagen: Danish National Institute of Social Research.

Rosenberg, S. (1989a), 'From Segmentation to Flexibility', *Labour and Society*, **14**, (4), 363–407.

Rosenberg, S. (ed.) (1989b), *The State and the Labour Market*, New York: Plenum Press.

Scheuer, S. (1989), 'Faglig organisering 1966 til 1987', Del I + II. *Økonomi og Politik*, no.2 and 3, Special Issues.

Sengenberger, W. (1981), 'Labour Market Segmentation and Business Cycle', in F. Wilkinson (ed.), *The Dynamic of Labor Market Segmentation*, New York: Academic Press. 243–259.

Sengenberger, W. (1988), 'Economic Development and Segmentation: The Case of the Federal Republic of Germany', Paper presented at the Conference on *Economic Development and Segmentation*, April, Notre Dame University.

Tarling, R. (ed.) (1987), *Flexibility in Labour Markets*, London: Academic Press.

Vejrup Hansen, P. (1985), *Arbejdskraftbevægelser og beskfætigelse*, Copenhagen: Danish National Institute of Social Research.

Wilkinson, F. (1987), 'Deregulation, Structural Labour Markets and Unemployment', In Pedersen P.J. and R. Lund (eds), *Unemployment: Theory, Policy and Structure*, Berlin: Walter de Grüyter, 167–186.

8.   A New Deal for Europe?

John Grahl and Paul Teague

A NEW COMPROMISE?

In Europe today several areas of political and economic debate raise the question of a reconstructed compromise between labour and capital. The question has been discussed most explicitly by the French regulation theorists, notably by Lipietz (1989), but it arises, in different ways within many types of discourse: work on unemployment and labour markets; on industrial organization and restructuring; on political agendas, both national and international. This kind of convergence suggests that the hypothesis of a new compromise may be a fruitful one – all that is attempted in this chapter is a preliminary, tentative exploration of some of the implications of that hypothesis.

The notion of a *new* compromise involves the rejection or obsolescence of an old one; it seems relatively uncontroversial to identify the latter with the post-war settlements which inaugurated three decades of rapid growth in West European countries within a clearly established institutional framework. It would be an exaggeration to say that the post-war order has collapsed or disappeared – only in Britain has the political consensus of the West European democracies been challenged in a fundamental way, and even there the basic mechanisms of the previous period continue to function. Nevertheless, if the old compromise has not been destroyed it has been profoundly destabilized. The empirical continuity of the institutions which embodied the settlement – welfare state, collective bargaining, patterns of mass consumption – no longer disguises a certain decline in their legitimacy, a questioning not so much of existing practice as of lines of economic and social advance. The economic background to this reappraisal is obviously the decline in economic growth rates from the mid-1970s onwards and the return of mass unemployment. Early attempts to reverse this decline involved Keynesian expansion with incomes policy as the main instrument for monetary stability. We might take the failure to make incomes policies work as signalling the degeneration of the old settlement. The social polarization which made such policies seem unacceptable both to labour and to capital announced a new phase of more open social and political conflict.

To use the notion of compromise at all implies the rejection not only of unlimited conflict but also of conflict resolution through a Carthaginian peace, where one party could simply impose its will on the other. On the side of labour there have been projects, usually of an extremely theoretical nature, for the imposition by political means of an extensive array of constraints on the autonomy of business enterprises. This was rarely other than a minority position but the collapse, in practice and in theory, of the economics of central planning, has forced its evacuation. The acceptance of decentralized production and exchange seems logically to require (especially within the Marxian intellectual tradition which inspired the anti-capitalist tendencies in European labour movements) the recognition of the categories to which they give rise: commodities, money and capital.

In practice the other side is also tempted by unilateral solutions. Although bargaining and negotiation as such are central to the neo-liberal views which have recently had so much influence on employer strategies, they are fully accepted only at the individual level. Neo-liberal doctrines have tended to justify the acceptance of high rates of unemployment at the same time as employers' representatives have pursued decentralizing bargaining strategies which would shift the determination of wages and conditions down to the local or enterprise level at which unemployment has the most intense impact. There is a Hobbesian strain in contemporary conservative thought: markets are sometimes seen, not so much as an efficient method of co-ordinating production, but rather as a necessary check on the unruliness of individuals. Thus the process of negotiation facing individual employees, menaced by social and economic exclusion and not supported by ties of solidarity, may preserve the form of compromise while emptying it of much it its content.

If a unilateral settlement by employers has not generally occurred this is largely because of the productive value of compromise itself within the enterprise. It is a change in the nature of work which is the possible basis of a new negotiated settlement within society. The Taylorist work regimes which controlled the efforts of the mass of employees in the leading sectors of western economies are no longer compatible with sustained increases in labour productivity; unless workers can be more thoroughly and responsibily engaged in their tasks, and these tasks themselves more broadly defined, in terms of results rather than functions, economic development in the broad sense will be blocked; the mere displacement of Taylorist work stations by robots may increase output volumes or lower costs but it makes no lasting contribution to development unless the redeployment of labour leads to qualitative advances in productive performance.

Already the notion of 'negotiated involvement' has found widespread confirmation in the practice of enterprises and in the approaches to personnel management which are emerging within them. At present both the negotiation and the involvement are confined within the enterprise, without social articulation or economy-wide organization. This limitation is the source of serious economic malfunctions; but it cannot be overcome by a simple extension of the corporatist negotiations of the past which are too centralized and aggregative. Nevertheless some economy-wide settlement will be needed for successful macroeconomic co-ordination of the new compromise and thus for the release of its developmental potential. Meanwhile other major uncertainties obscure the possible settlement. Which agents can carry out the negotiations? Have trade unions and labour movements been so weakened as to make them incapable of representing adequately the interests of workers? What is the arena of the settlement? Can the EC provide scope for forms of equilibration and co-ordination which are hardly possible at national level? What, finally, is the counterpart which will be offered in exchange for a comprehensive and thorough commitment of European workforces to a new phase of accumulation? The conclusion that emerges concerns the representation of labour: within a more integrated Western Europe it is implausible to suggest a revival of corporatist bargaining which would be inefficient both because of the scale of the economy and because of its complexity. It is therefore necessary to imagine more decentralized and pluralistic forms of labour representation. Clearly this kind of development poses the danger of fragmentation and incoherence but these can be overcome by appropriate unifying instances. The latter might be institutional, along a line of advance signalled by the Social Charter of the EC, and associative, through a dense set of links and alliances among unions and other organizations. Finally, a common ethos or ideology could be supplied by the notion of a responsible and active industrial citizenship.

NEW GEMEINSHAFT

One of the utopias of Andre Gorz, exploring the concept of a world freed from toil by technical advance, contains an anomalous survival from the past; a labour market. Why preserve anonymous, alienated labour when emancipation from scarcity and exploitation offers the alternative of self-determined, self-fulfilling activity within each community? Gorz (1982), with the wisdom of hindsight, preserves the labour market just as an *alternative* to the community, however ideal, and possibly as a refuge from the tyranny which, regardless of intentions, it might come to exert. It is an irony of contemporary neo-liberalism, for which the basic point of reference is the open society – civil society in the widest sense – that it has sponsored an economic programme which tends to just the kind of enclosure within petty communities which Gorz feared. The drive for labour flexibility aimed at strengthening the role of labour markets and the capacity of markets to organize and control productive activity, has in practice tended to closet employees within their own enterprises, within little communities increasingly isolated from each other.

There was always a certain ambiguity in the concept of labour flexibility. Much of the economic theory behind the flexibility agenda refers to the fluency with which labour *markets* operate, whether in the macroeconomic response of average wage levels to fluctuations in demand, or in the geographical and occupational mobility of workers in response to structural change. From the point of view of employers, however, the key issue was the flexible use of labour within the enterprise. What drove the programme forward, and gave it its resonance, was the need experienced by companies for a much deeper and more active commitment of workers to their tasks in order to clear the obstacles to productivity growth. The multiplication of dedicated functions, each requiring intense but highly focused attention and the disciplined observance of procedures laid down in advance, were no longer necessary supports for mechanization and for the expansion of output volumes. If the value added in production was to continue its long-term increase then this would have to be through abandoning narrowly specified job descriptions in order to make full use of the initiative and experience of each worker. Although the term flexibility ('functional flexibility' according to Atkinson's (1986) classification) is often used to describe the changes in work practice that are being sought, it is probably more accurate to speak of *involvement*.

The consequence of this kind of reform within the enterprise has been to decentralize and even fragment labour markets in ways which impair rather than enhance their efficiency in overall economic regulation. Bargaining becomes increasingly enterprise based, individuals being offered rewards for which the main reference is the pattern of relations within the enterprise itself. A good example is the tendency of bargains to tie remuneration, not to a physical measure of productivity, but to the financial performance of the employing enterprise. This kind of payment system is seen as corresponding to the need for a closer involvement of employees in the activity of the enterprise but clearly it tends to weaken the impact of general labour conditions on wage formation.

This outcome points to a general weakness in the neo-liberal programme, which aims to transfer economic responsibility from the state to civil society but often seems to work with a very impoverished notion of the latter. Society, considered as a mere agglomeration of economic agents is not intrinsically endowed with the capacity to perform complex feats of co-ordination and reorganization. Everything depends on the preparation and formation of the agents concerned and on the wealth of their interconnections. Institutional and associational structures, sometimes perceived as sources of barriers to pure market adjustment, are in fact necessary for the orientation of market agents.

The paradoxical and in many ways worrying nature of trends in labour markets can be seen in the emergence of 'human resource management' as the new paradigm of employee relations within the enterprise. In one sense there is a considerable enrichment in the content and scope of personnel management and in the notions of employee welfare which are used: career development, status, retraining at frequent intervals, are now seen as relevant to all permanent employees; there is a new and more intimate accommodation of employees' preferences in the design of the work-place and in working conditions; managements more readily accept the need for equal opportunities within the enterprise. But this humanization of employment remains within the confines of the enterprise as community: the same managements which adopt the human resources approach, frequently aim, at the same time, at a calm, slow but deliberate exclusion of trade unions and collective bargaining. This is not usually union-busting in the dramatic form seen in the US but there is a long-run perspective, an industrial relations *trajectory* in which trade union organization plays no part. It is not that unions are seen as imposing a monopoly price for labour; frequently the firms concerned will try to better the terms and conditions achieved in collective bargaining. Rather the union is perceived as an external constraint, an intrusion into the reordering of human relations within the enterprise as community. Trade union representatives in such a context are seen as anomalous, a source of discord and dislocation. This defensive kind of thinking has economic costs – the exclusion of external forces from employee relations tends to eliminate a valuable source of objective criticism and comparison, while isolating employees from a potentially rich source of information.

A growing literature explores the economic malfunctions induced by the hypertrophy of internal and the atrophy of external labour markets,

(Lindbeck and Snower, 1988). Formal analysis investigates a division of the workers into outsiders and insiders – the latter have a stable, long-term relationship with a given enterprise of just the kind that the 'human resource' approach seems likely to foster. The employment and pay of the insiders is protected from shocks on the goods market, with the not surprising result that the equilibrium of labour markets is impaired and unemployment tends to persist. In the limit, an excess supply of labour is unable to stimulate a wage reduction so that employment becomes simply demand determined, passively following fluctuations in the demand for final output. This is one basis for 'hysteresis' effects in unemployment – with the 'natural' or 'non-inflationary' rate of unemployment moving to follow the actual rate. This of course is a central example of rigidity in the external market, but one which is exacerbated by projects at enterprise level for maximum flexibility in the internal use of labour. Aoki (1990) refers to a similar problem as the 'dilemma of industrial democracy' but the dilemma arises from any close and exclusive involvement of employees in their employing enterprise.

The same group of models also reinforces notions of dualism in labour markets, although the simple dichotomy insider/outsider should not be taken too literally (as shown in the preceding chapter). Exclusions and divisions tend to multiply, so that even among those outside primary labour markets there are important differences in access to employment. Nevertheless the hypothesis of dualism is basically strengthened by the proliferation of enterprise strategies which attempt to shield a group of established workers against external fluctuations. The suggestion is that three quite different forms of analysis – the human resource approach to personnel management, theories of dualism in the labour market, and insider/outsider explanations of unemployment – show important convergences and can be related to the same group of tendencies in microeconomic behaviour: an attenuation of external relationships, whether market-based or not, among employees while the employment relationship between workers and their own enterprise becomes more intimate. The strength of this development is that it may tend to make fuller use of workers' capacities and thus unblock the path to productivity growth (the latter being measured economically, to include increased quality of services as well as increased volumes of goods). The corresponding weakness is in overall co-ordination, certainly in the labour market, perhaps in the goods market as well – paradoxically the increased independence of internal from external labour markets amplifies disturbances in the latter in ways which make 'insulation' strategies self-defeating. Of course it is not being suggested that internal labour markets are dispensable; on the contrary they are the inevitable consequence of the business enterprise itself, and of the need for long-term relations between employers and employees. What is at issue is the degree to which and the ways in which these unavoidable internal markets are constrained by external factors. (Thus there is no real inconsistency between the argument here and that of Boje in the previous chapter. Boje speaks of the 'decline' of internal labour markets, but by this he means their disorganization and loss of coherence rather than a general move to reliance on external markets. It is only for the more disadvantaged groups of workers that such a move is really important.)

As experience accumulates, the assessments that are made of flexibility regimes are increasingly negative, see Harrison and Bluestone (1990). A recent study of flexibility strategies by British companies reinforces the impression that they are essentially defensive – not linked to long-term development of either products or personnel, but seen even by managements themselves as a way of cutting costs and reducing exposure to financial or market shocks, see Atkinson (1986). Meanwhile the problems of training and of shortages of skilled labour have emerged as an object lesson in the limitations of enterprise-centred employment policies. Obviously there are simply externalities in training which necessitate a wider approach than that of a single company and which, in practice, cannot be removed by the extreme individualism which would throw the entire cost of training onto the employee. However, it is also relevant to the present argument that there are important informational aspects to the problem. Industry-wide training programmes imply objective, external, qualifications which, from the point of view of the isolated enterprise, may seem to be merely another constraint, see Fairley and Grahl (1983). The present question is whether effective co-ordination and communication is possible without such 'constraints' which are the necessary institutional supports of labour mobility. It is interesting to observe the accumulation of evidence for the superiority of German training practice over the pure flexibility strategies of Britain which seem increasingly like a form of neglect.

Today the necessity of business enterprise as a form of organization is not in question. But the contemporary cult of the enterprise seems to go further. Given that pure exchange relations, without institutional or social structures to underpin them, are an inadequate basis for economic co-ordination the enterprise comes to seem a refuge, caring and communitarian, from the danger and the anomy of society at large. A compromise is certainly reached between employers and, at the least, their core of privileged insider employees. But this compromise is not articulated throughout society and no longer has an economy-wide dimension. It was always clear that this outcome carried the risk of social exclusion; it now seems likely that it may also involve serious economic inefficiences.

BETWEEN FLEXIBILITY AND CORPORATISM

In contemporary discussion of labour markets corporatist forms of bargaining have emerged as the alternative to the new paradigm of flexibility. This is a completely logical response – it points to the actual achievements of specific types of social compromise and to their verifiable advantages when compared with the benefits claimed for enterprise level negotiations and for the dismantlement of economy-wide bargaining institutions. The theme of corporatism permits reference to the role of social compromise and of the integration of organized labour in the unprecedented economic success of the 'golden age'. If one is looking for an empirical basis from which to question labour flexibility and the neo-liberal agenda, there is no other real source of evidence.

Nevertheless, the simple polarity between corporatism and flexibility does not offer an adequate basis for a renewed social compromise simply because the established corporatist models are tied too closely to patterns of economic development which are now obsolete. In the context of the renewed drive for European integration the most developed models of corporatism seem to be confirmed to a periphery of small countries within which national labour market co-ordination is beleaguered both by external economic forces and by domestic social and political change. The following discussion does not aim to undermine the basic arguments made for organized employment bargaining, only to point out certain limits to the historically given corporatist models. Although a re-established employment compromise in Western Europe will certainly draw on these models it will also have to depart from them in several important respects.

One clear limitation of existing corporatist models is the scope of the bargaining process. Most of the discussion among economists has essentially concerned wage bargaining alone – the question is whether centralized wage bargaining can improve the trade-offs between un-employment and wage inflation. If one only considers negotiations between employers and employees, this reflects actual practice. According to Wilke (1990) it has been a consistent strategy of employers' organizations to keep other issues off the agenda – inability to deliver their membership on such questions as investment or output growth or even employment has been one way of tightening pressure on the key question of wage rates. Clearly wage rates cannot be completely isolated from the other questions; it is almost inevitable that wage structures in particular will be associated with wage levels in the bargaining process and this opens up the question of differentials. However, it does mean that the corporatist bargaining process may be too narrow to deal with the increasing involvement of workers with their tasks or the more complex counterpart which that involvement will require.

The impact of corporatist negotiations on wage structure has been, according to Rowthorn (1991), a key indicator of the comprehensiveness of the settlement and hence of its efficiency in combatting unemployment: the objective of reducing inequalities is linked to that of avoiding exclusions. Neglect of wage structure is then identified as a key weakness of Austrian corporatism relative to that of Scandinavia (at the same time Italy shows an anomalous ability to compress differentials in spite of a decentralized bargaining system, perhaps through the working of the *scala mobile* which institutionalized compensation for inflation). Rowthorn's results point to another fundamental limitation on some of the discussions of corporatism: its treatment of agency. Following a line of application of standard economic concepts to coalitions, well exemplified in the work of Olson (1982), corporatist and other centralized approaches to bargaining can be viewed simply as a way of aggregating individual interests. It seems very unlikely that this kind of interpretation is adequate. If, on the one hand, individual members take a purely instrumental view of the unions and federations which represent them then it becomes very difficult to see how powerful and stable conditions of interest are possible at all; on the other hand, the potency of centralized strategies cannot arise simply from the way they articulate given interests – they must also in some measure change the way in which interests are perceived and construct common interests in the process of expressing them. The more inclusive and egalitarian variants of corporatism do not reduce unemployment simply by improving the functioning of labour markets but also because they attach a higher value to full employment. There are corresponding dangers in the flexibility model which, by encouraging a parochial view of employee interests, may tend to dismantle the ethical and political supports of a wider social awareness. Political factors are also neglected in accounts of corporatism which abstract from the unavoidable presence of the government in centralized bargaining processes, whether or not this is formalized in tripartite negotiating structures. The most obvious implication is that governments aligned with labour can influence the bargaining process by altering the macroeconomic context in which it takes place, as was notably the case with the Rehn model in Sweden. The result is a very different kind of corporatism than will be found where governments are aligned with employers.

The two most fundamental economic limits on the corporatist models of the past are pointed out by Soskice (1989). The first results from the internationalization of economic life. This seems to be a crucial factor in many aspects of economic co-ordination. In several areas formal models suggest that asymmetries of information or high transaction costs make it advantageous to supplement purely contractual relationships with longer term formal and informal connections: this can be seen in employment, in finance, and in customer-supplier relations. Observation suggests, however, that the social basis of these supplementary relations is frequently national, whether because shared nationality improves communication or because it promotes the pooling of interests. Extension of these advantages to international economies seems impossible without dense networks of interconnections among agents in the countries concerned. On the other hand the continued internationalization of production and exchange may put tight constraints on the working of purely national supplements to exchange relations by undermining the structures of intermediation on which they depend. When, for example, companies have access to international credit markets their participation in more long-term and intimate national systems of credit allocation may continue only on a voluntary basis. Similar pressures clearly disturb corporatist labour bargaining within a national context.

The other limit on corporatist models, according to Soskice, results from new technologies and new patterns of output and can be associated here with the pressures for a more committed and responsible involvement of workers within each enterprise. This is a continuing source of differentiation which erodes the discipline on which centralized bargaining strategies have rested. It is true that decentralization is also the strategy favoured by many employers to take advantage of the changing balance of supply and demand in the labour market, but this is not the only force at work. Decentralization of aspects of bargaining also seems to rise from changes in the productive structure. In this context imposition of centrally determined bargaining outcomes can weaken the unions which adopt such strategies, to the point of undermining the links between unions and their members.

The present troubles of the Swedish economy symbolize the difficulties of centralized corporatist models. There have been problems in reaching centralized wage bargains which are consistent with balance of payments constraints while resort to devaluation is seen as damaging in a context of European economic integration. As its height the Rehn model of wage determination adjusted overall wage rates to trends in productivity and international competitiveness while the equalization of rates encouraged structural change and increased use of skilled labour. (Rowthorn suggests that the outcome was a labour market which imitated Walrasian equilibrium, although very high degrees of economic co-ordination are probably always 'imitations' in that they arise only when agents are orientated by powerful institutions as well as price signals.)

At their best, corporatist forms of bargaining not only stabilized labour markets; they combatted social and economic exclusion while promoting a rapid growth of output and productivity. These achievements depended on the establishment of objective, economy-wide, criteria for the use of labour which individual companies were constrained to apply. All these features remain essential requirements for a new social compromise: the challenge is to meet the same requirements within an international arena, and by forms of association which admit of a wider variety of individual outcomes.

REPRESENTATION OF LABOUR

A bargain can only be struck between negotiating agents. Is the trade union movement still a possible interlocutor in the process of social compromise? Can it still convincingly claim to represent the general interest of employees? Can it still commit its constituency to an agreed productive counterpart for concessions obtained in collective bargaining? The recent pressure on established trade union positions makes such questions a necessary aspect of any exploration of a renewed settlement.

In the 'golden age' of postwar growth, of course, trade unions enjoyed unprecedented power and influence. Through a complex set of bargains with governments and employees they both advanced the living standards of their members and established a range of workers' rights within the industrial order. Although the forms of these bargains varied widely organized labour was seen, everywhere in Western Europe, as a legitimate social institution and one of central importance. Today that centrality is being questioned even when it is not openly challenged. Persistantly high unemployment, changes in occupational and industrial structures, new managerial techniques as well as analysis (such as the 'Eurosclerosis' view, which attribute economic problems to inflexible labour markets), have all combined to put unions on the defensive. To varying degrees in different countries, trade unionism has been on the retreat throughout Western Europe for the last ten years. The focus of controversy is whether this retreat is temporary or permanent.

One view is that the decline of trade unionism is basically conjunctural. In support of this thesis it is argued first that union weakness is caused by high unemployment and sluggish growth and can be reversed in an economic recovery. Moreover, although it is conceded that industrial restructuring over the last decade has virtually eliminated the praetorian guards of organized labour in the coalfields, shipyards and so on, it is expected that recruits in the public and service sectors will take their place. Industrial conflict will spread radical militancy among white collar workers and transform them into a new proletariat. From this point of view trade unions will move back to the future as economic growth resumes, see Kelly (1989).

Although there certainly are conjunctural forces at work, they are inextricably linked to irreversible secular shifts which make this scenario of a rapid and complete recovery for organized labour highly implausible. One must consider in particular the ideological shifts which have undermined the traditional principles of trade unionism. The crisis of socialism makes it difficult for unions to see themselves as the bearers of a universal project for social transformation and as the pioneers of a better and higher order. The social philosophies which sustained working-class solidarity have thus tended to dissolve at the same time as industrial change has dispersed established concentrations of trade union power and attenuated the traditional ties of community among the working class. Even the rhetoric of traditional trade unionism has a hollow ring today when the practice of unions appeals more to a functional solidarity within the world of business than to an overarching movement. Quite logically also this loss of social objectives has reduced the political role of unions and their previous influence over general policy formation, so that their political aims now tend to be much more narrowly industrial.

Secondly, the move to more flexible production systems has undermined established bargaining practices. During the rapid industrial expansion of the 1950s and 1960s two contrasting models of industrial relations developed in Western Europe: on the one hand the adversarial bargaining characteristic of Britain and some Southern countries where wages and conditions were largely negotiated at sector or enterprise level; on the other hand the corporatist bargaining of Scandanavia and Germany where centralized wage restraint was traded against more favourable economic policies. Both models are inconsistent with flexible production which requires a sophisticated organizational intelligence, broader and higher skills and a closer, more intimate relationship between management and employees. Certainly the adversarial model is more thoroughly dislocated: a 'them and us' ethos and a pursuit of sectional demands are completely at odds with the new need for a wider sharing of responsibility and much more extensive communication within the enterprise. It also seems that existing corporatist models may be too centralized and bureaucratic to promote a deep and stable social compromise at enterprise level. Thus increasing incongruities between established trade union practice and new industrial relations agendas are encouraging employees to develop new, decentralized arrangements which threaten organized labour with continuing marginalization.

In the huge plants of the Fordist epoch, relatively homogeneous work tasks and their mechanical co-ordination within mass production provided a clear basis for trade union recruitment and organization. The emergence of more fragmented and dispersed productive structures has not only posed problems of recruitment for unions but also limited their ability to counter patterns of exclusion and disadvantage. Difficulties in penetrating ranks of precarious, peripheral workers or in formulating policies for the growing number of women in the labour force indicate the dimensions of this challenge.

Taken together, the decline of class politics, the emergence of a new industrial relations agenda and the fragmentation of the workforce suggest that unions can no longer be regarded as the sole agency for the promotion and protection of workers' rights and living standards. Increasingly they will share these functions with other forms of grouping and arrangements. Women's groups, for example, have done more to secure equal opportunities at the work-place than unions so that a plurality of representation in this sphere is now well established and likely to continue. If part-time and other 'atypical' workers continue to be beyond the reach of trade union organization then legislation and state regulation may be the main way of protecting their interests. Professional associations, which are now playing a greater role in defining standards for training in some occupations may be the most effective form of institution in developing advanced skill formation strategies. Social cohesion and economic equity may, in the long run, prove essential to the new industrial order but it is no longer plausible to suggest that the trade union movement alone can secure them.

New productive structures will also require substantial changes in the practice of the unions. Decentralization of union structures in Italy, increasing involvement of Swedish unions in firm-level skill formation, the recently signed National Economic and Social programme in Ireland which established new bargaining connections between the firm and the centre may all foreshadow a more general process of reform and adaptation (Sabel and Kern, 1990). The unions may in the end win back an important role, if not an exclusive one, in the construction of a new social compromise, but this will require both organizational changes and a thorough redefinition of their intermediary functions.

DESIGN FOR A MACROSYSTEM

Any lasting social compromise depends on general economic development and not simply on the labour market. Labour has an obvious
interest in a closer approach to full employment, but, for employers a
settlement will not seem advantageous unless a new model of accumulation opens the way to sustained expansion. The process of compromise
itself requires long-time horizons within which there is scope for mutual
gains rather than the pure distributional conflict that is implicit in a static
or short-term assessment of interests. Thus, both to engage employers in
social negotiations and to make the bargaining process meaningful, an
industrial settlement has to be embedded in a more comprehensive
economic order. For this reason some discussion of macroeconomic
themes is necessary. The exploration of macro–micro linkages is already
a central aspect of the response to neo-liberal doctrines and policies. It is
clear, in retrospect at least, that the neglect or misunderstanding of the
microeconomic bases of macroeconomic relationships was a key weakness in the Keynesian strategies of the early 1980s which, in both radical
and moderate versions, failed to provide a convincing path to economic
stabilization and renewal.

In the theoretical sphere, free-market conservatives established an
impressive lead by the work summarized in Phelps (1970) and the work
which grew out of it, especially that of the new classical macroeconomists.
An interpretation of inflation and unemployment was successfully
advanced which, if it did not directly justify the neo-liberal experiments
of the last decade, did help to make them plausible. Keynesian orthodoxy
attempted to reply, too often, in purely macroeconomic terms without
explaining why its own hypotheses, on pricing or output behaviour,
corresponded better to individual decisions at the level of the
household or the firm. In terms of policy it was often taken for granted
that micro behaviour could simply be constrained to correspond to
ambitiously expansionist macroeconomic strategies. The French left-
Keynesian experiment of 1981–83 rested on a purely fictional micro-
economics – a world of vertically integrated *filieres* where multinational
enterprises would cheerfully repatriate their activities and could be easily
induced to expand their workforces while their competitors were
shedding labour at dramatic speed.

Gradually these omissions and weaknesses have been corrected, at
least in theoretical terms. No survey can be undertaken here of a theme
which in itself covers a large part of contemporary economics but for
present purposes two important tendencies can be emphasized. On the
one hand there is the emergence of a New Keynesian research pro-

gramme, see Carlin and Soskice (1990): using the analytic tools of mainstream theory, but broadening its assumptions to reflect the context of limited information and imperfect competition in which micro-economic decisions are taken, New Keynesians attempt to construct more solid foundations for standard Keynesian macroeconomic positions. Particularly influential here was the theoretical deepening of Keynesian positions by US economists such as Okun (1981) and Tobin (1983). The achievements of New Keynesian theory still fall some way short of a full synthesis, which the very-complexity of the analytical work makes difficult, but they have already called into question the intellectual foundations of neo-liberal strategy. From the point of view of a new settlement a different approach to macro–micro interactions is particu-larly important, although in itself it is less central to contemporary economics. This may be described as the attempt to develop historical or evolutionist accounts of macroeconomic performance. Although this work makes less use of formal analytical techniques it tries to produce unified theories of macroeconomic systems in the course of structural change: the central hypotheses which are advanced concern the relation-ships between technical and organizational changes at the microlevel and consequent shifts in macrostructure. Labour markets are discussed (see, for example, the study by Boyer (1979) on the emergence and eventual decline of successive models of wage-formation); but the main focus is on goods markets or on the overall functioning of macrosystems. Three streams of thought will be distinguished here although their results are not mutually exclusive and there are interactions among them.

French regulationists have produced the most elaborate version of this kind of theory. Members of this tendency, represented in this book by the contribution of Coriat and Petit, use the notion of Fordist production to explain the characteristics of a period particularly favourable to Keynesian strategies of demand-led growth. The forms of organization and technology which gave rise to the mass production of standardized consumer goods provided a microeconomic basis which was highly conformable to Keynesian macroeconomics: on the one hand, the enterprises involved were particularly vulnerable to any decline in consumer spending; on the other hand, while the most important industrial enterprises pursued high volumes and economies of scale some of the most immediate limits on macroeconomic expansion could be suspended since higher consumption demand would lead to rapid productivity growth, and then, increased investment. Using Kaldorian models the regulationists proposed a kind of microeconomic foundation for Verdoorns law, according to which the countries pursuing the boldest Keynesian expansions would be rewarded by the most rapid improvement of their productive structures. At the same time a microeconomic explanation for the decline of the Keynesian era is found in the obstacles, social and technical, which eventually put an end to the corresponding enterprise strategy. These are the fragmentation of consumer markets, increasing difficulties in 'balancing' ever longer and more rigid production lines, profound employee resistance to the disciplines required for continuing productivity growth in such a context and the disturbance, by international forces, of national pricing systems which then failed to maintain profit margins.

These productivity/demand relationships are not the only ones explored by regulationists who have also, for example, produced a rich and original literature on monetary questions. However, their account of the macroeconomics of productivity growth is central to the challenging and complex research programme stimulated by regulationist theory. An early econometric study indicated that Western European economies were a long way from a new developmental logic to replace that of the post-war epoch (Boyer and Petit, 1981); since that time a range of quite heterogeneous research has used this hypothesis of a blocked productive system to explore possibilities of its renewal or supersession.

The second body of work can be considered as proposing a particular post-Fordist model based on the replacement of the rigid, dedicated production apparatus of the mass-production factory by smaller, decentralized, units able to accommodate wide variations in market requirements. Piore and Sabel's (1984) account of *flexible specialization* has provoked controversy: the value of such a sharply focused picture of contemporary economic transitions seems beyond dispute, even if many initial positions need correction or elaboration. On the question of macro–micro linkages the negative results reached in this context seem persuasive: Piore and Sabel suggest that the new more flexible production units will not give rise to such marked accelerator effects as have been found in the past, because investments at the microlevel are less vulnerable to demand shifts. It seems doubtful, however, that there will be a simple return to macroeconomic control by purely monetary means, on pre-Keynesian lines, as they also suggest. In recent years monetary policy has been a particularly potent instrument but this is more because of serious disorders in the financial system than because it offers adequate control over the investment process. One strength of the flexible specialization model is to emphasize the importance of the external relations of the enterprise – with its customers, its suppliers and, especially, with other firms in the same industry. Intra-industry relations are competitive but also, in many ways, collegiate because of shared resources and scale economies external to the firm. Forms of control bearing on these inter-firm networks, perhaps through the subsidy of common infrastructures, could be a possible policy response, rather than a simple return to reliance on monetary policy alone.

A third relevant body of work is supplied by the models of techno-logical trajectories developed by Dosi, Freeman and other writers associated with the Science Policy Research Unit at the University of Sussex (Dosi, Freeman, Nelson, Silverberg and Soete, 1988). This research does not concern the economics of science in any narrow sense; rather it takes technical change as the central source of uncertainty in economic life and examines the microeconomic and institutional processes by which that uncertainty is contained. If disequilibrium in economic systems reflects a situation in which agents are learning and adapting, then this literature uses a wide range of historical and empirical knowledge as the basis for a theory of disequilibrium behaviour. There are many macroeconomic implications – an example of particular relevance to the present argument is the account of structural crises by Freeman and Perez (1988): the emergence, diffusion and decline of 'techno-economic paradigms' is the basis of historical shifts in macro-economic relationships, such as investment functions.

There are several respects in which these approaches produce similar results: one suggestion common to all of them is that technical and social uncertainties may lie behind the cautious and defensive microbehaviour which, at present, impairs the macroperformance of Western Economies. Convincing *institutional* responses to changing patterns of technology and production may thus be the most direct route to sustained reductions in unemployment and inflation. However, the historical and evolutionary approach is not confined to such general judgements: for a more specific policy implication one can take the regulation school's notion of a *consumption norm*. A stable reference point for consumption behaviour, which shifts along a relatively predictable trajectory as productivity grows, is seen as a vital orientation for producers. Clearly such a norm is partly the work of convention, but it also has institutional supports which encourage the spread of certain consumer goods and services.

The saturation of western markets for some basic, highly standardized durables may today make feasible consumption norms more complex but this does not mean that norms can be dispensed with. Growing inequalities encourage high-income households to adopt consumption patterns based on the extravagant use of low-cost labour-intensive services. (Compare Davis, 1984, on 'overconsumption'). The resulting norms are intrinsically incapable of generalization through imitation and cannot support economic development through scale effects, whether by simple volume growth in yesterday's mass production factories, or by more complex externalities among the more decentralized production unit of the future. Neo-liberal economic strategies have regarded inequality as the means to restored efficiency. From the present point of view the widespread and sometimes dramatic increase in income dispersion which has occurred in many countries (see Davidson and Kregel, 1990), may itself be a critical barrier to macroeconomic stabilization.

The general argument then is that a potential settlement between employers and employees cannot be discussed in terms of the labour market alone. No settlement can last unless it is part of an overall *regime* (Glyn *et al.*, 1990) which fosters continued development of the whole economic system. This consideration may seem to make the settlement a hopelessly ambitious task. Labour bargaining obviously cannot cover every aspect of economic life. However, the discussion, by Glyn *et al.* of the postwar regimes indicates that they were not directly and consciously established by a process of social and political compromise, but were arrived at in various ways and from various decisions. The implication is not that the new settlement must be all-inclusive, but that the bargaining process is constrained by the emergence of particular productive possibilities and will only be successful if it adapts employment to a sustainable line of economic advance.

EC ARENA

Within the EC many of the conditions for a new, developmental compromise between labour and capital are close to being met. This is partly a matter of political traditions – together, Social Democratic and Christian Democratic formations, both orientated towards an institutionalized social settlement, have a large majority over the neo-liberal or leftist tendencies which might reject such a project or put impossible constraints upon it. But one can also detect the emergence of a European society in the sense of a rich set of associational links among individuals and organizations in different West European countries. Without such linkages, the patterns of communication, compensation and control which are needed to articulate an overall social settlement and make it effective at the micro-level are difficult to conceive. In economic terms a major programme of market-led integration is coming to an end and a new phase of institutional construction promises both to improve co-ordination in the EC economies and to open the process of co-ordination to social and political pressures.

Clearly the Community's Social Charter and the associated Action Programme have a very direct bearing on any projected settlement. Indeed the Charter can have little signifance apart from the openings it makes for a socially articulated compromise. The Charter and the Programme are weak on most questions of substance – on the minimum conditions that workers should obtain. Repeatedly concrete outcomes of bargaining are referred back to member states via the notion of subsidiarity. Charter and Programme seem much stronger when it is a question of the procedures by which these outcomes are achieved. The Action Programme resuscitates many of the Commission's previous proposals on communication, consultation and union recognition: these might not greatly alter existing procedures in any member country, but they would tend to block the exploitation of the 'big market' and the process of integration as a way for employers to escape existing obligations to inform and to negotiate. Another relatively strong point of the Charter concerns the dangers of exclusion and dualism in the labour market: the 'atypical' employment contracts which are designed to provide numerically flexible sources of labour are constrained to offer comparable terms to those enjoyed by permanent employees. In the same context it is worth noting that the projected statutes for a European Company also envisage constraints on employee relations and thus on the virtually absolute autonomy of enterprise-level bargaining in most versions of the flexibility model.

As Wedderburn (1990) points out in his commentary on the Charter, it is the tendencies of EC legislation and policy which are important, rather than the actual constraints on national bargaining practice at a particular moment in time, which are usually small and, in the case of the Charter itself, do not exist. What is in play are different European labour market projects; there is a clash of models rather than of policies. It is interesting, however, that the new instruments of Community policy – both Charter and Action Programme – create a great deal of scope for bargaining processes and that, if they rarely specify the outcome to be achieved in employment practice, they do clearly signal directions of advance – on wages, working conditions, training, consultation, equal opportunities and other issues. At the same time there is a shift to less direct and more decentralized constraints on bargaining than have been envisaged in the past. Frequently the EC Commission has attempted to sponsor a form of Euro-corporatism which would centralize aspects of bargaining for the Community as a whole. We have discussed elsewhere (Grahl and Teague, 1991) the weaknesses of this approach, among them the consistent inability of the employers' side to deliver its membership and its steadfast refusal to even attempt to do so. The more indirect and decentralized strategy purused at present through the Action Programme seems more realistic and more likely to succeed.

Direct labour market policies are not the only ones which bear on the construction of a new compromise. Of equal importance are the moves towards monetary integration which seem to be bringing to an end the prehistory of macroeconomic policy in the Community. Clearly a European Bank will not finance ambitious Keynesian experiments on a Community-wide basis; on the other hand it would permit a more effective defence of European economies from the external financial pressures which have been so damaging over the last decade and, merely by eliminating the competitive element in national monetary policies, make for easier and more stable credit. Refinancing policies, with an inevitable political element, will have to be defined: they can encourage social compromise by working to lengthen planning horizons and the development of creditor–debtor relationships.

Also of importance are the geographically constructed economic policies of the Community operated through the structural funds. The territorial criteria which are used, connecting with the evolution of models of industrial districts, see Goodman, Banford and Saynor (1989), allow for the assessment of productive structures going beyond the enterprise while still focusing on developmental issues rather than simple questions of welfare and redistribution.

Once again these possibilities are a long way from realization, although their relevance to the construction of a new settlement is clear. The principal constraint is not that the EC does not have competence over the policy areas involved – the community's powers are growing rapidly. A wide range of associations and other links among EC citizens, to guide and support legislative initiatives, and to take advantage of emerging institutional frameworks and bargaining rights, is the most important condition for developing the Community as the site of a new settlement. Recent strategies for integration have centred on the 1992 programme and the reinforcement of market relations. The response, in Polanyi's phrase the 'self-defence of society' against the effects of unconstrained market forces, more than ever requires a transnational dimension.

CONCLUSION

The premise of the argument presented in this chapter has been labour's acceptance of, and active engagement in, a new phase of private capital accumulation. What counterpart does this engagement attract? What will labour gain in return? It is already clear that business will pay well for the new degree of involvement and for the resolution of some of the old conflicts. Material rewards will not be lacking, although they will be distributed in a frighteningly unequal way, if there is no check on individual business policies. In any case, unco-ordinated enterprise-level bargaining will be unable to deliver even the sustained economic development which is the assumed basis of a new deal.

The implication of the argument is some notion of active industrial (or economic) citizenship (compare Marquand, 1990). This would be rooted in the new engagement of workers in their tasks but would develop a social dimension both to these productive responsibilities and to the pattern of rewards. Employees would consciously become a means by which economy-wide norms and social objectives were brought to bear on the enterprise. Through a plurality of associations they would both develop and transmit these criteria. They would also deploy the expertise needed to adapt business policy in appropriate ways. Some of the necessary conditions for such citizenship have been discussed. Communication within and between unions and other associations of workers would have to be much richer than at present, and would require unions to reform both structures and practices while deepening the concept of solidarity on which they are built. At the same time there is a need for a more basic form of communication – the straightforward mobility of larger numbers of workers among enterprises. The restoration of some balance between internal and external labour markets will hardly be achieved without many active labour market interventions but is indispensable to re-construct an objective environment in which business can function. The same kind of interventions tend to limit exclusions and dualism in labour markets but these dangers must also be directly attacked. Citizenship, as a shared condition, permitting inter-communication among producers, is not compatible with unlimited dispersions of rewards; nor can economic objectives be socially defined unless it is possible to discuss the needs of representative consumers whose welfare is considered relevant to the majority of agents. Finally, the structures and associations involved must today be international as must also the social articulation of production which they support.

This kind of project, for a wide industrial citizenship, presents novel and disturbing challenges because it must be sought essentially within civil society – legislation and public institutions can only enable the associations and initiatives which are needed, not supply them directly. Nevertheless, it is this pattern of advance which seems most likely, in contemporary Europe, to promote economic development while avoid-ing social regression.

REFERENCES

Aoki, M. (1990), 'The Dilemma of Industrial Democracy', in S. Marglin and J. Schor (eds), *The Golden Age of Capitalism*, Oxford: OUP.

Atkinson J. (1986), 'New Forms of Work Organisation', *IMS Report*, no 121, Brighton: Institute of Manpower Studies.

Boyer, R. (1979), 'Wage Formation in Historical Perspective: the French Experience', *Cambridge Journal of Economics*, 3, (2), 99–118.

Boyer, R. and P. Petit (1981), 'Employment and Productivity in the EEC', *Cambridge Journal of Economics*, 5, (1), 47–58.

Carlin, W. and D. Soskice, (1990), *Macroeconomics and the Wage Bargain*, Oxford: OUP.

Davis, M. (1984), 'The Political Economy of Late Imperial America', *New Left Review*, 143, 6–38.

Davidson, P. and J. Kregel (1990), *Macroeconomic Problems and Policies of Income Distribution*, Aldershot: Edward Elgar.

Dosi, G., C. Freeman, R. Nelson, G. Silverberg and L. Soete (1988), *Technical Change and Economic Theory*, London: Pinter.

Fairley, J. and J. Grahl (1983), 'Conservative Training Policy and the Alternatives', *Socialist Economic Review*, 3, 137–153.

Freeman, C. and C. Perez (1988), 'Structural Crises of Adjustment', in Dosi, *et al., op. cit.*

Glyn, A. *et al.* (1990), 'The Rise and Fall of the Golden Age', in S. Marglin and J. Schor (eds), The *Golden Age of Capitalism*, Oxford: OUP.

Goodman, E., J. Banford and P. Saynor (eds) (1989), *Small Firms and Industrial Districts in Italy*, London: Routledge.

Gorz, A. (1982), *Farewell to the Working Class*, London: Pluto.

Grahl, J. and P. Teague, (1991), 'European-level Collective Bargaining: a New Phase', *Relations Industrielles*, forthcoming.

Harrison, B. and B. Bluestone (1990), 'Wage Polarisation in the US and the Flexibility Debate', *Cambridge Journal of Economics*, 14, (3), 351–73.

Kelly, J. (1989), *Trade Unions and Socialist Politics*, London: Verso.

Lindbeck, A. and D. Snower (1988), *The Insider-Outsider Theory of Employment and Unemployment*, Cambridge, Mass : MIT.

Lipietz, A. (1989), *Choisir l'Audace*, Paris: la Decouverte.

Marquand, J. (1990), 'Living in Truth: Training and Economic Change', paper presented to EAEPE Conference, November, Hotel Montebello, Florence.

Okun, A. (1981), *Prices and Quantities : a Macroeconomic Analysis*, Oxford: Blackwell.

Olson, M. (1982), *The Rise and Decline of Nations*, New Haven: Yale University Press.

Phelps, E. (ed.) (1970), *Microeconomic Foundations of Employment and Inflation Theory*, New York: Norton.

Piore, M. and C. Sabel (1984), *The Second Industrial Divide*, New York: Basic Books.

Rowthorn, R. (1991), Social Corporatism and Labour Market Efficiency', in J. Pekkarinen *et al.* (eds), *Lessons from the Corporatist Experience*, Oxford: OUP, forthcoming.

Sabel, C. and H. Kern (1990), 'Trade Unions and Decentralised Production: a Sketch of Strategic Problems, *Mimeo*, Cambridge, Mass.: Department of Politics, MIT.

Soskice, D. (1989), 'Industrial Relations and Unemployment: the Case for Flexible Corporatism', in J. Kregel, *et al.* (eds), *Barriers to Full Employment*, New York: St. Martin's Press.

Tobin, J. (ed.) (1983), *Macroeconomics: Prices and Quantities*, Oxford: Blackwell.

Wedderburn, Lord (1990), *The Social Charter: European Company and Employment Rights*, London: Institute of Employment Rights.

Wilke, M. (1990), 'Societal Bargaining and Stability', *Mimeo:* Tilburg University, Department of Economics.

PART FOUR

European Monetary Union

9. European Monetary Arrangements and National Economic Sovereignty

John N. Smithin

INTRODUCTION

Since the publication of the Delors Report in 1989, and in tandem with the movement towards the 'completion of the internal market' by '1992', momentum towards eventual monetary union in the EC has gathered pace. The current case for such a development seems to depend partially on the view that a common currency will ultimately be necessary to gain the full benefits of economic integration; partially on a consensus that the current EMS of quasi-fixed exchange rates has been successful in some important respects (with an even greater degree of monetary inter-dependence then seen as the logical next step); and finally, in some quarters, as a prerequisite for pan-European political aspirations to become a reality.

Notwithstanding the current level of enthusiasm for monetary union, however, the purpose of this (and the following) chapter is to articulate some of the unfashionable counterarguments and caveats. The discussion here accepts the view that there will be positive benefits arising from a greater degree of economic integration as in the '1992' proposals, but will nonetheless point out some of the disadvantages of linking the trading arrangements either with an eventual currency union or, for that matter, with any 'irrevocable' fixed-exchange rate system.

To avoid misunderstanding, it should be stressed at the outset that the arguments will be of a somewhat different nature than those put forward by well-known monetarist critics of currency unions and fixed exchange rate systems, as in Walters (1990), Laidler (1990) or Friedman's (1953) classic statement. The traditional monetarist would favour national monetary autonomy essentially for the national authorities to be free to implement 'tight money' or tough anti-inflation policies in a single country, whereas the same autonomy is advocated here so that a national economy is free to avoid (as far as possible) excessive deflationary pressure emanating from the centre. Similarly, whereas traditional monetarists may fear that a supranational central bank would tend to spread *inflationary* pressure throughout the system (as in the case of the US Federal Reserve System, in its 'key currency' role during the Bretton Woods era), it is argued here that in the present circumstances, a supranational central bank in Europe would be more likely to spread *deflationary* pressure throughout the system (as, arguably, in the case of the Bundesbank in the current EMS).

It is an interesting sidelight on the contemporary European debate that much of the recent more sceptical commentary, about both existing and proposed monetary arrangements, has originated in jurisdictions such as the US and Canada which already possess federal political structures and customs and currency unions linking regions with diverse economic infrastructures. In comparison with their European counterparts, such discussions have been far more likely to stress matters such as the unresolved issue of what constitutes an optimal currency area, the differential impact of a centralized monetary policy on the regions, and the persistence of regional economic disparities within currency unions. Hence this chapter will make a number of references to the experiences of these jurisdictions.

POLITICAL DIMENSION

Although the main focus here is on the economic issues, an important preliminary point that must be conceded is that if the ultimate objective of proponents of monetary union is pan-European political union, then the proposed monetary arrangements are simply a logical and indispensable step in pursuit of that goal. In this case there is no effective purely economic argument which can be made against them.

It has been widely recognized, in fact, that a single currency, and control over monetary policy, are among the most important defining characteristics of national sovereignty. When a jurisdiction forfeits control over monetary policy, it abandons what is arguably the most important instrument it possesses to influence domestic economic conditions, and hence effectively abandons control over its own economic destiny. An obvious recent example was the monetary union between the two German states in 1990. As soon as this was completed, it was immediately recognized by most observers that the independent existence of the GDR was at an end, some months before the formal political unification. A more mundane illustration, in the context of the Canadian 'monetary union', is that even though the various provincial governments can pursue an independent fiscal policy and have significant independent powers in such areas as education, health, transport, housing and other fields, it is (rightly) never seriously suggested that this level of government can be held primarily responsible for general economic conditions, even in their own jurisdictions.

In the case of the EC, of course, a transfer of power and sovereignty from existing national governments to some new supra-national institutions is precisely what is advocated by the proponents of eventual political union in Europe, and it is impossible to dispute the logic of those who argue for monetary union on those grounds.

What is more questionable, however, is whether the hopes of those who see future political union as a means to an *economic* end, or who believe that the economic and political goals are fully compatible, are likely to be realized. Here the evidence from jurisdictions which have already achieved a federal structure and customs and monetary union is directly relevant. In jurisdictions such as the US and Canada, a continent-wide monetary union evidently has not depoliticized the debate over monetary policy, particularly that over the impact of monetary policy on the regions; has not eliminated significant regional economic disparities; and, at least in the case of contemporary Canada, has not even ensured the continuing stability of the political union itself.

In any event, the discussion which follows will take for granted the proposition that ultimate political union will indeed require monetary union, and focus instead on the economic case for either monetary union or at least a greater degree of fixity of exchange rates, in circumstances in which something less than a complete political union is contemplated.

MONETARIST CONNECTION

A remarkable feature of the current debate is the extent to which the most widely discussed arguments *both for and against* a greater degree of monetary integration in Europe have been based exclusively on a monetarist model. From the point of view adopted in this chapter this has had the unfortunate consequence of biasing the discussion of monetary policy and alternative exchange rate arrangements only towards the relationship between money and inflation. The *real* impact of monetary policy, on output, employment and growth is then typically neglected altogether or treated as a transitory phenomenon. Moreover, this bias has persisted even at a time when quite recent economic history has provided numerous dramatic examples of the impact of monetary policy on real economic variables, and after an eight-to-ten year period during which the traditional statistical relationships between growth rates of monetary aggregates and inflation had visibly broken down as a result of financial innovation and deregulation. Even though these developments have been widely discussed at the level of national monetary policies, as in the contributions by Friedman (1988) and Goodhart (1989), they seem to have had little impact on the debate over present or proposed monetary arrangements in Europe.

The reason that the standard arguments on both sides can be described as 'monetarist' is that in most cases they focus primarily on the objective of reducing national inflation rates to as low a figure as possible, and rely on the causal mechanisms implicit in the quantity theory of money to achieve this.

Monetarists who argue *against* an individual nation locking itself into a system of irrevocable fixed exchange rates still tend to rely on elements of what Zis (1989) has aptly called the 'pre-1973' case for flexible exchange rates, based on Friedman (1953) and a number of subsequent contributions in the tradition of the monetary approach to the balance of payments. Put briefly, the argument is that if control over the rate of growth of the money supply is necessary for control over the rate of inflation, a flexible exchange rate regime is necessary for individual nations to be able to control their own inflation rates. Alternatively, in a fixed exchange rate system, or *a fortiori* in a common currency area, defence of the existing exchange rate (or the absence of competing currencies) implies that the individual nation must accept the average inflation rate of the system as a whole. If the system-wide inflation rate happens to be low this would presumably be an acceptable outcome, but from the point of view of the original monetarist writers in the circumstances of the Bretton Woods era down to 1971–73, that particular fixed exchange regime was seen as responsible for spreading inflationary pressures throughout the world, given that the major player (the US) was itself pursuing an inflationary policy in the late 1960s and early 1970s. To avoid this type of experience an individual nation would therefore have to be prepared to float its currency and allow it to appreciate if necessary.

The monetarist case for *joining* a fixed exchange rate system is then just the obverse of this argument. If the major player in the system is regarded as committed to low inflation and 'sound money', and the domestic monetary authorities are not, it is argued that monetary discipline can be imposed on the domestic policy-makers by the requirement to maintain a fixed exchange rate. The debate in Britain in the late 1980s, prior to that nation finally joining the EMS in October 1990, provides numerous illustrations of this line of thinking. Clearly the Deutschmark was very much the lynchpin of the EMS as this had evolved at the time, and the policies of the Bundesbank were seen as having been responsible both for generating a low average rate of inflation within the EMS and the apparent convergence of national inflation rates among the EMS members. On the other hand, British social and political arrangements, such as the wage bargaining system and the lack of political independence of the Bank of England, were widely seen as being incapable on their own of delivering a rate of inflation to match that prevalent in continental Europe. For those in favour of entry to the EMS, the short-term solution to Britain's inflation problem was precisely to 'tie the hands' of the monetary authorities by EMS membership, relying on the defence of the exchange rate to impose anti-inflationary discipline. The long-term solution would be to remove the monetary policy debate from the British political arena altogether, by submitting to currency union and to the monetary policy of a supranational European central bank.

Of the two monetarist arguments, it is clearly the position of the flexible exchange rate advocates which is the more intellectually coherent. If low inflation is indeed the over-riding objective for a given society, then (in terms of the monetarist model of inflation) there should be no reason why domestic political and economic institutions cannot deliver it. If they do not do so in practice, there are presumably deeper social and political reasons why this society 'chooses' a higher inflation rate, and the alternative strategy of simply passing the responsibility on to some outside authority is unlikely to resolve the underlying conflicts. In the specific case of Britain, any potential conflict between, on the one hand, the often noted tendency of that society towards wage inflation and, on the other, a 'tight-money' policy on the German model, may be just as likely to result in unemployment and social distress as in a rapid social adjustment towards the norms of the other society. The result may well be simply a replay of the British government's own 'monetarist experiment' of the early 1980s, but with the responsibility for the resulting unemployment shifted elsewhere.

At an even more basic level, it is hard to locate the guarantee, from a monetarist point of view, that the authorities to whom the burden of monetary policy is shifted will always pursue the policies required of them. In the case of the existing EMS, how will the policy of the Bundesbank change, for example, in the new circumstances dictated by German unification? Even more pertinently, what is the likelihood that a future European central bank after currency union, which will be subject to Community-wide political pressures, will replicate the policies of the Bundesbank of the 1980s?

In the face of this type of uncertainty, the position of the more traditional monetarists, that with flexible exchange rate it should always be possible to pursue 'monetarism in one country' does provide an intellectual case that is less dependent on ephemeral factors and the current political climate. What it obviously does not do, however, is deal with the criticisms of monetarist policies themselves, whether pursued in an individual country or at the international level. Specifically, it does not deal adequately with the likely real impact of monetary policies, designed only with the objective of controlling overall inflation, in the concrete social, political and institutional circumstances of the differing societies and regions.

MONETARY POLICY, OUTPUT AND EMPLOYMENT

At the time (now more than 20 years ago) when a unique and stable 'Phillips curve' trade-off between inflation and unemployment was widely believed to exist, the apparently obvious argument for an individual nation to retain monetary autonomy would have been the ability to exploit that trade-off in some 'optimal' fashion. However, as Laidler (1990) and others have correctly pointed out, the demise of the Phillips curve, on both empirical and theoretical grounds, has effectively ruled out this line of argument. Nonetheless, it is misleading to move from this to the idea that the real effects of monetary policy can safely be neglected. Just as the 'stagflationary' episodes of the 1970s called into question the conventional wisdom on monetary economics of the 1950s and 1960s, the collapse of the monetary targeting experiments of the early 1980s, the recent rapid pace of financial innovation, and the role of high interest rates in the policy-induced recessions of the past decade have surely done the same for the rational expectations arguments for 'policy irrelevance' and monetary neutrality of the 1970s. Yet all this seems to have been ignored in the most prominent recent discussions of European monetary union.

An alternative approach to monetary economics, which comes to seem increasingly realistic in the current circumstances, is that found, for example, in the work of such 'Post Keynesian' economists as Kaldor (1970), (1982), and Moore (1988), and in some of the later work of Hicks (1982), (1986) and (1989). The essence of this approach is that the short-term rate of interest should be regarded as the important monetary control variable, and that money supplies (in the sense of the statistically defined monetary aggregates) respond endogenously, both to change in the interest rate and to exogenous shocks to the demand for credit at a given interest rate. This 'endogenous money' approach was not widely accepted at the zenith of the influence of the monetarist school and then the 'new classical' school, some 10 to 12 years ago. However, since then, the breakdown of monetary targeting and the obvious reversion of central banks around the world to an interest rate (and exchange rate) focus in the later part of the 1980s, have made it once again a subject for discussion even for economists previously associated with the alternative point of view, such as McCallum (1986), Barro (1989) and King and Plosser (1984).

Hicks (1982) made the argument in a clearcut fashion, when he extrapolated from trends in the financial system apparent at his time of writing and imagined the existence of a pure 'credit economy' in which there is no commodity or fiat money and the *only* exchange media consist of the (interest-bearing) liabilities of financial intermediaries. In such a system, the only way to discharge the payments function is by an exchange of debts, and the 'promises to pay' of the differing financial intermediaries or 'banks' will be acceptable to third parties in exchange for goods or services only if they in turn can be confident that others will also accept them in succeeding rounds of transactions. With the nebulous factors of 'confidence' and 'trust' looming so large it is easy to see that in any given system there will emerge one institution whose promises to pay are regarded as more reliable and hence more widely acceptable than any other. This *monocentre* (in Hicks's terminology) then becomes the lynchpin of the financial system, and, specifically, it will have a degree of market power over the setting of nominal interest rates, including its own deposit rate, which eventually enables it to conduct the 'monetary policy' of the system.

As a practical matter the administered interest rate will be in the first instance a nominal rate, but in conjuction with the existing inflation rate entrenched in the system this also implies a real rate. Moreover, it is always open to the monocentre to attempt to stabilize the real rate by adjusting the administered rate in response to changes in actual or expected inflation. A given policy with regard to short rates, if it is maintained for any length of time, will also influence long rates via the effect of expectations on the term structure.

In this view of the world, it tends to be argued that monetary policy is at least as important for real economic outcomes, such as levels of output and employment, and the rate of growth, as it is for inflation. Real effects occur not only as a result of short-run nominal rigidities, which would also be true of more traditional approaches, but also because of hysteresis effects which prolong economic downturns for longer periods than are assumed in 'natural rate' models, and, in the still longer run, via the impact of interest rate changes on investment, capital accumulation and growth. The eventual effect of monetary policy on inflation rates is not denied but is believed to occur via a somewhat more indirect mechanism than in the monetarist model. The immediate impact of a 'tight-money' (high interest rate) policy, for example, would be a recession, and this may have to be far longer lasting than is suggested in the monetarist description of the same process. The effect on inflation would only come later, after the recession had a chance to bite, and the impact of the downturn had begun to affect such factors as the wage bargaining process.

As argued by Smithin (1989), in examining the international or regional implications of this alternative view an important point is the identification of the crucial factors which would make a given financial centre a monocentre. Although, in principle, the monocentre is simply any institution, which could well be a private institution, whose promises to pay happen to be superior, in practice in the closed economy the government central bank will usually assume this role. Its promises to pay are ultimately backed by the coercive powers of the state, which will have both the tax system and legal tender laws at its disposal. In the international arena, however, such devices as acceptability in payment of taxes and legal restrictions will clearly not suffice. Instead, what the history of the international monetary system seems to show is that the emergence of world or regional 'monocentres' – financial centres which are sufficiently powerful to set the tone for interest rates in the region or the world as a whole – is based on the most crude indicators of national economic success. A country seems to be able to claim the position of a monocentre for its central bank basically if it has built up a large excess of net credits against outside nations on which it can draw in times of emergency. These claims may well be denominated in the currency of the monocentre itself, but they ultimately represent a claim against the real resources of other nations built up by a record of current account surpluses, reflected in capital outflow. Once a large credit position has been achieved, the promises to pay of the creditor become more trustworthy than those of immediate rivals, and status as a world or regional monocentre, with concomitant market power over interest rates, would follow.

Clear examples would be the obvious financial power of the UK and the Bank of England during the nineteenth century, and the US and the Federal Reserve for much of the twentieth century. Similarly, the recent (relative) decline in the importance of the US dollar in international financial transactions and the relative increase in the importance of both the Deutschmark and the yen, can also be traced to changes in the underlying international credit positions of the nations involved.

As for the discussion of appropriate exchange rate regimes it seems that a great deal will depend on the recent economic history of the system under discussion, and the stage of development reached by the various institutions involved. A first consideration is whether in the given historical situation a financial power has emerged which is truly 'monocentric' in the sense of dominating any rivals, as in the case of London and the Bank of England in the nineteenth century, or alternatively that a number of regional centres have evolved, each with a degree of power locally but competitive in the broader context.

In this latter case, which Hicks (1982) calls the 'polycentric' model, a fixed exchange rate regime between the different centres could potentially have an inherent deflationary bias. A centre which raises interest rates will attract funds from the other centres and force them to do the same, but a centre which lowers interest rates will have no such influence. In the monocentre case, however, system-wide monetary policy developments will be controlled in both directions. This model might apply not only at the global level in particular historical circumstances, but also within a regional currency bloc where one of the members is a dominant player. In either case, as far as the smaller countries are concerned (those most closely approximating the textbook case of the 'small open economy') it might even be possible to draw the conclusion that the nature of the exchange rate regime is essentially irrelevant. Although a change in the exchange rate regime may change the *mechanism* by which the small country adjusts to policy changes emanating from the monocentre, it will do nothing to remove the final necessity of adjustment.

However, another group of nations, those that might be termed 'medium size financial powers', will have important choices to make about their relationship to the financial superpower. In practice, even in situations where the world or regional economy is dominated by one powerful centre, there will still be intermediate cases of nations which may not be powerful enough to affect the fortunes of others, but which nonetheless have sufficient 'credit' to exercise a degree of interest rate autonomy if they chose. In such cases the nature of the exchange rate regime becomes crucially important. The retention of different currencies and the possibility of exchange rate changes will allow for the emergence of forward premia and risk premia (or discounts), and hence at least some scope for a different interest rate policy than the monocentre. Given the existence of such 'medium-sized open economies', even an absence of capital controls will not negate this conclusion (qualitatively) as 'perfect capital mobility' in the sense of the textbooks will not obtain unless the promises to pay under comparison are indeed perfect substitutes from all points of view. However, obviously, the imposition of capital controls will greatly enhance the _quantitative_ scope for an independent policy.

In the assumed circumstances, the decision to enter an irrevocably fixed exchange rate regime is essentially to submit to the hegemony of the monocentre, and the loss of whatever possibility of an independent policy continues to exist. If, as suggested here, monetary policy is indeed important for real economic outcomes, this may not be simply a matter of accepting a different inflation rate than the one which would be 'chosen' domestically but of accepting a different growth rate or unemployment level also. In particular, the medium-sized financial power forgoes a potential 'escape route' from deflationary pressure emanating from the centre, which might otherwise have been available.

In the case of the current EMS, these ideas, particularly the notion of a Hicksian monocentre, clearly go a long way towards explaining the hegemony of the Bundesbank within that system. They also bring out the point, however, that membership of such a system cannot be regarded simply as a desirable end in itself. The results depend entirely on the actual performance of the monocentre.

A number of important questions about the proposals for currency union and the European system of central banks (ESCB) also arise. A key issue is exactly how the new central bank might be expected to attain the postion of the monocentre. If this is to be achieved by government fiat, as in the closed economy case, this clearly implies that a situation _already exists_ in which political power is concentrated in some central authority, and the power of the national governments has effectively been reduced to provincial status. The alternative is a situation much like the old Bretton Woods system, in which the setting-up of the new central monetary authority is essentially a façade, and the real power to determine events rests with the original 'naturally selected' monocentre. In this case, the ESCB may well turn out to have much the same relationship to the Bundesbank as the IMF had to the US Federal Reserve System under Bretton Woods.

OPTIMAL CURRENCY AREAS?

The criticisms and caveats which can be raised about monetary union or greater exchange rate fixity have very often been met simply with what amounts to ridicule in recent public debate. As an example, consider the following rhetorical question from a recent editorial (August, 1990) in _The Economist_: 'Would America be a more open vibrant economy if the Louisiana franc, the New York lira, the Minnesota guilder and the Pennmark required changing on the state border?' A riposte in the same spirit might be that Louisiana, for one, may well have had a more prosperous economy if devaluation had been an option in the early 1980s, and would certainly have stood a much better chance of retaining its original language and culture if it had possessed monetary sovereignty in the past. More substantively, however, by postulating an extreme case (the 50 US states) in which most observers would agree that separate currencies are unviable, what such rhetorical devices set out to achieve is to by-pass the serious question of what actually constitutes an 'optimum currency area'.

This is an issue which was originally raised by Mundell (1961) thirty years ago, but has received surprisingly little attention in the current debate. Even in the case of the US, although it may well be agreed that an individual state does not constitute such an area, clearly this does not automatically mean that the existing currency union for the US as a whole, given its East–West, Rustbelt–Sunbelt and other regional divisions, is itself optimal just because it has existed historically.

Most expositions of the concept of the optimal currency area have essentially made the point that the area should comprise units which have both a similar economic infrastructure and a high degree of factor mobility (particularly labour mobility) between them. If economic conditions are dissimilar, unpredictable shifts in demand may well lead to situations in which the principal industries in one area are depressed while those in the other are booming. A common monetary policy which then focused on reducing inflationary pressures in the latter region (the likely outcome given the priorities of contemporary central bankers) would simply exacerbate the depression in the former. These regions are not therefore optimal currency areas and would benefit from some degree of exchange rate flexibility beween them. In the Canadian environment in recent years, problems of this nature have emerged as much more than a purely theoretical possibility. Many complaints about monetary policy during the late 1980s related precisely to the fact that the Bank of Canada was pursuing a 'tight money' (high interest rate) policy which was designed to restrain inflationary pressures in the industrial heartland of Ontario but which greatly worsened economic conditions in resource-based sectors of the economy in the West and East.

Fixed exchange rate proponents must argue that the inevitable discrepancies in regional economic performance can be ironed out by mobility of the factors of production rather than by separate monetary policies and exchange rate changes. This is why a high degree of factor mobility, and particularly labour mobility, is also one of the pre-conditions of the optimal currency area. When conditions in a given region are depressed, say by a reduction in the nominal demand for its products, one line of escape, if there are separate currencies, would be a depreciation. If this is ruled out because the region is involved in a currency union, the restoration of competitiveness then requires that there must be downward pressure on regional money wages and costs. This will surely be resisted, however, both for the traditional reasons, and because the linkages implicit in the currency union will encourage the use of bloc-wide comparisons of relativities and norms in wage bargaining. Both the resulting unemployment and the pressure for reductions in real incomes can then only be relieved by the migration of labour to the more prosperous regions. The real questions, therefore, are whether in practice there is likely to be sufficient labour mobility, and whether it is appropriate that all the burden of adjustment should either be on the migrants or, in the absence of migration, on those who stay behind and endure the rigours of unemployment and lower real wages.

The precedents from jurisdictions which already possess a currency union are not encouraging. In such countries large regional disparities in unemployment rates do persist even though quite substantial movements of labour and other factors certainly occur. These factor movements are simply not substantial enough. In both the US and Canada, for example, it could certainly be argued that there is traditionally a much more 'footloose' workforce than in the current EC. Yet the degree of factor mobility which does exist has clearly never been enough to provide an adequate adjustment mechanism for all regional disparities. It is necessary only to consider the case of Newfoundland or the Maritimes in Canada, for example, (with GDP per head in Newfoundland at 54 per cent of the national average, and an unemployment rate 2.5 times as large) or Appalachia in the US. Eichengreen (1990) also discusses in some detail the case of Puerto Rico, which is even more pertinent to the case of the EC, in that even though the island is a full member of the American 'customs and currency union' there are obviously linguistic and cultural barriers to full factor mobility, and these do seem to have had an impact.

From the European point of view, what these remarks imply is that some serious questions should be asked about whether the EC partners in the proposed EMU really do fulfil the requirements of the optimal currency area as set out in the textbooks. It is certainly possible to question whether the British economy, for example, given the disparate importance of the natural resources sector, and the continuing structural problems referred to earlier in this chapter, is really a good match for those of its Continental European neighbours. Similarly, there is also obviously something of a 'North–South' divide within the EC, which may be of sufficient magnitude to cause serious adjustment problems for the 'Southern' countries (and regions) when they finally have to accede to an irrevocable monetary union. It is difficult to avoid the impression that the awkward questions in this area have simply been pushed to one side in the momentum generated by the political debate.

Mention should also be made of a recent 'public finance' argument about optimal currency areas due to Canzoneri and Rogers (1990), which may be relevant to the situation of the 'Southern' EC countries. In tax systems which are not identical (with differences in the tax base, ease of collection and enforcement, administrative costs, and so on) the 'optimal' level of the inflation tax may need to be different also. If so, each jurisdiction would need a separate currency in order to achieve this. The argument is based on the standard monetarist view about the relationship between money and inflation, which was criticized above. Nonetheless, it is useful in making the point that the idea that inflation rates should *necessarily* converge is not automatically valid, given that the impact of differential inflation rates on competitiveness can be mediated by exchange rate changes.

FATE OF FLEXIBLE EXCHANGE RATES IN THE 1980s

A case can be made that the current positive evaluation of the EMS and the widespread enthusiasm for an even greater degree of monetary integration in Europe are both to some extent simply part of the legacy of the widely fluctuating exchange rates and global payments imbalances of the 1980s. At all levels there has been growing dissatisfaction with the existing regime of 'managed' floating exchange rates which has provided the environment for international finance since the break-up of the Bretton Woods system in the early 1970s. Hence, not only in Europe but also globally, there have been numerous suggestions for restoring a greater degree of fixity to exchange rates, including, for example, McKinnon's (1988) proposal for a common monetary standard between the US, Japan and Germany, and the proposal of Williamson and Miller (1987) for the establishment of 'target zones' for exchange rates. It will be argued here, however, that in many ways all these responses, including those in Europe, represent an inappropriate response to the actual events of the 1980s.

Up until the middle years of the past decade, it might have been more usual to argue that the *ad hoc* floating exchange rate regime which had emerged after 1973 had been working surprisingly well. It is true, of course, that exchange rate changes in practice were much larger than predicted by academic advocates of flexible exchange rates beforehand, and the phenomenon of exchange rate 'overshooting', as modelled by Dornbusch (1976), was recognized as the consequence of differential speeds of adjustment in asset and goods markets. Also, the 1970s were turbulent years for the world economy, primarily as a result of the two OPEC oil shocks. Nonetheless, after the floating of exchange rates, and the worldwide recessions of the early 1980s, the volume of world trade continued to grow, and it would be fair to say that individual importers and exporters quickly became accustomed to managing or hedging foreign exchange rate risk with the wide variety of financial instruments (forward contracts, financial futures, currency options) which became available.

The exchange rate gyrations of the 1980s, however, did a great deal to change the conventional wisdom. As in Marston (1988), economists were led to make a distinction between simple exchange rate 'volatility' (meaning the inevitable fluctuations around some norm or average exchange rate which occur as soon as exchange rates are free to move) and the much more serious problem of exchange rate 'misalignment'. The latter would be a persistant and cumulative departure from anything which might be recognized as an equilibrium exchange rate, meaning either a rate consistent with purchasing power parity or a rate which would achieve trade balance.

It has been usual to argue that the exchange risk associated with simple fluctuations around some norm can be laid off or hedged with the range of financial instruments currently available. However, this is *not* so in the case of persistent misalignment, and there were numerous apparent instances of this phenomenon during the course of the 1980s, such as the run-up of the US dollar to 1985 and the over-valuation of sterling in 1979–81. In these situations there was no effective way, *ex ante*, for the export industries on the ground to avoid serious miscalculations. In both cases, investments in plant and equipment, which had seemed viable based on expectations of economic fundamentals formed before the event, became progressively less so as the real effective values of the national currencies soared beyond any reasonable estimates of their 'equilibrium' values. Later, in 1986 and 1987, it was the turn of Japanese exporters to feel the pinch, as investments which had looked attractive when the yen was undervalued and the dollar over-valued became questionable as the dollar fell and the yen rose. The impossibility of making sensible business decisions in such an environment is what has led to the current climate in which a return to some sort of fixed exchange rate system seems desirable to many practitioners and economists, and naturally, within Europe, similar attitudes influence the current favourable evaluations of the performance of the EMS and the potential benefits of currency union.

The main criticism of this line of thinking, however, is that the focus on the exchange rate mechanism *per se* leads to a prescription which treats the symptom rather than the disease. The key point for discussion is whether the experience of the exchange rate misalignments of the 1980s was somehow inherent in the nature of the 'managed' floating system itself, or simply the result of pressures deriving from the unprecedented macroeconomic policy shifts of that decade, which might have caused trouble regardless of the exchange rate regime which was in place.

Turning the question around slightly, even when we consider the stable fixed exchange rate systems of the past, such as the gold standard era or Bretton Woods, it is a highly debatable point whether these 'worked' because of the inherent properties of fixed exchange rates, or simply because the major players in the system, the 'key currency' nations (or monocentres) were prepared to pursue the type of macroeconomic policies which allowed the system to continue.

It is certainly true, in both cases, that when the major players decided to pursue different policies the exchange rate systems themselves did nothing to constrain them. Both the gold standard and Bretton Woods, it could be argued, were broken up when the most important country in the system was forced to resort to 'easy money' policies to finance a war – World War I in the case of Britain in 1914, and Vietnam for the US in the late 1960s. In both instances the 'rules of the game' counted for nothing when the major players needed to suspend them. It could equally be argued that if the major players decide (whether for reasons of international altruism or domestic self-interest) to pursue policies which are sensible and stable and compatible with their neighbours, then a formal fixed exchange rate system would be superflous. Significant exchange rate misalignments would be less likely to occur, and over-shooting would be less of a problem if there were fewer disturbances in the first place.

Returning to the case of the 1980s, it seems obvious that the most important exchange rate misalignments occurred as a result of the monetary and fiscal policies pursued (in particular) by the US government. The 'tight money/loose fiscal' mix of the early part of the decade led to high interest rates, capital inflow and the subsequent overvaluation of the dollar. This in turn led to the large deficits on current account. It is true that capital movements were dominating balance of payments developments, but the capital movements themselves were driven by macroeconomics policy. Later in the decade, a more relaxed monetary policy was followed, interest rates were allowed to fall, and the budget deficit declined as percentage of GDP. The value of the US dollar fell as precipitously as it had risen, and after a lag the current account deficit fell also.

The point that needs to be made here is that assuming that domestic authorities were determined to pursue the same policies, it is doubtful whether the existence of a formal fixed exchange rate regime would have changed anything. In the actual circumstances, the policy shifts manifested themselves in misalignments of exchange rates, but had a fixed rate regime been in place they would simply have broken the system apart, like Bretton Woods.

A similar set of remarks applies to the EMS as it is currently constituted. From the point of view of those engaged in intra-European trade the motivation for a fixed exchange rate system within the European trading bloc is precisely the same as the case for fixed rates on a global scale. Fixed rates are believed to provide for a more stable environment for the conduct of trade, and to avoid the uncertainties associated with exchange rate fluctuations of the magnitude of those experienced generally in the 1980s. The point that must be stressed, however, is that the present EMS also stands or falls by the policies of its key currency nation.

As it stands the EMS is essentially a Deutschmark bloc, with the tight-money anti-inflation bias of the Bundesbank dominating European monetary developments. (What is meant by this is that *real* interest rates are kept relatively high. German nominal rates are often lower than elsewhere, but to the extent that the policy succeeds in keeping down inflation and nominal rate reductions do not fully compensate for this, real rates are kept high by historical standards.) The other nations in the system must acquiesce in this policy, and as long as the Bundesbank retains its traditional stance, this rules out, for example, the option of easier monetary policy to reduce domestic unemployment. As discussed earlier, in recent years this has actually been regarded as an advantage by governments in some European nations. They could hope to avoid the political fallout associated with tight-money policies by appealing to the technical requirements of EMS membership.

To make this observation is not to suggest that central banks should go to the opposite extreme of pursuing crudely 'inflationist' policies but it is possible to argue, for example, that the mass unemployment which persisted in continental Europe for much of the 1980s may have been less of a problem if the Bundesbank had softened its stance. More generally, whatever may have been the political priorities of the last decade or so, there is certainly room for debate about whether a monetary system with the potential for deflationary bias at the behest of a strong central bank will always be regarded by policy-makers and the public as necessarily desirable.

The point also remains that the continuity of a system like the EMS depends basically on the policies pursued by the monocentre, rather than on the properties of fixed exchange rate regimes themselves. It is the monocentre which will determine whether the system is deflationary or inflationary, and there is little or no guarantee either that those policies will always be reliable or that the monocentre will be responsive to the effects of its policies on those in the outlying regions.

In the case of complete monetary union with a European central bank, such a system, once established, would clearly be less likely to actually break up than a mere agreement on fixed rates. Once again, however, the performance of the total system and the impact on the regions will also be dependent on the performance of the new monocentre.

To sum up, if it is true that part of the current enthusiasm for rigidly fixed exchange rates is based on the experience of wildly misaligned exchange rates during the 1980s, then this response is somewhat perverse. What is actually being objected to is the economic damage arguably caused by the policies of the dominant central bank, the US Federal Reserve, together with the fiscal policies of the US government. However, the response of the supporters of irrevocably fixed exchange rates or currency unions is to advocate an even *greater* concentration of financial power, either regionally or globally, in a 'monocentre' which is even less politically accountable to those its policies affect. Moreover, to the extent that exchange rate changes could provide a potential 'safety net' for individual regions if things go wrong, the argument is also that the net should be removed.

ARE FIXED RATES NECESSARY FOR FREE TRADE?

A final observation needs to be made on the relationship of both the existing EMS and the planned EMU to the trading arrangements of the European Community. Viewed from the outside it is something of a mystery why the conventional wisdom in Europe holds that a common currency, or, at a minimum, a set of fixed exchange rates is necessary to support the proposed trading relationships. Indeed, Eichengreen (1990, p. 121 ff.), remarks that 'The belief that fixed exchange rates are needed to obtain the benefits of customs union is a recent and peculiarly European view'. He goes on to refer to an earlier literature which stressed that the benefits of an economic union could in fact be obtained with a wide variety of alternative exchange rate regimes, and also to note that other free-trade arrangements (such as the Canada–US FTA) pay little or no attention to the currency issue. It is suggested that some special features of the EC arrangements, in particular the Common Agricultural Policy (CAP), have historically predisposed the European debate towards a linkage of the two issues.

Clearly, also, the programme of the completion of the internal market as set out in the Single European Act has provided a proximate impulse. Padoa-Schioppa (1988) has been explicit about this in referring to the impossibility of reconciling what he calls the 'inconsistent quartet' of free trade, full capital mobility, fixed exchange rates, and national autonomy in the conduct of monetary policy. As the EC progresses on the first two of these items, he argues, it is clearly the fourth that will have to go, and the abdication of national control of monetary policy is also seen to imply at least some degree of restriction on national fiscal policies.

What is remarkable, however, is the short shrift given by not only Padoa-Schioppa but most other writers to the possibility of modifying the third element of the quartet instead. Nonetheless, as suggested above, as long as instruments for hedging foreign exchange risk are available, and, crucially, as long as severe misalignments are ruled out by reasonably sensible macroeconomic policy, it can be argued that there is really no reason why in principle the existence of different currencies subject to exchange rate changes should in itself provide any serious barrier to trade. It is not at all clear that the cost to society of 'insurance' through the provision of hedging instruments is any greater than the cost of maintaining a rigidly fixed exchange rate regime, where the latter include the dangers of deflationary bias inherent in the centralization of control over monetary policy.

There seems to be no genuinely compelling reason, in other words, why it is not possible to have a profitable trading relationship without relinquishing monetary sovereignty, as certainly seems to be envisaged in trade discussions in North America. Apart from Eichengreen's point about the CAP, the fact that the conventional wisdom in Europe does not recognize this may well be counted as another legacy of the avoidable exchange rate misalignments observed in the 1980s. Also, to the extent that the debate does not acknowledge how important the retention of monetary sovereignty can be, it further illustrates the influence of the 'monetarist' bias in the discussion of monetary policy in the past two decades. Both the short-term and longer-lasting effects of monetary policies on real economic prosperity are neglected, leaving the impression that the only impact of monetary policy is on the rate of inflation.

CONCLUSION

The premiss of this chapter is that the conduct of monetary policy, specifically control over interest rates, is one of the most important determinants of real economic outcomes such as the level of output and employment. Therefore, even in the context of supranational trading organizations such as the EC, it follows that those national economic authorities which retain political accountability for the economic well-being of their citizens might be well advised to retain control of monetary policy in so far as this is possible.

There is, of course, no guarantee that in any individual case the performance of the national authority would always be an improvement over that of a union-wide supranational central bank. However, the retention of separate national currencies, which either float or are at least subject to periodic revaluations, does at least allow for a possible 'escape route' from the straightjacket that centralized monetary policy could become. It is difficult to believe that the point will never arrive in the development of trading relationships at which the priorities of the regional or national unit will differ from those of policymakers at the centre. Also, it is an important consideration that national central banks may be at least somewhat more responsive to the political will of those directly affected by their policies. Although it is often suggested that one of the advantages of a supranational institution is that it is *more* removed from the political process (and therefore, presumably, free to impart a *deflationary* bias to its policies), the opposite view is taken here on the grounds of basic democratic principles.

It is not suggested, of course, that either central banks or international organizations should be unconcerned with inflation, and elsewhere (Smithin, 1990), I have suggested alternative national monetary rules (specifically, real interest rate rules) which might both reduce the influence of the monetary authorities on real economic outcomes and also at least contribute to keeping inflationary pressures in bounds. However, there is an implied judgement in these remarks that in recent years central bankers have tended to overemphasize the role of the monetary authorities in controlling inflation and to neglect the real impact of their policies. In present circumstances, these tendencies would likely be reinforced by setting up a supranational monetary authority remote from the political process.

Moreover, in the specific case of the EC, it is unlikely that the proposed monetary union (or indeed the existing EMS) will actually fulfil the requirements of an optimum currency area. Therefore a monetary policy which is appropriate for one or more important regions at any given time need not be appropriate for all. Experience from the existing currency unions in North America has shown that even with reasonably complete customs unions and internal capital mobility, labour mobility (though substantial) has still not been adequate to mediate all regional disparities. Sooner or later, therefore, situations will arise in which devaluations or revaluations of separate currencies (if they existed) would come to seem a relatively low cost method of dealing with regional payments imbalances.

The view that the substantial benefits of the 'completion of the international market' of the EC cannot be obtained without monetary integration has not been subject to critical scrutiny. Similarly, fears that the substantial exchange rate misalignments such as those of the 1980s are an inevitable consequence of moving away from rigidly fixed exchange rate regimes essentially misinterpret the policy-driven causes of those alignments.

It would certainly be true that commitments by trading partners to pursue the stable macroeconomic policies which would prevent dramatic exchange rate changes themselves imply a 'loss of sovereignty' in some degree. In normal times they will dictate very much the same policy responses regardless of the nature of the exchange rate regime. However, there is a qualitative difference between these informal constraints and the irrevocable loss of both economic and national sovereignty which is implied in the concept of formal monetary integration.

REFERENCES

Barro, R. (1989), 'Interest Rate Targeting', *Journal of Monetary Economics*, **23**, (1), 3–30.

Canzoneri, M.B. and C.A. Rogers (1990), 'Is the European Community an Optimal Currency Area? Optimal Taxation Versus the Cost of Multiple Currencies', *American Economic Review*, **80**, (3), 419–433.

Dornbusch, R. (1976), 'Expectations and Exchange Rate Dynamics', *Journal of Political Economy*, **84**, (6), 1161–1176.

The Economist (1990), 'The Flaw in Thatcher's Europe', August 11, 14–15.

Eichengreen, B. (1990), 'One Money for Europe? Lessons From the US Currency Union', *Economic Policy*, No. 10, 117–187.

Friedman, B.M. (1988), 'Lessons on Monetary Policy from the 1980s', *Journal of Economic Perspectives*, **2**, (3) 51–72.

Friedman, M. (1953), 'The Case for Flexible Exchange Rates', in *Essays in positive economics*, Chicago: University of Chicago Press.

Goodhart, C.A.E. (1989), 'The Conduct of Monetary Policy', *Economic Journal*, **99**, (396), 293–346.

Hicks, J.R. (1982), 'The Credit Economy', in *Money, Interest and Wages: Collected Essays in Economic Theory*, Oxford: Basil Blackwell, Vol. 2.

Hicks, J.R. (1986), 'Managing Without Money', in *Chung-Hua Series of Lectures by Invited Eminent Economists*, Tapei: Academia Sinica.

Hicks, J.R. (1989), *A Market Theory of Money*, Oxford: Oxford University Press.

Kaldor, N. (1970), 'The New Monetarism', *Lloyds Bank Review*, No. 97, 1–18.

Kaldor, N. (1982), *The Scourge of Monetarism*, Oxford: Oxford University Press.

King, R.G., and C.I. Plosser (1984), 'Money, Credit and Prices in a Real Business Cycle', *American Economic Review*, **LXXIV**, 363–380.

Laidler, D.E.W. (1990), *Taking Money Seriously*, London: Philip Allan.

Marston, R.C. (1988), 'Exchange Rate Policy Reconsidered', *Economic Impact*, No. 62.

McCallum, B.T. (1986), 'Some Issues Concerning Interest Rate Pegging, Price Level Determinacy, and the Real Bills Doctrine', *Journal of Monetary Economics*, No. 17, 135–160.

McKinnon, R. (1988), 'Monetary and Exchange Rate Policies for International Stability', *Journal of Economic Perspectives*, **2**, (1), 83–103.

Moore, B.J. (1988), *Horizontalists and Verticalists: the Macroeconomics of Credit Money*, Cambridge: Cambridge University Press.

Mundell, R. (1961), 'A Theory of Optimal Currency Areas', *American Economic Review*, **LI**, (4), 657–665.

National Institute Economic Review (1990), 'The European Monetary System and the MTFS', No. 131, 3–5.

Padoa-Schioppa, T. (1988), 'The European Monetary System: a Long-Term View', in F. Giavazzi, S. Micossi and M. Miller (eds), *The European monetary system*, Cambridge: Cambridge University Press.

Smithin, J.N. (1989) 'Hicksian Monetary Economics and Contemporary Financial Innovation', *Review of Political Economy*, **1**, (2), 192–207.

Smithin, J.N. (1990), *Macroeconomics after Thatcher and Reagan: the Conservative Policy Revolution in Retrospect*, Aldershot: Edward Elgar.

Walters, A.A. (1990), *Sterling in Danger*, London: Fontana.

Williamson, J., and M. Miller (1987), *Targets and Indicators: a Blueprint for the International Coordination of Economic Policy*, Washington, DC: Institute for International Economics.

Zis, G. (1989), 'Is There Still a Case for Flexible Exchange Rates?' *British Review of Economic Issues*, Spring.

10. 'Leap before you Look': The Implications of EMU for the Future of the EC

John Williams, Karel Williams and Colin Haslam

INTRODUCTION

European Monetary Union (EMU) is a set of proposals which has yet to be negotiated by member governments before being implemented and operated. In early 1991, the only certainty is that the issues and the agenda will change, perhaps rapidly and unpredictably, in the coming year. The best intellectual starting point is the official Commission plan for EMU which was originally published in April 1989. It treats EMU primarily as an instrument of monetary integration, but naturally aspects of economic union are also involved.

The Delors plan envisaged progress to full EMU in three stages. Stage I is a (hard) Exchange Rate Mechanism (ERM) where all currency parities are defended and devaluation is avoided as far as possible. Stage II is a transitional period of institutional construction which sets up the Euro Fed or a new supranational central bank and gives the Council of Ministers a new role in supervising national budget deficits. While in Stage III the institutions are used actively to move from irrevocably locked exchange rates to full monetary union around a new single community currency supported by binding rules about budget deficits.

This grand scheme for building and operating new European institutions has 'sound money' as its clear superordinate goal. In the original Delors report the sole declared objective of monetary policy is 'price stability'. Maintenance of employment, balanced growth or other desirable objectives are simply not mentioned. This crucial operational objective is built into the design of the new institutions. Thus the constitutional status of the Euro Fed as a politically independent central bank is specifically provided for: 'the (Euro Fed's) . . . council should be independent of instructions from national governments and community authorities', and this arrangement is then explicitly linked to the prime objective of safeguarding sound money.

If the content of the EMU plan is new, its form recapitulates the Commission's earlier successes; there are important homologies between the new plan for EMU and the old single market programme. A seven year timetable is again used as a tactical device to cut short discussion and capitalize on agreement in principle. The single market programme began in 1985 and will be completed in 1992. Stage one of monetary union began in 1990 and the Commission now wants the Euro Fed in place by 1994 so that agreement on the new single currency is concluded in 1997. If the single currency is the main objective in its new plan the Commission is still committed to two track progress with the major headline programme complemented by a much less tightly defined and timetabled subscript; as 1992 was shadowed by social Europe, so EMU is shadowed by a project of political union. The status of this second political project is completely unclear because the stages and objectives of political union have never been defined in a programmatic official document like the Delors Report.

If the EMU plan is a recapitulation, it also represents the Commission's preferred next step in its plan for building Europe. The old single market was about promoting economic integration and EMU should deliver a further instalment of economic integration. No doubt monetary union has been privileged as the next step partly because it promises a new kind of irreversibility; if the single currency is achieved, national governments will find it very difficult to withdraw or re-negotiate their association with other members. At the same time, monetary union is publicly presented by Padoa-Schioppa (1987) and others as an inevitable next step because the free movement of capital (after removal of exchange controls under the 1992 programme) is incompatible with fixed exchange rates and can only be safeguarded by full union around a single currency. This argument is fairly dubious because, as Giavazzi (1990) has argued, the most important controls on capital have already been relaxed in France and Italy. Nevertheless, an important symbolic connection is maintained by the timetabling of the two programmes; stage one of EMU began in July 1990, the date when most EC countries were committed to lifting remaining exchange controls.

What the Commission represents as an inevitable economic next step is also in political terms a quantum leap. For the first time, the Commission is playing at *Ordnungspolitik* with a grand plan that would quickly abolish all national currencies and create a new politically independent central bank. The brilliant political success of the economically negligible 1992 programme plus the personal identification of Jacques Delors with the EMU project has encouraged the Commission to up the stakes and gamble on success: failure to bring off EMU could put back the process of building Europe.

The 1992 programme was a matter of removing non-tariff barriers in a Europe where all governments had long since accepted trade without tariffs. This old programme did not directly threaten any government, promised a diffuse general benefit to European consumers and could be represented as a healthy challenge to which Community enterprises should respond. The EMU plan involves creating new institutions in the area of monetary policy which has great real and symbolic importance to national governments which have hitherto been sovereign in this area. The awkward fact is that the new institutions plus a single currency could involve a permanent loss of sovereignty for all twelve governments. If the Commission is to succeed it must keep other plans off the table and it must deal with the pragmatic objection that full EMU is premature given the divergence of monetary and real performance. As we will argue below, the first of these tactical objectives is easier to achieve than the second.

The only alternative so far defined is the minimalist British plan for a hard ECU which would circulate as a parallel currency. This plan is discussed with a certain fondness by some economists because it would allow market forces to determine whether, when and how monetary union was achieved. For that reason the British plan is anathema to the Commission which is opposed to any scheme that does not have a strong institutional basis and does not meet the test of irreversibility: as long as individual currencies survive, a national government could withdraw from ERM and a hard ECU scheme if its interests were threatened. From this perspective the aim must be a *single currency* rather than a regime of irrevocably fixed exchange rates. If such concerns account for the Commission's hostility to the hard ECU, there is also little enthusiasm from the member states. Among other EC governments, only the Spanish government shows any interest in the British plan for a hard ECU. The British scheme will probably be relegated to a footnote in history because of German opposition based on the belief that it is not hard enough. As Karl Pohl, the outgoing chairman of the Bundesbank, recently observed, the hard ECU is 'an idea whose time has gone'.

If alternative plans can be dismissed, the pragmatic objections to EMU are an altogether more serious problem for the Commission. How can EMU be possible as long as there is divergence both of inflation rates and economic performance amongst EC member states? The German Bundesbank and the Federal Government alike have long taken the position that EMU without convergence means Germany's tight monetary policy must be relaxed or a politically unsustainable amount of deflation must be inflicted on the periphery. If this price is too high for the Germans, then the logic of the situation is a two-tier Europe where full monetary union is reserved for an inner group of countries (Germany, Belgium, Netherlands and, maybe, France) which can manage the necessary convergence. For the Commision, this would be a very unwelcome development because any scheme which creates two classes of member state does not meet the test of building Europe.

The outcome remains uncertain but by early 1991 the bright confident morning of EMU is over. After a first inter-governmental conference at Rome in September 1990, the newspapers reported that only four national governments supported the Delors plan and timetable; the list of enthusiasts included France and Italy but significantly did not include Germany (*Financial Times*, 1990a). After a second inter-governmental conference at Rome in December 1990, Delors publicly complained that all the governments were reneging on their commitment to timetabled progress and none of them were sound on EMU: 'ask the German, the Spaniard, the Dutchman, the Frenchman what they think (of EMU) in the bottom of their hearts' (*Financial Times*, 1990b). As the timetable deadlines grow closer, so national governments are increasingly reluctant to put their weight behind the Delors plan and there is growing disagreement about the timing, form and content of EMU.

If the Rome meeting disappointed the Commission, the national governments could quite reasonably reply that they had achieved a broad political consensus which unites left and right, north and south, around participation in hard ERM and the ultimate goal of a single currency. All EC governments accept the desirability of a hard ERM with locked exchange rates: ten of the twelve are participating in ERM on this basis. Furthermore, no EC government is now opposed to the desirability, in principle, of full monetary union.

The political consensus holds amidst the present confusions, partly because it is supported by a remarkable consensus of expert opinion among European economists. In Britain, for example, sterling's October 1990 entry into a hard ERM was universally applauded by city and academic economists, although there were some misgivings that a central rate of 2.95 against the Deutschmarks was too high for British industry. And the university professors are now asking for the institutional next step of a 'politically independent central bank'; this was unanimously supported in a recent 'round-robin' letter to the *Independent* by 22 academics with a variety of political and discursive affiliations. A small minority of economists on the far right question the wisdom of hard ERM and EMU, but they occupy positions which give them little influence over outcomes. Alan Walters (1990) continues to argue the case for floating exchange rates, but he is an ex-adviser to a former British prime minister.

Against this background, the aim here is to continue the theme of the previous chapter and question the prevailing orthodoxy about the economic desirability and political practicality of proceeding through hard ERM to full EMU. In the next section we analyse the terrain of the economic argument before turning to examine the likely economic consequences of hard ERM and EMU. In the final section we take a broader view of the economic alternatives and question the political priority of monetary union. Our conclusion is that, in economic policy terms, the Commission and the mainstream economists are encouraging national governments to 'leap before you look'. Seldom in the history of economic policy has the case for such a fundamental change in regime been accepted on such flimsy justifications and with so little evidence. In broader political terms, we conclude the Commission's EMU project has a cart-before-the-horse flavour; rapid and durable EMU ahead of real convergence which depends partly on the political precondition of a strong federal Europe.

TERRAIN OF THE ECONOMIC ARGUMENT

The Commission published its official economic justification of the Delors plan in a special number of *European Economy* (1990). As a statement of the case for hard ERM and EMU, this is an authoritative and classic text. The terrain of the argument in this text is of considerable interest because it represents a political shift and a theoretical break with earlier Commission texts. Politically, *European Economy* (*EE*) is a shift to the right because it envisages a Community where the objective of employment has no priority and deflationary discipline operates without the counterweight of credible regional policy. Theoretically, *EE* is a break because it operates within a specifically monetarist problematic that sets EMU in a theatre of representations where it has the power to transform expectations and behaviour.

The political shift is most easily registered by comparing *EE* with the Cecchini Report. This is instructive because *EE* relates to the EMU project as Cecchini related to the earlier 1992 project. As we have argued elsewhere (Cutler *et al.*, 1989, pp. 2–3), Cecchini was a right wing text where liberal collectivism survives as a series of residual gestures; in the *EE* text the gestures are no longer thought necessary. This point can be established by considering the difference between Cecchini and *EE* on two key issues: the first issue concerns the balance between reflation and deflation, which is an indicator of differences about the status of employment as a policy objective; the second issue concerns the scope and role of regional policy, which is an indicator of differences about the proper scope of government redistribution.

The objective of full employment may have been written into the original Treaty of Rome but it has never figured prominently in the Commission's hierarchy of objectives. Nevertheless, co-ordinated reflation was rather unconvincingly added on in Cecchini enabling the Commission to claim 1992 meant job gain rather than job loss. But, by the early 1990s, the objective of employment has been demoted by the EC, so *EE* can be robust about the need for fiscal deflation as the corollary of monetary union. Budgetary discipline is essential because the balance of payments constraint on national fiscal policy is removed by EMU and loose fiscal policy would spill over to undermine the policy stance of the Euro Fed and other national governments:

> Unsustainable budgetary positions in a member State, ultimately leading to either default or debt monetization would be a major threat to the overall monetary stability.
>
> *European Economy* (1990, p. 100)

Of course, the inter-connection between monetary and fiscal policy is such that the Commission must consider the possibility that the interests of (international) monetary policy could be undermined by (national) fiscal policy. But, in *EE*, the concern is exclusively with the possibility that tight monetary policy might be frustrated by loose fiscal policy: the reverse case is never considered. Furthermore, loose fiscal policy is operationally defined in an extraordinarily restrictive way. Whatever the starting point and whatever the objectives of expenditure, *any* rise in the debt to GDP ratio is labelled 'unsustainable' (*European Economy*, 1990, p. 103); and, whatever the rate of increase, any debt ratio above 100 per cent of GDP 'should imperatively be stabilized' (*European Economy*, 1990, p. 109). On this basis the list of EC countries needing deflationary treatment for loose fiscal policies includes Greece, Italy, Portugal, Belgium, Ireland and the Netherlands.

Behind this *EE* position on public debt is an overwhelming prejudice against public expenditure and, even more, against redistributive expenditure through instruments like regional policy. Again the contrast with Cecchini is instructive because Cecchini included the then obligatory reference to regional policy even though its chosen instruments, the Social Funds, were palpably inadequate for the task (Cutler *et al.* Chapter 3). However, *EE* dispenses with such gestures and is deeply suspicious of supranational redistribution which like other forms of government involves the 'risks of weakening incentives for production activity and creates a state welfare dependency' (*European Economy*, 1990, p. 227). The success of the weaker peripheral economies depends on their own commitment to 'generalized modernization' which has to 'extend very deeply and acquire socio-political as well as purely economic dimensions' (*European Economy*, 1990, p. 227). More specifically, their economic success depends on a 'comprehensive and credible change of regime' which effectively means the marketization of everything:

> There is a widespread concensus on some elements, such as a unified and open Europe-sized market; national policies of enterprise reform, aimed at the introduction of market discipline mechanisms in all sectors of the economy; labour market regulatory reform, aimed at more flexibility, efficiency and employment; modernization of tax systems and stability-orientated and transparent monetary and budgetary policies
>
> *European Economy* (1990, pp. 225–6)

In this context, the task of national policy makers is re-defined; policy is not about securing final outcomes or managing adjustment processes, it is about creating a framework of opportunities which the appropriately motivated can exploit. Thus, *EE* is agnostic about whether the weaker, peripheral economies will generally lose through EMU (*European Economy*, 1990, p. 220). Without any supporting argument or evidence, the variable success of these national economies is attributed to differences in national government commitment to modernization:

> convergence has not occurred uniformly . . . suggesting that the adequacy of domestic economic policies play a crucial role
>
> *European Economy* (1990, p. 220)

Within this circular form of argument, the theory and its policy prescriptions cannot fail: if the economic results are disappointing, it is because national government has not created the appropriate framework and/or other economic actors are not responding appropriately as in the case of South Italian workers who obtain wages that are too high in relation to the North (*European Economy*, 1990, p. 220).

The same philosophy of theory immunized against disproof, and policy as the framework of opportunity, is applied to the *EE* discussion of the benefits of EMU. Like the more general economists' debate, the *EE* report is not only about money but also operates within a monetarist problematic that has two notable features. First, as Smithin observes in chapter 9, within the monetarist problematic, the objective of sound money is privileged and the real economic objectives of output, employment and growth are demoted. *EE* tries to cover this over with the assertion that 'on average, high inflation countries have a higher unemployment rate and a lower income per capita' (*European Economy*, 1990, p. 22). Even if this proposition is true of most of the industrialized countries since World War II, it does not of course justify the inference that converting high-inflation countries to low-inflation countries will generate more employment and higher growth rates. Secondly, within the monetarist problematic, monetary policy is privileged as an active primary kind of intervention. The logic of the *EE* position on national debt is that fiscal policy must ultimately play a passive secondary role. If, for example, GDP fell during recession, a prudent national government would keep its debt burden sustainable by cutting back economic and social expenditure.

Within this problematic, EMU and hard ERM are key instruments which can deliver the master objective of price stability through institutional and representational mechanisms. The main institutional demand is for a politically independent central bank which has price stability as its sole objective:

> Monetary policy is vulnerable . . . unless the central bank has political independence, board members with long and secure tenure, and statutes establishing an explicit duty to give priority to price stability.
>
> *European Economy* (1990, p. 22)

A properly structured and institutionalized Euro Fed would eliminate national political cycles which occur because democratically elected governments succumb to electoral needs 'which may at times make it attractive to exploit short term gains against longer term costs' (*European Economy* (1990) p.22). In this, and other ways, the Euro Fed can be beneficial because it will take the politics out of economics.

The hard ERM offers less than full EMU, but can still be beneficial because ERM would operate on expectations in a kind of theatre of representations. *EE* argues that 'expectations are at the heart of the inflation process' (*European Economy*, 1990, p. 21). As wage bargainers realize that excessive wage rises are not underwritten by devaluation, they will modify expectations and behaviour. The cost in terms of output and employment need not be high if expectations are transformed and this transformation is a powerful argument for going all the way to EMU which is likely to be more representationally effective. The advantage of EMU is that it:

> will not be a mere unilateral commitment to exchange rate stability, but rather an institutional change whose impact should be clear for all agents (especially with the adoption of a single currency)
>
> *European Economy* (1990, p. 46)

The institutional and representational mechanisms together define a supply side programme for making reality like economic theory. We are asked to believe that EMU-type monetary policy is an enormously powerful instrument for good; through monetary policy, a Keynesian real economy which is all political interests and economic stickiness can be turned back into a smoothly-adjusting neo-classical economy. The whole programme has a long pre-history in right wing economic thought on the causes and cures for inflation. Consider, for example, Hayek's postion in *The Constitution of Liberty*:

> The process is sometimes described as though wage increases directly produced inflation. This is not correct. If the supply of money and credit were not expanded, the wage increases would rapidly lead to unemployment. But under the influence of a doctrine that represents it as a duty of the monetary authorities to provide enough money to secure full employment at a given wage level, it is politically inevitable that each round of wage increases should lead to further inflation
>
> Hayek (1960, p. 281)

If the monetary authorities do not accommodate the wage bargainers, then the inflationary spiral will be halted; what could be simpler and more self-evident?

In this kind of supply side economics, monetary policy (via ERM and EMU) occupies the same place as incomes policy in the centrism of twenty years ago: it blocks unreasonable wage demands as a means of reasserting the bourgeois value of sound money and enforcing the working-class value of deferred gratification. The political authorities may be equally enthusiastic for the new monetary instrument but are less convinced of its effectiveness: they thus publicize the new constraints but warn of failure to heed them. Thus the Governor of the Bank of England welcomes sterling's entry into ERM but warns employers:

> henceforth companies can have no grounds for expecting a lower exchange rate to validate any failure to control costs . . . If companies recognize that they are operating under a changed regime, the benefits of lower inflation will acrue sooner and at lower cost in terms of lost output, than would otherwise be expected. But if they fail to recognize the constraints under which they now operate the outcome will prove painful for them
>
> Bank Briefing (1990, p. 1)

The political line may be familiar, but the difference is that if the new monetary policy techniques do not work to transform behaviour through expectations then monetarist theory and policy prescriptions will not be discredited as Keynesianism was by the failure of incomes policy twenty years ago. In the theatre of representations, a failure of policy only reflects on the unreasonableness of the actors who set wages. Thus the monetarist fix comes with a small print health warning on the side of the package. The *EE* study implies at several points that if the benefits do not materialize, it will be because the economic actors do not grasp the opportunities. The role of economists is to rehearse the arguments for the monetarist solution while repeating the health warning about side effects. Thus, a recent article supports EMU and then concludes:

> UK industry has been looking to the ERM as a haven of stability, but unless it adopts its practices rapidly, entry will make industry, less, not more, competitive in the European market
>
> Currie and Williamson (1990, p. 16)

For those who are concerned with processes and policy outcomes, this whole position is bizarre. The idea that institutionalized EMU can take the politics out of economics is crushingly naive as the 1990 inter-governmental conferences illustrated. Perhaps the politicians will not deliver the kind of full-blooded politically independent central bank which the economists favour. In any event, the political independence of existing national central banks is always qualified and limited: the case of the Bundesbank's 1990 capitulation on one for one German monetary union is a perfect illustration of the limits of independence. The national governments may also decide that the experiments of a hard ERM and the single currency are only worth attempting (or persisting with) if there is a reasonable assurance that locked exchange rates will take out inflation without too high a price in terms of their national output and employment loss. It is to this issue that we turn in the next section.

ECONOMIC EFFECTS OF HARD ERM AND EMU

It is difficult to discuss the consequences of hard ERM or EMU because the form and content of these arrangements has yet to be defined. This uncertainty about future EC rules and structures is increased by uncertainty about the economic conduct and performance of re-united Germany. This last point is important because, as Smithin in Chapter 9 of this work observes, the trajectory of every exchange and payments system depends on the conduct and performance of the major players. And there can be no doubt that Germany is the major player in any future European system. The former Federal Republic had a one-third share of EC 12 intra-European manufactured exports and thereby earned a huge trade surplus which pushed most other EC members into or near payments deficit.

Under pressure of German re-unification, the Germans have maintained relatively tight monetary policy but relaxed their fiscal policy stance. Chancellor Kohl's government has reluctantly taxed West Germany for the support and reconstruction of East Germany and next year's fiscal deficit is estimated at 5 per cent of GDP. At the same time the long-established German trade surplus has been dramatically reduced as West German consumer goods are diverted to East Germany where indigenous firms had hitherto supplied the market. If these developments raise the German inflation rate, their immediate effect would be to make monetary union easier because nominal convergence becomes less of a problem for the weaker economies. But the longer-term implications are unclear. The East German *Länder* must for some considerable time be supported as pensioners, while Germany puts together a productive partnership which in the long run is likely to reinforce the centralization of EC production around the Rhine Corridor.

If these complications do not figure much in the current debate about ERM and EMU, that is because the orthodox pro-EMU positon does not rest on any solid empirical basis. European economists and politicians have declared themselves in favour of fundamental changes without any empirical analysis of the past benefits of hard ERM or the future benefits of EMU. All the European countries are being encouraged to leap into the dark because Europe has little recent experience of fixed exchange rate systems which block devaluation. Hard ERM has only operated in this way for the past four years in the later 1980s. Between 1981 and 1985, the lira was repeatedly devalued in small bites by a total of more than 20 per cent. In this period, the ERM was a crawling peg system which offered the Italians partial compensation for their higher rates of inflation. And the maintenance of hard ERM through the first half of the 1990s is by no means absolutely certain. With the entrance of sterling in October 1990, the ERM took on the new burden of supporting a weak major trading currency. Although the EC would represent any devaluation of the pound as a once and for all special case, any devaluation would set a precedent.

When arguing the case for 1992, the Commission produced a forward looking economic analysis of the gains that would be realized from the removal of non-tariff barriers. But, significantly, the Commission has not tried to repeat the exercise for its new initiative on hard ERM and EMU. Cecchini provided estimated measures of the overall Europe-wide gains from the removal of NTBs. But *EE* does not provide anything comparable for EMU. Occasional illustrative estimates of specific gains are provided, often in 'as much as' form. But these estimates cannot be added up to provide a total of overall Europe-wide gains from ERM and EMU.

The earlier exercise of adding up benefits has not been repeated for fairly obvious reasons. Despite a massive commitment of academic and consultancy resources, the Commission lost the argument about the size of the economic benefits from 1992. The Commission's critics (Neuburger, 1989; Geroski, 1988; Cutler *et al.*, 1989) showed that the supposed benefits were exaggerated by Cecchini and the costs were likely to be distributed unevenly amongst member countries. More fundamentally, the exercise cannot be repeated because it is practically impossible to find large positive benefits using any orthodox form of economic analysis of the comparative static or dynamic effects of hard ERM or EMU. It is, for example, extraordinarily difficult to measure the effects of cheaper capital in weaker peripheral countries which at present pay some kind of risk premium for their capital. The only easy to measure gain is the direct cost saving realized by exporters who must hedge their transactions as long as there is a risk of currency fluctuation. These direct savings turn out to be completely trivial. A recent CBI (1990, pp. 6–8), survey suggests that the elimination of hedging by British exporters to Europe would save £100 million in the first year; this direct saving amounts to just 0.5 per cent of the total sales value of British exports.

The case for hard ERM and EMU must therefore rest on the predicted dynamic effects on the rate of inflation which are higher in the weaker countries. As we have noted, the orthodox prediction is that inflation must come down because credible policy will influence the expectations and behaviour of wage setters. This form of prediction rests on a very peculiar view of economic behaviour which almost entirely abstracts from differences in national institutions and circumstances (European Economy, 1990, p. 150). Thus the orthodoxy does not seriously consider the effects of variations in labour market institutions, nor such factors as the size of the non-tradeable goods sector, the balance between intra- and extra-European trade or the strategies of national manufacturing firms about where and how to compete.

The importance of these considerations can be illustrated by considering the British national case where the stylized orthodox prescription is hardly relevant. Less than one quarter of the British workforce is employed in the manufacturing sector which is the main source of tradeable goods. And only half of Britain's manufacturing exports go to Europe where exchange rates are to be locked. More fundamentally, the orthodox view presumes that the efforts of national manufacturing firms are directed towards competing through export to other European countries. This hardly fits the case of those 'hollowed out' British giant firms which are shifting out of manufacturing and/or building up American operations through acquisition (Williams, *et al.*, 1990). In

British manufacturing, problems about controlling costs will only result in more hollowing out.

In this kind of complex national case, the representational effects and the impact on wage-setting expectations are likely to be muted: the effects on wage-setting behaviour may well be negligible, while the results in terms of performance may be perverse. In so far as the adjustment of behaviour does proceed on orthodox lines, it is likely to be at the expense of considerable social injustice. The burden of wage adjustment will generally be carried by that minority of each national workforce which is engaged in intra-European trade. Some groups in exposed competitive activities will be asked directly to take real wage cuts in the form of wage increases below the rate of inflation.

At this point, the advocate of hard ERM and EMU could reply that the sole objective was lower inflation rates and that adherence to a hardening ERM has reduced the inflation differentials of weaker European countries *vis-à-vis* Germany. As Table 10.1 shows, it is undoubtedly true that inflation differentials have narrowed.

Table 10.1   Inflation rates in Germany, France and Italy

	France v Germany difference (%)	Italy v Germany difference (%)
1983	+6.5	+12.0
1988	+1.5	+ 3.5

But Barrell's (1990, p.71) econometric study for the NIESR suggests that lower inflation rates were obtained at considerable cost in terms of lost output and increased unemployment: the job loss is estimated at 700 000 in France and one million in Italy. Barrell's results are particularly striking in the Italian case because large-scale job loss occurred here despite structural reform with the effective removal of the *'scala mobile'* wage indexation system.

The implication of this econometric study is that, even with structural reform, wage-setting actors do not adjust their expectations and behaviour quickly enough. In this case, we would protest that the remaining weaker, high-inflation countries in Europe are unsuitable cases for monetarist treatment. Countries like Spain start from rates of unemployment which are already scandalously high; a country with around 20 per cent unemployment cannot afford *any* rise in unemployment. Countries like Britain have decentralized wage bargaining systems; a country whose labour market institutions subvert incomes policy is unlikely to find that these institutions smoothly generate the behaviour required by a hard ERM.

If the weaker peripheral economies do not adjust labour market expectations and behaviour, then orthodox theorists concede that the burden of adjustment must fall on output and employment. As we do not expect adjustment, we predict that hard ERM will depress output and employment in these economies and open up real divergence in income per capita and unemployment rates across the EC. This is (more) bad news for weaker peripheral economies because the Commission's own evidence suggests that rapid EC wide growth is a necessary precondition of real convergence (*European Economy*, 1990, p. 212).

The doggedly orthodox might still argue that these are transitional costs because expectations and behaviour will adjust in the long run. But, on the available American and Canadian experience, this is dubious. As discussed in the previous chapter, the US and Canada have long experience of long-established currency unions over large and diverse economic areas. It is noticeable that American and Canadian economists are much less sanguine about the benefits of EMU than their European counterparts; North American economists, like Smithin (1990, pp. 19–20) and Eichengreen (1990, pp. 134–9) are unimpressed by nominal convergence and are worried by the absence of long-run real economic convergence. Here, currency union has been associated with large persistent differences in regional income per capita and unemployment rates. Eichengreen (1990, pp. 159–64) emphasizes the persistance of regional unemployment differences in the US despite large-scale labour mobility across a more linguistically and culturally homogeneous population than the EC. The outcome in Europe is uncertain but it does seem inconceivable that hard ERM and EMU would work to reduce real economic divergence.

BURDEN OF ADJUSTMENT

No doubt the debate on the consequences of ERM and EMU will continue. But a good deal of modern economics has turned in on itself and the economists' contributions to the debate on this large issue will be conducted within a narrow technical frame which blocks out the political, the social and the institutional. If this makes insight into fundamental choices elusive, it was not always so. Much can still be learnt from earlier work generated at an equally significant turning point in the first half of the 1940s, when Keynes was wrestling with the problems of reconstructing a system of international exchange and payments. Our own position is not Keynesian because we believe that Keynes presented a lop-sided demand side explanation of the inter-war debacle when he implied that 'the difficulty . . . (was) the lack of markets as a result of restrictive policies throughout the world' (Keynes, 1980, p. 48). Keynes's acute intelligence can be used to deconstruct the current supply side banalities about frameworks of opportunity.

The details of Keynes's proposals for a post war international Currency Union are no longer of any interest. But Keynes's broad guiding principles and his reflection on the desiderata of an ideal exchange and payments system remain relevant. The first of Keynes's principles relates to the need for symmetry in adjustment. He criticized previous systems of free convertibility because they threw 'the main burden of adjustment on the country which is in the *debtor* position on the international balance of payments' (Keynes, 1980, p. 27). The result in the case of a system like the pre-1914 gold standard was 'to force adjustments in the direction most disruptive of social order and to throw the burden on the countries least able to support it, making the poor poorer' (Keynes, 1980, p. 29). Keynes's proposals differed 'by putting at least as much pressure of adjustment on the creditor country as on the debtor' (Keynes, 1980, pp. 48–9). If Keynes's first requirement was redistribution of the burden of adjustment, his second parallel requirement was for an exchange and payments system which had an expansionary rather than a contractionary bias. Thus, Keynes claimed his 'plan aims at the substitution of an expansionist, in place of a contractionist, pressure on world trade' (Keynes, 1980, p.74). On this issue, he somewhat optimistically informed a leading British trade unionist, Bevin, that 'no responsible person today contemplated the use of the old weapons, deflation enforced by dear money, resulting in unemployment as a means of restoring international equilibrium' (Keynes, 1980, p. 142).

In laying down these principles, Keynes's overall objective was entirely in accord with liberal economics: his aim was not to attack but to safeguard free trade. 'It is a great advantage of the proposed Currency Union that it restores unfettered multilateral clearing between its members . . .' (Keynes, 1980, p. 51). In this respect the prescriptions of Keynes for the international economy matched those of his earlier work in the *General Theory* on the domestic economy: the aim was to ensure the unfettered continuance of liberal capitalism. The main threat was capitalism's inherent tendency towards a degree of unemployment and instability that might be unsupportable in a democratic context. Keynes's analysis suggested that, both nationally and internationally, this threat could be offset with a minimal intervention after which the economic system could be left to operate efficiently and equitably. Thus, externally, if deflation and contraction were avoided, the international economy could expand and, within a multilateral trading system, everyone would benefit. Keynes was optimistic about the rationality of the existing international division of labour which was still then largely between industrial countries and primary producers and he had no doubt that, in a multilateral system, the benefits of trade would be distributed fairly. The productive circle of mutual benefit could finally be closed by the recreation of nineteenth-century patterns of investment whereby creditor industrial countries recycled funds into productive investment in primary producing countries.

If we share Keynes's concern about the likely instability of an unfettered capitalist system, we do not share his unquenchable liberal optimism about the general benefits of trade. This difference only strengthens our misgivings about ERM/EMU in the form in which it is proposed in the Delors plan and justified in *EE*: the mechanisms of this plan throw the main burden of adjustment on the already weaker, peripheral countries. From a Keynesian perspective, Delors-style EMU has two great defects: first, this plan does not require, and probably positively blocks, any adjustment at the strong centre; secondly, this plan has inbuilt contractionist tendencies which are embodied in the general emphasis on 'monetary soundness'. Worse still, twenty years of EC experience of free trade does not support Keynes's optimism about the international division of labour and the benefits of trade. From our point of view, a third defect of the Delors plan is that it does nothing to counter the centralization of production within the Community as discussed in Chapter 3 of this work. In the discussion which follows, we will consider each of the three key economic defects of the Delors plan in turn, before finally drawing out the political implications of our economic analysis.

The existing debate on EMU is more or less exclusively preoccupied with the way in which, under hard ERM and EMU, the peripheral countries lose the possibility of devaluation: the fears of some weaker countries about the costs of this are simply the mirror image of the hopes of *EE* about the benefits of blocking devaluation. Nothing is said about the possibility of revaluation at the centre which will, of course, cease to exist as an option when and if full EMU is achieved. The loss of the devaluation option, just like the planned single currency, raises lively political fears about the loss of sovereignty in the weaker countries. Superficially, in economic terms, the renunciation of nominal exchange rate adjustment is symmetrical and equal: the strong lose the possibility of revaluation at the same time as the weak renounce the possibility of devaluation. The fact that the strong are, as Keynes observed, usually reluctant to revalue while the weak are often forced into devaluation gives the game away.

The behavioural difference between strong and weak countries reflects political power differences and a basic asymmetry between the effects of devaluation at the periphery and revaluation at the centre. Devaluation of nominal exchange rates at the periphery may improve price and cost competitiveness subject to J-curve effects and various perversities. However, improved price and cost competitiveness is not an automatic key to success in manufacturing trade if unfavourable non-price characteristics limit sales, and the perversities are important. To a country like Britain, although overvaluation is a significant burden, devaluation may bring few positive benefits. In 1989, Turner calculated that a 50 per cent devaluation of the *real* exchange rate would be required to eliminate the trade deficit (William and Haslam, 1989, p. 16). Revaluation at the centre is likely to be a sharper, more effective instrument, because it more or less directly hits the profits of manufacturing enterprises through its effects on margins and sales volume: however favourable the non-price characteristics foreign consumers will be reluctant to accept large price increases. The appreciation of the yen in the 1980s reduced Japanese manufacturing profits as a percentage of assets by 32 per cent in the period 1984–85 and forced the Japanese to transfer manufacturing production to other parts of the Pacific rim and North America. A similar process might be the most effective way of persuading the Germans to manufacture outside Germany: in the EC free trade area, there is at present no pressure for them to do so, nor would there be under the Commission's schemes for ERM and EMU. In the context of the present imbalance of manufacturing output, the blocking of revaluation at the centre involves the loss of a more effective mechanism for redress, than does the blocking of devaluation at the periphery.

This important point is invisible in the existing debate for much the same reasons as the contractionist bias in the Delors plan. The 1992 plan for removing non-tariff barriers powerfully reinforced the idea of free competition across a level field: the implication is that the weaker countries should not rely on artificial aids such as exchange rate manipulation but commit themselves to emulating the free market success of Germany which is a model for all. 'Contractionism' is not posed as a problem because the success of the German economy, in *EE* as in other texts, is confidently attributed to the German pursuit of sound money: the implication is that what has been good for Germany will be good for all the rest. It is hard to know where to begin in criticizing this farrago of confusions. Germany (like Japan) is the national economy which least fits the free market stereotype. More obviously market economies like the US and UK have much worse economic performance; the whole argument about the general benefits of sound money rests on illegitimate generalization from a single case which involves the logical fallacy of composition as well as a crude *post hoc ergo propter hoc* fallacy; even if we heroically assume that sound money is a major cause of German success, it is by no means obvious that its extension will be good for all the other EC countries.

Furthermore, the heroic assumption is not justified because it rests on a (mis)reading of the German case which only illustrates the slippery opportunism of modern economic discourse. As we have seen in *EE*, those who plan policy frameworks of opportunity offer no guarantee that the outcome in particular cases will be favourable. However, when the outcome is favourable, success is always attributable to the influence of the policy variable which is identified in the *a priori* of the discourse. So it is in the misreading of German economic success which in the *EE* and other texts, illegitimately abstracts monetary policy and institutions from everything else in the economy. In Germany this leaves out national peculiarities such as the supportive relation between banks and industrial firms, a distinctive system of labour relations and a long tradition of education and vocational training. The active direct cause of German success is the superior productive competence of German engineering firms, a success which is unexplained and inexplicable in any orthodox theory of prices and costs. On this productive basis, the Germans have built a unique division of responsibility between public authorities and private capital: the Federal Government and the Bundesbank have generally maintained restrictive, contractionist fiscal and monetary policies and left competent German manufacturers to seek their own reflationary solution by expanding their export sales to European and world markets. This makes it literally impossible for Germany to act as a model for all the other European countries: most of them lack the German level of manufacturing competence and all the EC countries can hardly succeed by running a large surplus on intra-EC trade.

If the German case is misread (as free market success based on sound money), that not only suppresses the issue of contractionism, but also obscures the international division of labour which can always be rationalized as the efficient result of free competition across the level field. In our view, the industrial division of labour within the EC is, or should be, a cause for concern. Nearly three-fifths of EC trade is intra-industrial trade which involves the competitive exchange of differentiated products, above all consumer goods like cars, kitchen machines and brown goods. This pattern of trade supports a substantial centralization of production: with 18 per cent of EC 12 population, the old West Germany had 38 per cent of manufacturing production. The most affluent regions of Europe are concentrated in the Federal Republic and along the Rhine Corridor.

Against this background, we would argue that what Europe needs is an exchange system which promotes decentralization of production through revaluation at the centre. It is hard to compensate for the loss of revaluation as a primary adjustment mechanism because none of the secondary mechanisms of redistribution can do the job in the EC as it exists and is now planned. The original Delors plan for EMU paid lip service to EC regional policy and suggested the EC structural funds could be used to soften the negative effects of monetary discipline on the periphery. As we have argued elsewhere (Cutle *et al.*, 1989, chapter 3), existing regional policy is completely inadequate to the task of correcting the present scale of intra-European inequalities. The much-vaunted doubling of the structural funds between 1988 and 1993 promises more than it delivers: twice very little is still not very much. The fact is that the EC budget remains pathetically limited when its total for all purposes is just over one per cent of Community GDP. As part of its drive to European political unity, the Commission champions strong monetary institutions at the centre but it does not plan to construct a strong federal power. The contrast between EC and a strong federal system like the US is very marked: the American Federal Government has the resources to underwrite a quarter of local state expenditure. Curiously, too, Germany is not here seen as a model: the Federal Republic of Germany has extensive provisions for redistribution to poorer *Länder*.

If revaluation at the centre is blocked and as long as the EC is a financially weak federal power, it is hard to envisage the reduction of substantial regional disparities in both income levels and rates of unemployment. The whole case for EMU rests on the supposition that Europe is or can be something like an optimal currency area. The arcane literature on optimal currency areas assumes that, if the economic infrastructure in various regional or national units is dissimilar, then adjustment will be made through labour mobility. As Smithin in Chapter 9 and Eichengreen (1990) argue, the adjustment mechanisms do not work in the US where linguistic and cultural barriers to labour migration are small. The labour migration 'solution' is much less likely in the EC where only one country, Eire, has significant net migration and that migration is to the British mainland which shares a language and a culture. Hard ERM and EMU puts all the burden of adjustment on wages and costs in the weaker, peripheral countries and the result is likely to be a jammed economy, rather than smooth, semi-automatic market adjustments. If

EMU were achieved, perhaps the US (rather than Germany) shows us our European future: sustained poor economic performance in association with persistent disparities. The more exact analogy would be Canada, which shows us a future where economic divergence and cultural diversity together put the maintenance of the political union itself into question.

CONCLUSION

In the final analysis, it is this political hazard of EMU which is most threatening. At a strictly economic level, EMU raises the issue of what neo-Keynesians, for example, Dow and Chick (1988), discuss as the centralization of banking power and the imposition of an unsuitable contractionist monetary regime on the periphery. In a broader political perspective, the issue is the terms on which (supra-national) centralized power over money and many other economic and social policy objects can be rendered acceptable to the (national) participants. The intergovernmental conference in Rome in December 1990 signalled very clearly the dangers which are involved. Up to the summer of 1990 – the beginning of phase one of the Delors plan – it had looked as if the Commission was going to be able to move effortlessly up a gear from the single-market programme to the single currency objective. Only Britain was opposed to the principle of EMU and that represented no insuperable obstacle. During the second half of 1990 several national governments began to express misgivings about the pace and nature of the Delors plan for EMU. The emergence of these tensions at so early a stage in the EMU negotiations should be seen as a salutary warning.

Their significance is underlined when it is remembered that the ultimate objective is to build Europe as a stable, cohesive political unit. If stability is to be maintained, it is essential to maintain cohesion and this can only be done by ensuring every national player has a stake and derives positive benefits from federation. In our view, the current Delors plan for hard ERM followed by EMU fails this key political test. Even if the Commission can persuade the national governments to leap before they look, our prediction is that the economic distribution of costs and benefits will be so unequal that the political institutions of hard ERM and EMU will not hold. The political damage may then spill over into other policy areas and issues.

Some part of these consequences may be evaded or softened by a less purely monetarist approach. The 'binding limits' on each country's fiscal deficits could be made less fierce, the burden of adjustments be spread more equitably, the contractionist bias relaxed or reversed. Nonetheless the logic of the position is not simply that Europe needs a different scheme for monetary union: Europe also needs a different order of priorities between economic and political *ordnungspolitik*. For the basic pre-condition of cohesion cannot be met by the re-design of one subsystem like the exchange and payments system; cohesion more generally requires a strong, democratic, federal European government which has substantial financial resources that allow re-distribution to lagging nations and regions. Political union should therefore be presented as the initial pre-condition of EMU, rather than as an ill-defined optional corollary. Hard ERM and EMU are not, in themselves, a sensible way of building Europe. If the Commission perseveres with its misconceived strategic order of priorities, the political consequences of the Delors plan may yet turn out to be more unfortunate than the economic consequences. In both the 1992 programme and the current plan for EMU, the Commission has, for presentational reasons, tended to bury its political subtext in what appear to be economic texts: it is time to make the ultimate political aim the explicit starting point.

REFERENCES

Barrell, R. (1990), 'Has the EMS Changed Wage and Price Behaviour in Europe?' *National Institute Economic Review*, Nov., 64–71.

Bank Briefing (1990), 'The ERM Discipline', Bank of England, London, November.

CBI (1990), *The Exchange Rate Mechanism and UK Manufacturing Exports*, London: Price Waterhouse.

Cecchini, P. (1988), *1992 – The European Challenge: the Benefits of a Single Market*, Aldershot: Wildwood House.

Currie, D. and P. Williamson, (1990), 'Will ERM Entry Make British Companies More Competitive?' *Business Strategy Review*, **1**, (3), 1–17.

Cutler, T., K. Williams, and J. Williams (1989), *1992 – the Struggle for Europe*, Oxford: Berg.

Dow, S. and V. Chick (1988), 'A Post-Keynesian Perspective of the Relation Between Banking and Regional Development', *Thames Papers in Political Economy*, Spring, Division of Economics, Thames Polytechnic.

Eichengreen, B. (1990), 'One Money for Europe? Lessons from the US Currency Union', *Economic Policy*, April, 119–75.

European Economy (1990), 'One Market, One Money', No. 44, October.

Financial Times (1990a), 'EC Ministers Fall Out Over Speed of Monetary Union', 10 Sept.

Financial Times (1990b), 'Delors Fears Finance Ministers May Back Down on EMU', 18 Dec.

Geroski, P.A. (1988), '1992 and European Industrial Structure in the Twenty-First Century', *Mimeo*, London Business School.

Giavazzi, F. (1990), *Capital Controls are Gone: will the EMS Survive?* London: Centre for Economic Policy Research.

Hayek, F. (1960), *The Constitution of Liberty*. London: Routledge.

Keynes, J.M. (1980), *Collected Works*, vol. XXV, London: Macmillan.

Neuberger, H. (1989), *The Economics of 1992*, London: Socialist Group of European Parliament.

Padoa-Schioppa, T. (1987), *Efficiency, Stability and Equity: of the European Community*, Oxford: Oxford University Press.

Smithin, J.N. (1990), *European Monetary Arrangements and National Economic Sovereignty: a Canadian Perspective*, Ontario: York University.

Walters, A. (1990), *Sterling in danger: Economic Consequences of Fixed Exchange Rates*, London: Fontana.

Williams, K. and C. Haslam (1989), 'A Leaky Shelter', *New Statesman*, 27 Oct.

Williams, K., J. Williams, and C. Haslam (1990), 'The Hollowing out of British manufacturing and its implications for policy', *Economy and Society*, **19**, (4), 456–90.

Index

235